ACCESS ALL AREAS

a user's guide to the
art of urban exploration

by Ninjalicious

The book is set in the typeface Concorde.

Printed in Canada.

Library and Archives Canada Cataloguing in Publication

Ninjalicious, 1973-
    Access all areas : a user's guide to the art of urban exploration / by Ninjalicious.

Includes index.
ISBN 0-9737787-0-9

        1. Cities and towns--Guidebooks.   2. Industrial buildings--Guidebooks. 3. Architecture and tourism. I. Title.

NA6400.N55 2005   725'.4   C2005-904038-6

First Edition

For Liz

CONTENTS

STATEMENT

This book is a guide for hobbyists. It is intended to enhance and enlighten the reader's appreciation of his or her landscape, and is written with great respect for the sites described herein. We are staunch defenders of these sites and will battle for their conservation. Our tourism is not one of exploitation, but rather of reverence.

We are not doctors; we cannot guarantee your long-term safety in the face of certain environmental hazards you may encounter in your exploration. Similarly, we are not lawyers; we cannot advise you of the legality of various expeditions nor can we reassure you that the legal climate where you live will not contort your good or harmless intentions out of fear.

The safety and protection of those who practice the art of exploring, and the appreciation and preservation of those sites they explore, are the foremost concerns of this book.

INTRODUCTION

This book is meant as an introduction to the hobby of urban exploration, a sort of interior tourism that allows the curious-minded to discover a world of behind-the-scenes sights like forgotten subbasements, engine rooms, rooftops, abandoned mineshafts, secret tunnels, abandoned factories and other places not designed for public usage. Urban exploration is a thrilling, mind-expanding hobby that encourages our natural instincts to explore and play in our own environment. Urban exploration inspires people to create their own adventures, like when they were kids, instead of buying the pre-packaged adventures too many of us settle for. And it nurtures a sense of wonder in the everyday spaces we inhabit that few local history books could ever hope to recreate. Perhaps because the hobby combines straightforward appreciation of a site's aesthetic beauty and historical significance with elements of risk and creative problem solving, explorers can feel a vivid, exhilarating awareness of the urban environment that can be almost overwhelming in its intensity during and following an enjoyable expedition. It's a rush.

For too many people, urban living consists of mindless travel between work, shopping and home, oblivious to the countless wonders a city offers. Most people think the only things worth looking at in our cities and towns are those safe and sanitized attractions that require an admission fee. Their alertness has atrophied due to the lack of any real adventure in their lives, and their senses have dulled to help them cope with the cacophony of noise and meaningless spectacle that surrounds them. It's no wonder people feel unfulfilled and uninvolved as they are corralled through the maze of velvet ropes on their way out through the gift shop.

Rather than passively consuming entertainment, urban explorers strive to actually create authentic experiences, by making discoveries that allow them to participate in the secret workings of cities and structures, and to appreciate fantastic, obscure spaces that might otherwise go completely neglected. There's certainly more to the hobby than just having a good time: the new and deeper perspectives explorers can get from standing atop the city, or peering up at it from underground, or just coming to appreciate the extent and complexity of the world behind the scenes, are truly incredible. But it's also just unbelievably fun. When you fully embrace the urban exploration mindset, the city becomes a wonderful playground, and playing in it seems like working your way through a fun and challenging adventure game — except it's real.

Urban exploration is an incredibly enlightening hobby, and the world would be a better place if more people thought of themselves as urban explorers. In part, this guide is intended to encourage more people to engage in the harmless exploration of the urban environment I've always promoted in *Infiltration*. In addition, I hope this guide will help expand some people's definition of urban exploration, so that they can broaden their horizons and enjoy the hobby more. Since abandoned buildings are probably the most obvious and photogenic places explorers frequent, many have begun to think of the hobby as encompassing little more than exploring abandoned buildings, with maybe the occasional tunnel thrown in for good measure. As I hope to point out in this guide, such places are wonderful and beautiful, but they aren't the end-all-and-be-all of urban exploration. Structures and infrastructures are interesting in all phases of their life cycles, and places that are under construction or in use can hold as much wonder, beauty and opportunity for adventure as abandoned places.

As I've disclaimed before, I don't pretend to be the world's most talented or most experienced urban explorer, just an enthusiastic chronicler and booster of the hobby. As well as spending a lot of time exploring a wide variety of settings myself, I've also spent a decade corresponding with a few hundred explorers worldwide and paying close attention to their expedition reports. Much of my advice in this guide is based on what I've heard from others. It's mainly written for people who are relatively new to the hobby, but I hope experienced explorers will get something out of it nonetheless, even if it's just the inspiration to write better guidebooks of their own.

Hey, What Are You Doing Down There?
So, what is and isn't urban exploration? Speaking broadly, urban exploration consists of seeking out, visiting and documenting interesting human-made spaces, most typically abandoned buildings, construction sites, active buildings, stormwater drains, utility tunnels and transit tunnels, though with lots of other possibilities on top of those basics. The areas explorers are interested in are usually neglected by or off-limits to the general public, though there are some exceptions to this, and it's certainly not the case that urban exploration always involves trespassing. Explorers flock to opportunities to see interesting buildings and tunnels

that are temporarily opened to the public, and most are quick to take advantage of chances to visit special areas with permission from friends and relatives. Explorers are also quick to take advantage of legal grey areas, such as touring stormwater drains which in certain municipalities isn't technically illegal. So, exploring isn't synonymous with recreational trespassing.

While urban exploration is often grouped with or even called "infiltration" or "urban adventure", in reality those are three different activities that share a great degree of overlap. All three are great, and many people who enjoy one branch enjoy them all, but they have some distinctions.

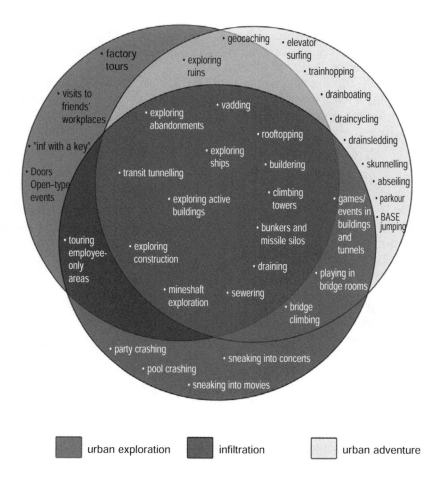

urban exploration   infiltration   urban adventure

Sneaking into a pool, a movie theatre or a concert is infiltration, but it isn't really urban exploration, since your primary goal isn't to see a place but to engage in or watch another activity. Often with infiltration the focus is on overcoming a human element, sometimes just for the strategic pleasure of doing so. Playing hide-and-go-seek in an abandoned building or climbing up a bridge for the joy of the climb is urban adventure, but it isn't really urban exploration, since it's more about playing somewhere cool rather than exploring somewhere cool. With urban adventure–type activities, the challenges (if there are challenges beyond having a good time) are usually self-imposed, rather than being simply the price one must pay in order to view a particular location. They're often more stunt-oriented and focussed on the fantastic final picture or story of the adventurer's achievement. On the previous page is a rough Venn diagram showing where different infiltration/urban adventure/urban exploration activities might fall in relation to one another.

While infiltration and urban adventure are both worth checking out (indeed, infiltration's even worth publishing a whole zine about, in my humble opinion), this book is primarily concerned with the activities that fall into the top left circle: those that are focussed on finding, exploring and documenting locations off the beaten path.

The Risk to Reward Ratio

It's probably fair to describe urban exploration as a somewhat dangerous hobby, though it's less dangerous than many would have you believe. From what I've heard anecdotally, only a couple of self-described urban explorers have ever died while exploring, so statistically speaking urban exploration is slightly less likely to kill you than lawn bowling. But explorers do get injured or trapped from time to time, and if we weren't extremely careful we'd probably get killed every once in a while.

One common argument against urban exploration is that someone might get hurt and then society would be responsible for saving them, but if this logic worked for urban exploration, it would presumably hold true for far more dangerous activities like white water rafting, contact sports, bungee jumping, parachute diving, downhill skiing, driving, cycling or mountain climbing, which all have much higher fatality rates. Yet people do those things all the time, and as long as they get proper permission from the authorities, no one condemns them for risking their lives and the lives of those around them. What the people who say urban exploration is wrong and bad because it's dangerous really mean is that it's wrong and bad because it's dangerous and they didn't get permission. This is a weird way to think.

In life, there are needless risks and acceptable risks. If practiced carefully, urban exploration need involve only acceptable risks, but all exploration activities should be evaluated in terms of the risk to reward ratio. This hobby isn't about stunts, and something doesn't become more worthwhile simply because it's more dangerous. It makes sense to run through a gauntlet if the reward awaiting you at the end is likely to be a really tasty slice of fresh, warm, homemade blueberry pie topped with high-quality ice cream with little bits of vanilla bean in it and everything, but it's foolish to do so if it's likely that all that's waiting for you at the end is a dried-up slice of generic, store-bought apple pie. You can get that anywhere. My parents buy it all the time. It's not that good.

Similarly, don't try to climb over a razor wire fence and run past a pack of hungry dogs unless you're confident that they're guarding something pretty incredible, because you're going to be really annoyed if you lose a foot just so you can stare at a nondescript electrical closet. While it's true that danger isn't the ultimate evil, this hobby isn't about the quest for danger so much as a willingness to accept certain levels of danger in the course of the quest to discover and document forgotten or neglected realms. You know, like Indiana Jones or Lara Croft, but without the stealing.

Conventional wisdom holds that tension is bad and to be avoided, so many people will suggest that a good way to choose the right risk to reward ratio is to do only what you feel comfortable with. In my humble opinion, this advice is on par with telling an aspiring Olympic athlete to exercise only until he or she feels tired. It is good and healthy to push yourself a little and to do things that make you slightly uncomfortable. If you continually stretch the boundaries of your comfort zone by doing things that make you a little nervous and a little uneasy, you'll gradually expand the range of activities with which you feel comfortable. (This is how that whole "gateway drug" business works, too, I think, but you should go exploring instead of doing drugs — both activities are addictive and mind-expanding, but exploration is cheaper.) Most people feel extremely nervous the first time they climb a fence into a construction site or stroll past an employee into an off-limits area. But after you've done these things a dozen times they become second nature, allowing you to save your stores of nerve for larger challenges.

To be clear, I'm not suggesting that you fully abandon your comfort zone and leap towards what terrifies you. If you're claustrophobic and afraid of the dark, don't try to cure yourself by single-handedly wriggling through a narrow drain without a flashlight late one night — the mantra "mind over matter" may lose some of its potency once you're enveloped in darkness and finding it difficult to breathe. Nor should you assume you're braver or more rational than you actually are: don't suddenly realize that your morbid fear of insane ghosts with chainsaws isn't as suppressed as you thought it was when you're deep in the tunnel system under an abandoned asylum. Rather, figure out with what you are and are not comfortable and gradually work on getting more comfortable with some of the things that make you nervous. This strategy works because when you have a realistic idea of your strengths and weaknesses, your common sense will function much more reliably. It's when you start deceiving yourself and telling yourself that you're the biggest bad-ass in town, when in reality you're easily shaken, that your common sense starts becoming unreliable. Get an honest picture of what you can and cannot handle, both mentally and physically. People get caught or hurt less because they were doing something that made them nervous or scared than because they did not have an informed and realistic sense of their capabilities.

A lot of people, including a lot of people I've gone exploring with, deny their own nervousness because they think it's embarrassing, but personally I much prefer to go exploring with people who get nervous and admit it. Nervousness is like fire. If it gets out of hand, it can consume and destroy you, but if you keep a little bit of it under your control, it can help guide the way. Look at the word itself: nerv-ous. It means fearful, but it also means full of nerves.

When you're exploring, your nerves are your allies. Being full of nerves makes you acutely aware of your surroundings, and that is both a very pleasant and a very useful state of mind. If you are keeping quiet and moving carefully, while looking and listening intensely, you are much less likely to fall into an unseen hole or run into an unexpected guard. One reason I hesitate to explore in large groups is that people tend to relax when they're around three or four friends, because they feel secure in a group and perhaps also because they don't want the others to see that they're nervous. But five relaxed people are a hell of a lot more likely to run into trouble than two nervous people.

TRAINING

As tempting as it is to quickly gather up your ten closest friends and head into the subway tunnels on your inaugural expedition, that's a recipe for disaster. As in videogames, you should start with basic training missions to get a feel for the controls before you attempt "apocalypse"-level difficulty. While most explorers train themselves by just going out there and exploring, a little advance training doesn't hurt, and knowing what you're doing could keep you from making things worse for yourself and others later on. At the very least, it's a good idea to know what you and your cohorts are and aren't capable of before your skills are tested under more stressful conditions.

Training involves both off-the-job and on-the-job pursuits. Off-the-job, exercising and practicing certain exploration-related skills need not be tedious; if you do it with games and competitions, it can be a lot of fun in itself. On-the-job training is even more likely to hold your attention, since it is actual exploring, just in a setting where you're unlikely to face injuries or other punishments if something goes wrong. And sometimes you make some pretty interesting finds on those little practice missions before you level up.

Fitness

Urban exploration isn't a sport — anything that requires so much nerdy research and geeky aesthetic sensibility doesn't fit with our culture's understanding of a sport — but it can occasionally require some physical fitness. Endurance, strength, speed, balance and flexibility are all useful to explorers. Endurance will take you those four kilometres up the storm drain to the waterfall, or get you up that 34th flight of stairs that takes you to the roof. Strength will help you pull open that door that's rusted shut, or hoist yourself up onto that ladder that's dangling two feet overhead. Speed will help you run away when the alarm sounds, or when someone decides to chase you. Balance will help you walk along the rafters without falling five storeys to your death. Being flexible and in good shape will help you make it through those awkward climbs and squeezes and make you less likely to strain muscles or otherwise injure yourself while exploring.

There's an additional benefit to exercise. While the world of public spaces is increasingly built to comfortably accommodate people who are

Occasionally explorers have to squeeze themselves through inhumanly small spaces in order to get to their goal.

between 50 and 100 pounds over-weight, the world behind the scenes hasn't yet caught up to this exciting new trend. Being skinny is a major asset for an explorer. If you haven't done a lot of exploring you may not appreciate just how often you'll come across spaces where just a couple inches of surplus girth will make the difference between tri-umph and defeat. Explorers squeeze, or try to squeeze, their way through slightly ajar windows, between pipes in steam tunnels, through narrow hatches, up air ducts, through tiny chatieres ("cat holes") carved into stone or bricks, between stairs in staircases, through the metal grates of storm drains and into all manner of tight tunnels never meant to accommodate people. In these situations, the only thing more frustrating than being the only one in your group who can squeeze through a particular opening is being the only one who can't. If you're significantly heavier than the rest of the people you go exploring with, you may want to bring a good book.

Giving Up Smoking
While it's certainly true that many explorers smoke, smoking and exploring aren't very compatible, for a number of reasons. People who insist on smoking while exploring can potentially create a number of problems for their group. Smoke and lit cigarettes reduce your stealth-iness. Dropped ashes and cigarette butts leave clear signs that someone was present. Improperly extinguished cigarettes are a fire hazard in old wooden buildings.

Even smokers who are smart enough not to smoke while they're exploring face a few disadvantages. People who smoke regularly gener-ally have diminished senses of smell, and tend to get out of breath more easily than non-smokers. Many smokers have coughs that are prone to happen at the wrong time. According to many scientists, smokers are at least four times as likely to suffer health problems due to asbestos as non-smokers — some estimates are a lot higher. So, smoking and exploring aren't ideally matched to one another.

Climbing

The ability to climb fences and walls is among the most useful skills an explorer can cultivate, and it's not a tricky one to practice. Climbing trees is pretty fun, and it's also decent climbing practice, at least a decent warm-up to the more advanced practice you would have to pay to get in a climbing gym or at the Y. The basic concepts of searching for, finding, evaluating and then finally employing different hand- and footholds, while navigating a vertical path towards the top, are the same whether you're climbing a tree, a rock wall, a mountain or a building. If you dislike nature, or don't have access to it, you can practice your climbing skills in a playground. This doesn't involve just crawling up the tube slide backwards; there are also monkey bars to fool around on and swing sets to climb.

After you've graduated from this first level, grab a friend and find some fences that you won't get in trouble for climbing — maybe a wooden house fence, wire fencing around a local basketball or tennis court or the vertical steel bars fencing in a local school — and just practice safely hauling yourself up and over. Practice

Ethan demonstrates the proper technique for chimneying up a building, with the back to the wall and his legs pushing.

both solo climbing and climbing with the help of a friend. Experiment to see if a running start helps you or not. Pay attention to how your clothing and footwear affect your climb — if you find a wire fence with narrow spacing in which you simply can't get a foothold, try taking off your shoes and tucking in your socks between your big toe and the rest of your foot for an improvised set of tabi socks. Try sticking a board between the links in a chain link fence to make an improvised step. Try climbing with and without gloves. Notice how you occasional-

Ensure that you have hands and feet before attempting a difficult climb.

ly need to employ different climbing tactics on different sides of the same fence: getting out isn't always as easy as getting in. Work on your speed — maybe have your friend pretend to chase you over the fence. Move from shorter fences to taller fences, and from easier ones to harder ones. If anyone comes along and asks what you're doing, just say you're practicing climbing — there's no law against that. (Throwing a ball over a fence also provides a good excuse for you to climb over and retrieve it, but you probably won't need an excuse.)

For your next trick, work on rope climbing. Even if you hated it when you were in gym like I did, you'll find that being able to shimmy up a rope can be a truly useful skill in situations where getting up to a second-storey window or a fire escape is the only possible way into a building. After you get to the point where you can use a knotted rope to help to climb up the side of a building without too much trouble, try free climbing the rope without bracing yourself on anything. Practice dismounting from the rope onto a staircase or fire escape. You can either work on this until you think you're good enough at it to do it while exploring, or just admit to yourself that you're not much of a rope climber. The one thing you don't want is to assume that you'll be able to climb a rope while exploring without any problems, only to find out you just don't have it in you when it's too late.

Playing Games
Being successful in urban exploration requires a huge variety of skills, ranging from hiding to climbing to fast-talking, and sometimes it's helpful to cultivate those skills while you aren't actively exploring. Hobbies tan-

gentially related to urban exploration, such as trainhopping, geocaching, parkour and buildering (see Glossary for definitions), can all teach handy skills useful in exploration. So can simpler fun-oriented pursuits. Hide-and-seek is a classic urban exploration training game. The basic idea behind hide-and-seek is for one person, dubbed "it", to count to a preset number (say, 30) while all the other participants scurry off and hide anywhere they wish within a given area. Then they are sought. For explorers' purposes, this game works especially well when played indoors somewhere with multiple levels, and tweaked in such a way as to allow stealthy players to move from their hiding places and sneak back to "home" and become "safe" (this propagandistic terminology was clearly worked out by parents). In another hide-and-seek variant, played in the dark and sometimes called Bloody Murder, each person who is caught treacherously joins the "dark side" and aids her captor in seeking out her erstwhile colleagues in concealment. This game is totally awesome.

My friend Sean and I used to play a game of our own invention called Can't Be Seen. It probably should have had a cooler name, but oh well, at least it's memorable. Wearing dark clothes and equipped with two-way walkie-talkies and flashlights, we would attempt to travel across town by as direct a route as possible without anyone spotting us. There was no precise way to measure our level of success, since people who did see us probably didn't realize the greatness of their achievement and thus generally failed to tell us they'd spotted us. But we usually knew and admitted to ourselves when we'd screwed up and taken too long to dive behind the hedges or roll beneath the truck, and we kept a mental tally of our failures. This was not only one of the most fun games of all time, it was also a risk-free way to practice our skills at orienteering, running, hiding, scouting ahead, moving stealthily and communicating either silently or with walkie-talkies. Only its two-dimensional nature, and the difficulty of playing it in a highly populated urban setting, keep it from being the perfect urban exploration training game. It is, however, fun.

Laser tag is also fun. While urban exploration does not generally involve the use of futuristic weaponry, it does involve hiding, moving stealthily, navigating complex multi-level mazes and thinking three-dimensionally. Paintball, while a little more messy, painful and expensive, teaches many of the same skills as laser tag, including working as a team. The only big problem with the shooting games is their focus on aim. Aim is one of the few skills that's of not much use to explorers. An old-fashioned game of capture the flag, played in an urban setting, might be better training. Capture the flag is cheaper and requires less silly clothing and expensive equipment, and it's damn good exercise, especially if you're competitive.

On-the-Job
It would be nice if we could all train until we were in peak physical and mental condition, but of course it's tough to resist the temptation to get out onto, or under, the street and put your skills to the test in a realistic setting. Until such time as proper urban exploration training academies can be founded worldwide, you can improvise by on-the-job training through minor missions that aren't likely to result in anyone being hospitalized or arrested, but still provide useful experience in sneaking and seeking. (Please don't be an idiot and head into active subway tunnels on your first expedition.)

It's easy to arrange small missions that won't have any real negative consequences if you screw up. At your own school or workplace, or in any interesting buildings your friends or family can get you into legitimately, try to examine the interesting areas while not being seen by anyone. Hide your visitor pass or employee badge and then try to map out the whole building without being questioned. When you get a lapel pin at a museum, a hand stamp at a concert, a temporary visitor pass at an office or any sort of similar visible proof of valid admission, conceal it and then try to talk your way around its absence without showing your receipt or pass to anyone unless it is absolutely demanded. When you go out of town, sneak around your own hotel and, when dealing with employees, don't offer any proof that you're a hotel guest unless you must. These kinds of exercises offer you good practice at sneaking, looking innocent, fast-talking and dealing with stressful situations without actually putting you at risk.

While on-the-job training missions can certainly be quite challenging, the line between practice missions and real missions can be drawn at the point where the external obstacles become greater than the self-imposed obstacles. In those situations, do away with any artificial handicaps, prepare fully and focus on performing as well as you possibly can. You will not get additional shadowpoints because you wore a blindfold while you tried to sneak into a train tunnel at night — you will just get caught or hurt, thereby making things worse for not only yourself but for everyone else. By being careful while you're exploring, you're doing a favour to the whole urban exploration community.

RECRUITING

It can be very helpful to find a few friends you can drag along on your expeditions. While one person can often do an excellent and thorough scouting job, in most situations you shouldn't do much intensive exploring alone, since the areas we visit are often areas where you won't be found for a while. There are a few exceptions, of course, and you'll probably find you make more and more exceptions the more you want to get somewhere and the less your friends do, but try not to make too many.

Besides the safety benefits of having someone else along to give you a hand if you get into trouble (or to go get help if you accidentally get into real trouble), there are also the exploratory benefits of having someone to give you a boost, to hold something open while you climb through or to keep an eye out while you do something suspicious. You also have someone else who can open something after you've loosened it. Having an extra pair of eyes and ears is extremely handy, and having someone else's common sense is invaluable, especially if yours, like mine, tends to get muted when you're excited about something. Many of the best expeditions I've been on wouldn't have been possible if I'd been going solo, and in quite a few other cases I've had a sense that I could have found some fantastic places if only I'd had someone else with me. Exploring is also more fun with a friend or two.

Numbers

While I strongly recommend bringing one or two friends along, I'm not keen on exploring in large groups. There are plusses to such groups, sure: it's fun to be around a lot of people, and it feels safe knowing that you'll probably outnumber any unpleasant people you might encounter. (Whether or not it is actually any safer is debatable, but it certainly feels that way.) You can also draw upon a larger skill set if, for example, your group has an expert climber, an expert sneaker, an expert cartographer, an expert photographer, an expert fast-talker and an expert... strong guy. (You don't need a cleric.) But when you enter in force it really feels more like an invasion than an infiltration. The sense of danger and stealth evaporates. The group can only move as quickly as its slowest member, sneak as quietly as its noisiest member, squeeze through openings as small as its largest member and, often, behave as intelligently as its stupidest member. It only takes one person deciding to see what a button does to ruin the trip for everyone! Similarly, if one person in the group does something stupid like steal or break something, the rest of the group is likely to be punished more harshly on that person's account. It's tougher to keep a large group focussed, so people may hurry ahead to shine their flashlights on something they find interesting, wander away to have a smoke or hang back to take some flash photographs. It's common for larger groups to inadvertently break down into several smaller groups, making things more chaotic. Unless everyone in the group is experienced and focussed, the odds of six people sneaking past a guard without being noticed are very slim. Not surprisingly, large exploring groups tend to get busted disproportionately often.

There may be strength in numbers, but there is stealth in keeping those numbers small, and when you're exploring stealth beats strength any day.

Another consideration regarding numbers is the number of initiates one should bring along on expeditions. While it is certainly noble for you to share the joy of exploring with people who are new to the hobby, unless you're visiting somewhere quite simple and safe, I'd recommend not bringing more than one novice on any given expedition. On tricky trips, new explorers need to be watched and tutored carefully, so you can keep them quiet with frequent shushing, repeatedly remind them not to take or damage anything, warn them to conceal their flashlight beam, tell them to not to smoke while you're tunnelling, caution them about cameras and alarms, explain why it's a bad idea to take flash photographs on a rooftop at night, advise them not to take needless risks and so on. Things that seem like common sense to experienced explorers are often nowhere near as commonsensical as you might suppose, and you don't want to put yourself in a situation where you're worrying more about the people you're with than the obstacles of the place that you're exploring.

Sex

A nice thing to be, if you are one, or a nice thing to bring along, if you can get one, is a girl. If you are a guy, you may want to ask a member of the fairer sex to come along with you when you explore inhabited buildings, particularly places like churches and hotels. Except in a few scenarios — such as at construction sites, or in monasteries — women generally come under much less suspicion than men, since it's a well documented fact that girls are made of sugar and spice and everything nice. Who would risk getting mud on that? For most people, the idea of a woman deliberately going somewhere she's not supposed to be just doesn't make any sense. Capitalize on this ignorance! At the risk of making broad generalizations, women are also nice to have along since they tend to be better at fast-talking than men, and tend to have better instincts and intuition than men. While I don't believe in ESP or anything like that, I do believe that some people are better at picking up vibes than others, and personally I tend to trust those vibes. Trusting my own intuition and the intuition of others — especially women — has saved me from bad situations on multiple occasions.

If you are a woman, you may want to ask a member of the not-as-fair sex to come along with you when you explore unpopulated or highly underpopulated areas. This is not because you need someone else to act as your bodyguard, but simply because creeps are more likely to be creepy when they encounter a woman (or a group of women) without male accompaniment. It's tough to say exactly why this is, though it probably has something to do with sexism and cowardice. And, to keep things fair by making a broad generalization in favour of men, guys I've explored with tend to be better with three-dimensional spatial relationships than women I've explored with, and thus are generally better at navigating and mapping complex structures and systems. It's tough to say why this is... maybe videogames?

Age

Most active explorers are between the ages of 15 and 35, though there are many people older than this who occasionally dabble in the hobby, and most people get their first taste of wandering into storm drains, construction sites and abandoned buildings when they are kids, before their sense of adventure has been blunted and dulled by consumer culture. (It always saddens me when someone reads *Infiltration* and says to me, "Wow, this is so cool! I used to do this when I was younger, and it was the best!" They don't know why they stopped.

Most people are probably mature enough to start exploring by their early teens, and probably aren't too old until past retirement age, and then only because of the physical restrictions. I love looking at old buildings with old people, because they match, and older people often have great stories and a wonderful appreciation for the way places used to be. I generally don't go exploring with people under 18 any more, but this isn't because I don't enjoy exploring with them; it's just because I don't want to be charged with endangering a minor or corrupting the youth. (So: youth, be obedient. Elders, come with me.)

Younger explorers face some advantages and some disadvantages. Obviously younger people have the advantage of near-endless endurance and enthusiasm, but they're also more likely to suffer from problems with impatience and overconfidence. These are all huge stereotypes, of course, but there's still something to them. On the plus side, a group consisting entirely of teenagers is much more likely to be casually dismissed as a bunch of bored kids than a group of people in their late 20s and 30s. On the minus side, a group of three or more teenagers is likely to attract some attention from guards, employees or nosy people generally, and is likely to get shooed out of places like offices or public buildings more quickly than older explorers might. Teenagers asking for directions at a concierge or a security desk are much more likely to be treated with suspicion.

A group of explorers in their late 20s and early 30s, conversely, has a much easier time walking through hotels, convention centres, office buildings and most other occupied spaces without being noticed, because people are much quicker to assume that adults are somewhere on business — which is widely perceived to be the only legitimate reason to be anywhere — and to know what they're doing. The drawback is that when older explorers *do* get caught they're less likely to be dismissed as bored kids and more likely to be considered improperly socialized adults in need of reprogramming. They are thus more likely to have to explain themselves to authorities that can't imagine why anyone would do something as bizarre as wander around appreciating interesting structures. Middle-aged and older people probably get even more slack in this department, simply because they're more likely to be deemed harmless, sweet and grandparenty.

Appearance

It's sadly superficial, alas, but when you're visiting a populated place, it's not a good idea to bring along people who will get noticed. Biased and awful though it is, it just doesn't make sense to take people with attention-getting tattoos, piercings, haircuts, hair colours or clothes — unless, of course, they're willing and able to adapt and throw their personal style out the window for the evening. Unfortunately, this excludes a lot of cool people, but we can only hope that the joy they get from having a pink mohawk equals or exceeds the joy they would have taken from sneaking into a bank tower at night, because they can't have both.

Moustaches and beards, as distinguished or funny as they can be, aren't great accessories for urban explorers. Not only do they provide a handy distinguishing feature guards can look for when they're plucking your image off the surveillance videotapes, but people just naturally tend to regard men with facial hair with greater suspicion, wondering exactly what they have to hide. The bad cowboy always had a moustache. The good cowboy didn't. As a more practical consideration, respirators work better on clean-shaven faces, meaning that those utility tunnel explorers without moustaches and beards are less likely to die of asbestosis. Explorers who don't already have facial hair should probably stay that way, and those who aren't too attached to their moustaches, beards, permastubble, soul-patches, van dykes, goatees or muttonchop sideburns may want to consider giving them up.

Those with hair flair are lucky to have the option of getting rid of it; unfortunately, some people are going to have a lot of trouble becoming great explorers of inhabited spaces through absolutely no fault of their own. Subtle or overt biases against dark-skinned people run pretty deep in many places, and biases against Middle Eastern–looking people are in the midst of an unfortunate renaissance. While no one should abandon the idea of going exploring based solely on their skin colour or ethnicity, people with darker complexions should be aware that they face longer odds of going through doors unnoticed. This is sad but undeniably true.

Ethics

Beyond the "do not enter" signs and outside the protected zone, you and your friends are free to behave as you really are, and you don't want to disappoint yourselves. When you're considering potential exploratory partners, try to enlist people who you know have firm consciences. Keep in mind that these people will not necessarily be your traditional goody-goodies; a lot of people who usually behave well do so because they're mindlessly obeying rules and laws, not because they're carefully considering which actions are helpful and right and which are harmful and wrong. People who think laws are more important than ethics are exactly the sorts who will wander into an abandoned area and be so confused by their sudden freedom and lack of supervision that they'll start breaking windows and urinating on the floor. Law-free zone, right? That means they can do anything they feel like, right?

Wrong, of course, which is why it's important to seek out people with positive ethics, who will show respect for sites by not breaking anything, taking anything, defacing anything or even littering while exploring. From what I've seen, people who don't use the law as a substitute for their own moral compass tend to develop stronger consciences and greater self-discipline simply through greater use — kind of like how trees that grow outside are stronger than trees that grow indoors, because they've been blown by the wind often enough that they've learned to stand straight on their own. Some people have the idea that urban explorers are generally troublemakers and ne'er-do-wells; on the contrary, I would say that urban explorers are generally better behaved, more considerate and more polite than the vast majority of the population, if perhaps slightly more inclined towards geekiness and social awkwardness. In any meeting of a group of experienced explorers, the conversation is likely to frequently turn to ethics, since explorers care a great deal about these issues and feel it's important to continually consider what is right and what is wrong.

So, when you're enlisting fellow explorers, it's a good idea to avoid people who seem more excited by the opportunity to be naughty and "anarchistic" than by the opportunity to discover and appreciate some cool places. People who have been vandals, thieves or all-purpose troublemakers in the past can certainly reform and make good explorers: a lot of people who engage in that sort of nonsense when they're younger aren't really eager to deface and destroy so much as they're eager to rebel and have some non-commercial fun. If you can show them the light, offer them a more constructive way to channel their energies and teach them the all-important skill of appreciating without tagging or taking, more power to you.

Unfortunately, when a lot of people first start exploring they feel like they have to claim some souvenir or treasure from a site in order to make the experience real, or tangible, or worthwhile. They can't help it — they've been raised in a world built around gift shops. I was certainly guilty of this simple thinking in my younger days. But the broader urban exploration community has quite wisely adopted the Sierra Club's motto of "take nothing but pictures, leave nothing but footprints." The advantages to this mindset, both to individual explorers and to the hobby as a whole, are innumerable. When you take a cool relic from a site, you not only vastly increase the potential charges against you if you are caught, you also up the odds that security will be increased in the future. More importantly, you diminish the experience for all future explorers and damage the reputation of the urban exploration community as a whole.

There's no need to make exploration about souvenirs. What was cool about *Raiders of the Lost Ark* was not that dumb ark — it was the running through the tunnels and avoiding the traps and dodging the Nazis and sneaking into all those cool places. You don't need to take any souvenirs to make both the experience and the site your own; if anything, you diminish your ownership of the place by defacing it or taking away a piece of it. The quotation I use to explain this Zennish own-without-acquiring mindset is from comedian Steven Wright: "I have a large seashell collection which I keep scattered all over the beaches of the world... maybe you've seen it?"

You share a similar collection of relics scattered all around the buildings of the world, and you won't make them any more yours just by depriving everyone else. You'll reduce yourselves into mere robbers in the eyes of anyone who catches you. So, make sure both you and the people you're with remember that ethics don't disappear on the far side of the "do not enter" sign — if anything, they become more important.

For this reason, it's not a good idea to explore with strangers. I'm not saying that I haven't done it, repeatedly — merely that it's not a good idea, as I've found from experience. You have no idea what criminal record a stranger might have, how crazy they'll be, how willing they'll be to compromise their ethics in "certain situations" (such as when they *really, really* feel like it — some ridiculous people actually think the intensity of their desire factors into the ethical equation) or what sort of bizarre reactions they'll have to a tense situation. (Abandoning you? Crying? Confessing? Panicking? Freezing up? They all happen.) It's much more difficult to tell a fellow explorer to go put something back or stop writing his or her name on the wall than it is if everyone just understands in advance that nothing will be taken or damaged, period. Go with people you trust, who you know will treat both the location and their fellow explorers with respect. Go with people whose reactions you can anticipate.

Christianity and most world religions sum up their moral principles with a "golden rule", usually summed up as "do unto others as you would have them do unto you". This is good, but I like the Jewish take on the rule even better: "Whatever is harmful to yourself, do not to your fellow person. That is the whole of the law, the rest is merely a commentary."

SNEAKING

Sneaking around is a lot of fun, but it's important to remember that real-life sneaking is different from videogame sneaking. In games like Elevator Action, Impossible Mission and Thief, being seen is always bad so you should always be sneaking. In real life, where most people are not enemy agents or evil robots (or at least so they'd have you think), it's not so much being seen that's bad as being seen engaging in certain suspicious activities. Being seen walking down a public hallway or waiting for a passenger elevator is almost always fine, because people do that kind of thing. Being seen climbing a ladder or peering through a keyhole is bad, because people don't do that kind of thing unless they're up to something.

The trick, then, is to only be stealthy when you need to be. While it's always smart to have an idea whether or not there's someone behind you, you really don't need to keep looking over your shoulder unless you're getting ready to try a few doors, and you really don't need to tiptoe down a hallway unless... well, actually, you never need to tiptoe down a hallway. Tiptoeing is a scam invented by security forces so they'd be able to spot potential troublemakers more easily. You can walk quietly without making yourself look like a complete freak.

Moving Silently
When most people think of stealth they think of crouching low and hiding in the shadows, but staying silent is just as important. If you spend a lot of time trying to move silently, you'll come to loathe certain types of floors, particularly creaky wooden floors. (And if you have to sneak around outside, you'll come to absolutely despise dry leaves and gravel.) Conversely, you'll find that while linoleum and plastic tiles may not look all that attractive, they certainly are good for sneaking about on. Rugs and carpets can also be good, provided they aren't resting atop creaky wooden floors. When you're dealing with a creaky floor, try to find the part of the floor that creaks the least — generally, floors and stairs are most secure near the walls and in the spots above floor joists (that is, where the rows of nails are). You move more quietly when your muscles are relaxed, so try to move fluidly and use all your joints. Wear shoes with soft soles if you're able. Try not to cough or sneeze. Pay attention to air vents that might carry your voice elsewhere. Turn off your cell phone and your radio.

No matter how much of a ninja you are, you're probably going to make at least some noise while you're moving about. This probably won't be a problem as long as you don't make noise in the steady, recognizable pattern of approaching footfalls, which millions of years of evolution have trained people to listen for. People working late at night can ignore the occasional click or swish as long as they don't hear a series of clicks and swishes that adds up to a mental image of someone stealthily moving down a darkened hallway toward them with a knife. If at some point you feel you've accidentally made too much noise, pause for a short while to give whomever you're sneaking past time to forget about it. If the people you're sneaking around are occasionally getting up and down, you may want to pace your movement so you're moving when they're moving, as they're unlikely to hear your quiet motion atop their own deafening activity.

Moving Stealthily

As fun as it is to behave like a ninja, in my experience that whole staying-low-and-slinking-unseen-from-shadow-to-shadow business doesn't really have much practical application for urban exploration, except in a few situations, such as when one is approaching a building from the outside at night. While it would certainly be thrilling to constantly crouch, hide and slither along on your belly beneath the rug, for our variety of sneaking, spies make better role models than ninjas. In the sort of settings most explorers visit, moving stealthily mainly requires you to move slowly and steadily (since more rapid movement is more likely to attract the eye), keep to the darker parts of the passage or room, pay close attention to other people's possible lines of sight and choose those paths that will least expose you to any observers. Don't turn the lights on or off — leave them as they are. If the area is very dark and you don't want to risk bringing out a light source, just wait patiently for a few minutes and let your eyes adjust to the darkness. Pay attention to your shadows and your reflections. Walk near walls instead of out in the open, don't pass directly in front of windows, avoid being backlit and try not to look tremendously suspicious while you're doing all of this.

When you're sneaking through even a very sparsely populated area, you'll look very suspicious if it's obvious that you're constantly looking around and peering over your shoulder. Even in situations where you plan not to be seen at all, bear in mind that that is merely plan A, and that plan A disappears as soon as you realize you're on camera or someone's walking behind you. So, even while you're actively pursuing plan A, you should try not to jeopardize plan B, which is to hide in plain sight, being seen but ignored. This means that even as you attempt to move through the site unseen, you should try to avoid suspicious behaviour like crouching, hiding, climbing, checking doors or constantly looking over your shoulder. It's quite possible to walk quietly and stealthily without behaving in such a way that you might as well be wearing a bright yellow shirt that says SKULKER.

Hiding

In some situations, acting like you're supposed to be somewhere, or like you're merely lost, isn't an option. When you hear someone coming but feel you won't be able to either explain your presence or get away, you may want to consider hiding. It's risky, since if you're caught you're really caught, but it normally works, since no one actually expects someone to be hiding unless they're in the middle of a game of hide-and-seek. Quickly slipping behind a door or ducking behind a machine has worked for me on many occasions. In most cases, the person who shows up has no interest in finding you or anyone else — they're just going about their business. By hiding, you're really doing them a favour, by keeping them from being distracted from their important task, and if you can just wait them out for a minute or two, you'll have no trouble either leaving or continuing your exploration unimpeded.

Of course, finding a decent hiding spot really only works when you have a moment of advance warning, as when you hear approaching conversation, or whistling, or keys jingling, or a door being opened. When someone just suddenly turns the corner ahead of you while you're in a darkened utility tunnel two levels underground, or suddenly appears at the far end of an unlit warehouse, don't run for non-existent cover: extinguish your light, stop moving and hope for the best. Movement is the first thing the human eye notices. The second is the human form, so attempt to disguise your silhouette and shadow if possible. If you're able, gradually put your gloved hands over your face or pull your hat down low to hide your eyes and most of your face. If the person leaves the area temporarily, then you have an opportunity to hide or get out of there, but otherwise just stay still until you're confronted. Then you can decide if you want to try to talk your way out of the situation or run for it.

Concealing Light
Urban exploration involves a great deal of wandering around in unlit or insufficiently lit areas while looking for things, but it also involves a lot of trying not to stand out or be seen. For this reason, many explorers worry about methods to reduce or conceal light from their flashlights.

Those fancying themselves secret agents or covert operatives swear by multicoloured gels and filters, contending that using a red lens filter will make light from your flashlight less visible, less reflective and less likely to destroy your night vision. Others find that red light is really only ideal in pitch-black environments, while blue or green light works better in dimly lit areas or in the changing light conditions associated with buildings and tunnels.

Personally, I'm too cheap to go in for such solutions when I can get roughly the same effect just by squeezing a packet of McDonald's ketchup on the lens of my Maglite, even if I have to deal with the sweet tomato smell for the rest of the evening. If you don't care for ketchup, you can employ the simple and old-fashioned technique of just shining the light through the cracks in your fingers, which muffles the light and turns it red, and also gives you a great degree of control over exactly how much light you project in any given room. Placing a coloured balloon, a handkerchief or piece of cloth over the lens does the same trick. Obviously, you need only limit your light this way when you're near windows in a building at night; in a drain, tunnel, basement or enclosed area, you should aim to see all that you can see, and for this, bright white light is your friend. Bright white light also gives you the most realistic sense of perspective, which can keep you from falling down holes and the like, so don't play commando when you don't have to.

Don't Leave a Trace
Naturally, it doesn't do much good to sneak around noiseless and unseen if anyone can just follow your footprints to find you. Although I've mentioned explorers use the motto, "take nothing but pictures, leave nothing but footprints," you really shouldn't leave any footprints, either. If you're outside, favour hard surfaces like metal and rock over pliable surfaces like mud and snow. If you have to walk in mud or snow, try to walk inside the footprints other people have already left behind or leave a false trail. Once inside, dry your feet and do your best to keep them dry. If you go through a damp area, like a moist steam tunnel, try to avoid the puddles. When you can't avoid getting wet, dry your feet off

at the first opportunity so you don't leave a trail behind you. While it's true that your wet footprints will dry up fairly quickly in a hot steam tunnel, you will likely leave a distinctive foot-shaped clean spot on the floor even after the moisture evaporates.

Similarly, in a dirty construction or renovation site, try to avoid leaving handprints or footprints in the dust. When you emerge from the area, wipe away your dirty footprints, especially all around a door or any other sort of operable entrance, as there's no need to draw attention to where you went in or came out. If there's a mat, shaking it out is a good way to conceal footprints quickly.

Incidentally, people who patrol and work in buildings are nowhere near as careful about concealing their footprints as urban explorers tend to be, and these sorts of signs can be glaringly obvious and helpful pointers as to what entrances to use and what doors to pay attention to inside. They also give decent clues about which areas to avoid.

SOCIAL ENGINEERING

Social engineering is a term urban explorers have adopted from the computer hacking community. Hackers use the term to refer to that portion of their craft that deals with talking to people offline, usually over the phone but occasionally in person, in order to get them to allow access or reveal information about their networks. Explorers use the term the same way, though most of our social engineering is accomplished in person, and we're after information about and access to physical systems rather than computer systems. Social engineering skills come into play when you're talking to an employee in the hope of finding out about some tunnels, trying to convince an archivist to allow you access to the blueprints of a particular site, bluffing your way into an event, scamming your way past the front desk, talking someone into holding the door open for you, explaining to a security guard why you're on the roof and in dozens of other similar scenarios. If you intend to explore where there are people present, you must become good at dealing with people.

The best advice I can give you about the ancient art of social engineering is to read and reread Dale Carnegie's classic book *How to Win Friends and Influence People*. Though it's slightly dated, having been written in the 1930s, Carnegie's popular guide provides useful, solid, sincere tips on how to be the kind of person that other people will like, trust and respond to. I strongly recommend you pick up a copy for yourself, but since I know most of you won't (you lazy bastards), I offer this quick summary of the book's most important concepts:

People are self-interested. To get someone to do something for you, show how doing so will help them help themselves. Because people are self-interested, letting them know how they will benefit will motivate them more than simply telling them how much you would appreciate it, how disappointed you would be if they don't or how it is fair. A big part of self-interest is laziness. As Liz once put it to me, "People have rules against everything, unless they like you and breaking the rules would make their lives easier."

People crave attention. Be a good listener and let the other person do the talking. The best way to make other people interested in you is not by convincing them that you are fascinating but by being genuinely interested in them. Always remember and use someone's name when you speak to them, and remember and refer to other details that are important to them.

People crave appreciation and a feeling of importance. Find what is good and interesting in other people (and there's always something), and then emphatically express your sincere appreciation with real compliments, not false flattery. Emphasize the other person's achievements. Attribute good ideas and successes to the other person when possible. Never criticize the other person directly.

People want to be right. Respond positively and reassuringly, and get them doing the same. Don't contradict or argue with people, since you can never really win. Instead, make yourself see their point of view and work out a mutually acceptable solution. Admit when you are wrong and take the blame yourself even when you could share it with others.

Yes, Carnegie would have you become a pretty humble and unassertive person, and this sort of advice might be difficult for you to take if you have a strong ego or a dominating personality. But a little humility can go a long way when you're dealing with people who want to feel important, and it's often easier to get what you want with diplomacy, politeness and subtlety than with stubbornness, intimidation and bluntness.

If a security guard tells you you're breaking the law by being somewhere and you know you're not, what good can it possibly do for you to argue with her? If she doesn't believe you, she'll be angry with you; if you successfully convince her that she's mistaken or foolish, she'll resent you. Realistically, what the law says is irrelevant. If she wants to punish you she'll find a way to do it, legally or illegally, and it's a pretty sure thing that she's going to want to punish you if you contradict her. Your best bet is to show her that you are humble and likable. Apologize. Say you didn't realize you were breaking the law but now you understand that you were in the wrong; convince her that she'll benefit from not punishing you and that her idea (well, technically yours, but who's counting) of letting you off with a warning makes sense, and that you're deeply grateful for her generosity in not going through the whole hassle of talking to her supervisor, writing up reports, calling in the police and all of that rigmarole. (And what's it like for her being a security officer here, anyhow? It sounds hard, but she must have a lot of good stories about catching dumb kids looking for tunnels and stuff.) In the words of a wise t-shirt, diplomacy is the art of letting other people have your way. People who are unable to check their egos are exactly the kind who are eventually going to wind up locking horns with employees, guards or police officers, and they aren't going to come out ahead.

An additional tip I picked up from James Howard Kunstler, another author whose books are worth reading, although more for their thoughts on urban planning than their insights on social engineering, is that in any room containing 100 people, 99 of them each think that they are the only one in the room who doesn't have his or her act together. He's absolutely right, and bearing Kunstler's Law in mind will help you become the one person who does. Your attitude and bearing should express your absolute confidence in your right to be there. If you can't look like a regular worker, look like a visiting supervisor. In the wise words of explorer Wes Modes, "Look important and people will assume that you are."

Telephone Research
As mentioned, for computer hackers, social engineering is usually something done over the phone with the goal of gaining information about or additional access to a given system. While urban explorers do most of our social engineering in person, there are some instances when a little advance research over the phone can be helpful, especially if one is trying to get into a more tricky occupied location. For example, you could call up a commercial building posing as a potential tenant to ask about security policies, the regular building hours and the hours during which services are provided for tenants. If you're going to bluff your way in, it might be helpful to find out the name of the building manager, or the name of a person coordinating an event on the premises. In most cases, knowing a name or two will get you ridiculously far. Once at the location, dropping the names of other employees, or casually using acronyms or other jargon that an authorized person would know, provides subtle reassurance that you are legit, while not actually requiring you to misrepresent yourself.

Appearance
On most explorations you simply want to dress so that you don't stand out from the crowd, but on expeditions that will rely on social engineering you may need to do more than just blend in. You may want to actually appear a cut above the rest. If the circumstances warrant it and your age and appearance will allow you to pull it off, try to look like management, by grooming carefully and dressing in proper business

attire and nice shoes (a shoeshine kit is a great investment for people who explore a lot of active sites.) Enlightened as we believe ourselves to be, human beings simply can't help but judge people on their appearance. Guards and employees are more reluctant to hassle someone with the ability to punish them, and tend to let those who look powerful or influential go about their business unimpeded. At the very least, if they ask "Can I help you?" they're likely to actually be wondering whether or not they can help you, rather than simply using a polite euphemism for "What the hell are you doing here?"

Let Them Do the Talking
While I'm a big advocate of properly researching a place to get the inside scoop on how to act like you're supposed to be there, sometimes it's also necessary, or at least fun, to fly by the seat of your pants. In such cases, you may suddenly find yourself questioned by someone, or needing to speak with someone in order to get through a particular barrier, without having any real idea what might be a plausible reason for you to be there.

In such a case, I recommend just stalling for time and letting the person you're talking to supply your excuse for you. People hate uncomfortable silences and confusing situations and will often rush to supply the information they're looking for themselves. Good stalling phrases include: "I hope you can help me"; "I'm not sure exactly what the procedure is here"; "Do I need to show you some ID?"; "I didn't even know I was going to have to speak to anyone about this" or something of that sort. After you say one of these lines, wait for a response. People generally want to believe that the people around them are rational, so they'll more or less tell you the most rational reason they can conceive of for your presence — "Are you here for the class?"; "You must be looking for Mark"; "Are you one of today's volunteers?"; "I guess you're looking for the way to the observation level"; etc. You don't have to come up with a good reason — you just have to agree to the one they devise for you. Once you perfect the skill of stalling without seeming like you're stalling, this will work for you quite often.

Sometimes sounding prematurely defeated or overly repentant works, by making the other person eager to reassure you. Your saying "I'm really sorry, I thought the lounge might be open to all hotel guests; this is embarrassing.... I'll just go", or "I'm so stupid, I don't know why it didn't occur to me that taking a shortcut through the basement was a security problem, I was just trying to get to my car without going out into the cold and didn't realize, oh my god I probably set off an alarm, I apologize so much..." is likely to prompt the person you're talking to to not only reassure you that you've done nothing wrong but to help you get exactly where you want to go as a way of demonstrating that there are no hard feelings.

Smiling

I know what you're thinking. You're thinking: "Smiling? Smiling gets its own section? I know about smiling! I don't need to learn about smiling! This is an outrage! I want a section about [insert thing you want a section about here], not some section about smiling! Maybe I don't feel like smiling, because I am just a big, fat, complaining jerk!"

While I certainly respect your concerns, and I do admit that this point about smiling is quite straightforward, it is so crucial to your success as an explorer that it really does merit its own section, if only to stress the point.

Smiling is the human equivalent of tail wagging: it tells all those mean dogs you'll encounter out there not only that you're friendly and pleasant, but also that you're calm and confident about your right to be somewhere. A smile says you're at ease, your guard is down, you're on your home turf, you're safe and surrounded by loved ones, you're so very relaxed... ahhhhh, naptime.

Okay I'm back. When you are exploring a populated area, it's usually a good idea to carry around a cheerful, contented expression on your face at all times, even if you don't feel that way at all. Psychological research has demonstrated that having a cheerful facial expression will actually help you *feel* happy; you wouldn't think emotions would flow from your face to your brain, but it turns out they do, so that shows what you know. Your face and brain should be on the same cheerful channel. The thought running through your head should be, "I'm happy, because I belong here." If you pass someone, offer a friendly nod or quick "hi", "good morning" or "how are ya". Don't go much beyond this — you don't want to leave much of an impression, or come off like a giddy freak. You just want to radiate calm contentedness.

Negative emotions have no place on your face. When you pass someone in the hallway and worry that they know you're not supposed to be there, you must smile at them. When someone suddenly stumbles upon you in a slightly off-limits area and you're upset at being found, you must flash him or her a winning smile. When someone scowls at you and asks if they can help you and the first response that pops into your head is "only by minding your own business," you must strain to force those immensely heavy corners of your mouth aloft as you respond by thanking them and requesting directions. Your more natural nervous reactions — like keeping your eyes low, clearing your throat often, fidgeting, jumping at noises, abruptly turning away when you spot people or cameras, etc. — are much more likely to lead to trouble than just walking towards the potential trouble with a clean conscience, confidence and a cheerful disposition. Remember, you belong here and you're not doing anyone any harm.

This all probably seems obvious, and you probably assume that you would have kept on smiling whether I'd devoted a whole section to the subject or not. (Really, you need to get over that.) Indeed, you probably think you're smart enough to have figured out this smiling business all by your lonesome. But frankly I'm not so sure. Pay attention to yourself the next time you're lurking around some grey areas in a sub-basement and I think you'll find that your default expression is not really that cheerful or friendly, but rather a look of concentration or even wariness, perhaps changing to a startled expression if you encounter someone. I know these are my default expressions unless I really make a conscious effort to smile, and from what I've seen most other explorers are the same.

When I'm out with other explorers, I often find I have to remind them that we aren't doing anything wrong, because their body language is crying out that they feel timid and guilty. It's actually pretty tough to smile when you're feeling nervous and have your guard up, and especially tough to smile when you encounter people whom you regard as opponents in a tense strategic struggle. But it's a really good idea, so you should always try to remind yourself to do it.

Confidence

Of course, there's more to projecting confidence than just smiling — it's quite possible to smile and still look nervous, and it's also possible to look unhappy while still looking confident. Fortunately, cultivating self-assured body language takes only slightly more effort than smiling. Basically, to look self-assured, you should try to behave like a stereotypical Texan. Walk big, with a bit of swagger. Smile and wave at people who make even tentative eye contact. Gesture a lot when you speak and use broad gestures. Stretch your arms out to point at things. If you have occasion to speak with anyone, trim meek stalling phrases like "I guess" and "or whatever" from your vocabulary. Speak loudly and laugh frequently. Basically, make it clear as can be that you're not trying to hide or go unnoticed, but that you want to share all that you have to offer with the world. Obviously, you only need to behave like this when people who might question your presence are around, or when you're on camera.

Another important aspect of projecting confidence is looking like you know where you're going, especially whenever it's likely that you're being personally or electronically supervised. The basic trick here is to continually move forward at a steady pace — like a shark, but smarter. Don't enter a building and stand around looking confusedly for the coolest way to go, just pick a direction and start walking. It's not necessary that you move quickly, just steadily. You want to convey the idea that the building is basically a second home to you, so you should have no need to slow down to read a sign, take something in, do any double-takes or (especially) do any really elaborate, over-the-top spit-takes. You should look like it's all old news to you and you're sleepwalking through it just like everyone else. Don't try any doors that might be locked, or you'll look confused. Don't slow down to take a second look at a slightly ajar door unless you intend to walk right through it. Don't backtrack — act as if wherever you wind up is exactly where you wanted to go. Slip out of super spy mode and just let doors slam behind you instead of carefully easing them shut — careful people often look like they're up to something. If you wind up at a payphone or a washroom, pretend to use it. If you wind up at a dead end, whip out your cell phone and look like you were just seeking out a quiet corner from which you could make a call. As long as you always look like you know where you're going and what you're doing, it's unlikely that anyone will try to "help" you.

It's simple and cliché, but absolutely true: if you're confident you know what you're doing, they will be too.

Being Polite, Friendly and Helpful

Being polite, friendly and helpful will take you pretty far. Being polite costs nothing but a few seconds of time, so there's really no reason at all not to be polite all the time. Like smiling and acting confidently, politeness may not come naturally, particularly if you're thinking of the people you encounter as your adversaries. Being an outsider on someone else's turf, you may feel the need to project toughness, and you may even feel vaguely hostile and confrontational. But while it's true that the people around you are your opponents, you should treat them like your closest allies. Try complimenting the building in such a way as to give them credit for the place: "This is an incredible building you have here. I bet your roof has the best view in town." Asking a janitor you run into in a service corridor, "Excuse me, I'm sorry to bother you, but could you please tell me how to get to the atrium?" is so much more likely to yield positive results than "I need to get to the atrium" or "I'm looking for the atrium...?" While you'll probably get the information you need regardless of how you ask, if you ask politely you might get the longer version with additional helpful information, or at least get on the person's good side.

Being polite is a great start, but if you can go a step further and actually be outgoing, friendly and interested in the other person you'll be even further along. Obviously, this is a difficult task for more introverted explorers, but just try to think of it as working on your charisma score. Striking up conversations with people who have a more widely acknowledged right to be on site than you can provide you with a lot of useful information. Go a step beyond "Hi, how are you, nice weather" and actually get them talking. Simple leads like "Long day?"; "So, do people who work here still get lost?"; or "You must be fed up with people asking for directions all the time" express your friendliness and invite them to start talking (specifically, to start complaining, which is something most people love to do, and something which brings you at least slightly into their confidence). People with incredibly boring jobs, like custodians, ticket takers and security guards, may find it quite refreshing to have an opportunity to interact with someone who treats them like a human being.

Occasionally, you'll get a golden opportunity and see a worker who could use a hand. Whether it's something as simple as holding a door open for them or something slightly more advanced like helping them carry a ladder down the stairs, you should never pass up an opportunity to help a worker out. When you do this, the proper technique is not to say "Want a hand?" — an offer that most people will politely decline by instinct — but to simply grab hold and start helping. Not only will this eliminate any suspicion they might have felt towards you, it will make them feel like they owe you one. You don't actually have to cash this favour in, of course, since being helpful is just a nice thing to do, but it's still nice to know it's there if you need it. And who knows, maybe you'll wind up carrying that ladder all the way down to the locked basement. It's often amazing who has the keys that open the magic doors. (And there's a good chance it will be the one person you piss off.)

When you're not in the mood to behave kindly, it does no harm to act a little with the goal of becoming sincere. Being polite, friendly and helpful with employees, guards and even just regular people using the building takes little effort, makes the world a better place and will occasionally help you with your explorations, so you may as well do it every time.

Credibility Props

Credibility props are simple objects that in some way radiate believability and belonging. As an actor uses a stethoscope to indicate that he's a doctor or a gavel to indicate that he's a judge, explorers use props, like clipboards, key rings and tool belts, as a means of claiming to belong somewhere without having to say a word. Using simple credibility props, one can acquire near-universal trust and respect without doing a thing to deserve it and without making a false claim of any sort. And you may be surprised at just how authoritative holding a clipboard can make you feel.

There's no way to make an exhaustive list of useful credibility props, because the items that might prove useful vary drastically from place to place and situation to situation. You just have to get a sense of what will work where and get good at improvising. In a parking garage, a set of keys is a good prop. In a mechanical area, a tool belt and a well-stocked key ring work. In a field outside a patrolled abandoned building, a bird-watching guide is a handy thing to have in hand. At a construction site, a worn or carried hard hat or safety vest will help you blend in. At a TV or radio station, a clipboard clearly indicates your belongingness. If you're trying to get into a hotel pool, a towel is a good prop. Sometimes temporarily picking up a prop on location — for example, grabbing a broom or a mop to look more like a janitor — can work well, but you take the risk of being charged with theft if you happen to wind up in a confrontation with completely unreasonable people.

In places like hotels, corporate offices and similar institutions, it's often a good idea to carry a file folder or a blank sheet of paper around with you until you get the opportunity to trade up to an even better credibility prop, like a company prospectus, a map of the site or something written on a tenant company's letterhead. Or write down a fake name and room number on a piece of paper and carry that around until you stumble upon an actual company directory, and then trade up to a real name and room number. If you see a listing of daily events in a hotel, feel free to pick one that sounds fun; write down its name, location and time in your date book; and then refer to that entry as you ask a nearby hotel employee to show you how to get there. If you think it's necessary, arrive with fake business cards — either ones you've made for yourself, or just fun ones you've found in your travels. For some weird reason, people always feel more trusting of someone after that person has handed them a business card. As the *Kids in the Hall* once pointed out, it's sort of businesspeople's equivalent of smelling each other's crotches.

You should also consider the credibility issue when you're deciding how to carry your stuff. In most cases infiltration is easiest when you're carrying nothing, since people without baggage look less likely to be thieves or troublemakers, but often you'll want to bring along a tripod, a sandwich or something else that you don't want stuffed down your pants all evening. In such cases, think about where you're going. A backpack is great if you're poking around a college, but a briefcase or an attaché case (either of which can be purchased for a couple of dollars at a garage sale or a thrift store) will blend in better if you're heading to a more businesslike setting. Even a shopping bag, preferably from an upscale store, will work better than a backpack in many situations, since a bag marks you as a moneyed consumer and therefore harmless. If you're out with a ratty backpack when the exploring urge hits, see if you can get a big bag from some rich person store, and then carry your backpack around in that. A small suitcase can be appropriate at a hotel or a transit hub. If you're heading to a more blue-collar site, a metal lunchbox or small plastic cooler will easily store a camera, a flashlight, a first aid kit and more. Don't default to a backpack just because it's easiest for you.

Perhaps the most important credibility prop of all these days is the cell phone. Even though everyone on earth has one these days, if you're dressed appropriately, a cell phone can still help you convey the sense that you are important and businesslike and have way too many demands on your time to speak with every employee in the building who wonders if he or she can help you. Pagers and PDAs do the job of conveying importance, but they don't give you quite as much excuse to seem completely oblivious to the world around you as a cell phone. When you're wandering through a lobby or looking around for an elevator, a cell phone gives you a perfect cover for seeming distracted, confused, irritable, curt or even entirely non-responsive, since most people who use cell phones a lot are annoying jerks. (An unfair generalization perhaps, but what are the odds that anyone who uses a cell phone a lot is going to read this?) People will generally not bother you while you're talking on a cell phone. On top of these advantages, being on a cell phone provides a good excuse for wandering away from noisy populated areas, down the stairs or off into the darkened hallways, or for looking for an area with better reception, like the roof. Even if you can't afford, or simply don't want, a working cell phone, you might still consider taking along a broken one as a credibility prop.

Be-Right-Back Props
Speaking of broken cell phones, another sort of prop, with far less common applications, is the be-right-back prop. These are cheap items, obtained at garage sales or thrift stores for a dollar or so, that seem like the sort of item no one would leave behind, but that you can actually easily abandon. Obvious examples include a jacket, a book, a broken cell phone or a purse. Anything of perceived value that doesn't look like a bomb will do. If you leave your jacket or shopping bag on your chair in the waiting room while you wander away, the receptionist will just naturally assume that you're not going far and that you'll be back in a moment, while in actuality you're long gone, having snuck down to the basement and taken the steam tunnels halfway to Mexico. People such as receptionists, guards and other employees will generally worry less about the possibility of you wandering off if they think you've left some of your possessions behind as collateral, particularly if they assume that those possessions contain some ID. While these disposable props are only handy in a few fairly specialized situations, when they're handy they're really handy.

Disguise
What can compare to the joy of slowly peeling off your fake head and confronting your archnemesis deep within the sanctity of his or her secret underground lair, after having duped him or her into thinking that you were his or her trusted henchperson? Not much, let me tell you, not much. And yet disguises need not be quite this elaborate to

be useful to an explorer. Indeed, most disguises explorers use are extremely simple, stopping well short of the phoney moustache, let alone the prosthetic face.

One basic variety of disguise that explorers use fairly often to some degree involves simply not looking like yourself, so that any video footage or eyewitness accounts of your exploits will not be connected back to you. This kind of low-level disguise can be useful if you're exploring your own school or workplace, for example, or if you're exploring a building from which you've been banned on a previous occasion. Merely wearing a different jacket than you normally would is a disguise of a sort. Most people recognize you by your eyes and hair, so temporary hair dye, sunglasses or weak non-prescription glasses can help you out; if you have the option, you could also temporarily grow or shave off some facial hair for the occasion. If you had long hair before, put it up and tuck it into a hat; if it was up, take it down.

Another sort of disguise is more geared to fitting in than to active deception. You're hardly committing fraud if you dress up like a student, a churchgoer, a businessman or a tourist in order to make people less inclined to notice you in your setting of choice. Such costumes take minimum effort and involve minimum risk.

Using the same sort of disguise, but to a greater degree, allows you to very strongly imply that you have permission to be somewhere, while still stopping short of actually making a dishonest claim or actually impersonating someone. While it is illegal in most places to disguise yourself as a cop or a security guard, it isn't illegal to look like a construction worker, an electrician or a maintenance worker. If you're wearing workpants and a tool belt and people assume you're a maintenance worker, well, that's tragic but it can't be helped. A few different-coloured hard hats, safety vests and jumpsuits can go a long way. Ebay and Goodwill are both very helpful in this regard, and you'll also often find hard hats and safety vests lying around a construction site. They're pretty cheap, so they aren't usually kept locked up. If you borrow such items, make sure you remember the "returning" part of the borrowing, and bear in mind that if you get caught before you've returned them you're probably going to be charged with theft rather than borrowing.

In theory, pizza delivery or courier company uniforms could be useful for getting past front desks, but I'm unable to confirm or deny that this works, having never heard any believable stories.

Excuses

Know your story. Many infiltrations will involve at least some interaction with other people, so unless you're excellent at thinking on your feet, you should have a detailed, realistic story of what you're up to in mind before you get there, and anyone you're exploring with should have the same story. At the very least, you should know the name and location of the person or business you're pretending to visit. Again, writing this down on a slip of paper makes for a quick and simple prop.

Of course, there's more to this than just having everyone in the group memorize a clever story in advance. You need to be adaptable and adjust the story as you go along. If your plan is to look for the utility tunnel network under a particular building, "We're just looking for a shortcut to the parking garage" is a great story to start out with, but don't forget to change your story when you move on to try to seek out the pool, visit an abandoned wing, crash a party or look for the roof. Make sure everyone in your group knows the updated story and behaves appropriately. There's more to this than just having the excuse memorized: you should be in character. A group of three young men riding up an elevator with other people shouldn't just be smiling shyly and staring at their shoes, they should be talking to each other about the fake meeting they're going to. Similarly, two contractors walking around a construction site shouldn't be lurking quietly and giving each other subtle hand signals — they should be making notes, talking to each other loudly and confidently and pointing things out to each other. A little acting goes a long way.

Explorers get a lot of mileage out of the same handful of vague, tried-and-true excuses: trying to find the keys you dropped down this hole, looking for a washroom, here for the conference, looking for a payphone, looking for the exit, getting a little exercise, looking for the parking garage, waiting for a friend, on the way out, looking for Dr. Emil's office, heading to the vending machine, looking for a place to have a smoke, getting a breath of fresh air, lost... basically anything straightforward and hard to disprove will work. More concrete excuses involving false claims ("I'm a courier"; "I just got a job in your shipping department"; "I'm here for an appointment") are too easy for a guard or employee to check up on and disprove, especially if you see they're carrying a radio or phone.

When I go exploring with other people, I sometimes like to ask them out of the blue every now and then, "So if a guard came up to you right now and asked you what you were doing here, what would you say?" All too often, they've got nothing ready and are totally unable to improvise. Perhaps half the time, they do have an excuse, but it's much too easy to disprove. "I'm staying in room 1310" is likely to generate one of the three following responses: (1) "May I see your room key, please?"; (2) "Can I have your name please, so I can just check that with the front desk?"; (3) "This hotel doesn't have a room 1310, please come with me." You're not *staying* at the hotel — that's too easy to disprove. You're visiting friends who are staying at the hotel, and have no idea what room they're in. You were coming for dinner at the restaurant in the hotel. You're at the hotel for the convention (provided you know the name of a convention happening in the hotel that day). You parked underneath the hotel on your way to a nearby show. Or something more straightforward, like, you wanted to show your friend how beautiful the hotel you stayed in was or you wanted to see the view of the city from the top of the hotel. Stick with excuses they can disbelieve, if they want, but that they will find difficult to prove false.

My general practice, which I would recommend to any explorer, is not to lie any more than you have to, even when it would be entirely legal to do so. This has some practical benefits, but mostly I suggest this just because I think it's lousy behaviour to abuse someone's trust. Yes, it curtails your freedom of action a little, but hey, that whole placing-ethics-above-laws dealie has to go both ways. (But, you ask, is there a real ethical difference between directly lying to people and merely deceiving them? Personally I think lying's considerably nastier than misleading, since it takes advantage of people's trust rather than people's assumptions, but I'll leave you to consider the issue for yourself.)

In my opinion, misleading can be a great substitute for lying if you're fairly quick on your feet, since doing a good job at being misleading can often save you the trouble of having to lie. Suppose you're riding up in an elevator with a bunch of businessmen who you've just piggybacked in with in order to bypass the security desk and one happens to ask if you work in the building. While your easiest and most obvious reply would probably be "I'm just a temp helping out in marketing" or something of that sort, it's preferable to respond with something misleading but not dishonest, like "Not when I don't have to!" (As an added plus, people never bust you once you've made them laugh... even if it's only with the sort of lame humour that's only funny in the rarefied environment of an office building.) This sort of indirect reply also eliminates the chance that they'll respond, "But this company doesn't have a marketing department", or "I thought Claire was on holiday this week" or something of that sort. Lying as little as possible also has the practical benefit of keeping you from mixing your story up and getting caught by your lies.

In many cases it will be to your advantage for you to initiate the conversation, rather than waiting for the other person to do so. One of the basic principles of chess, and most strategic games, is equally true of social engineering: take the lead and make your opponent react to you, instead of you reacting to your opponent. If you stroll right up to the security desk and politely but confidently ask how to get to the conference level, they don't *need* to stop you and ask you if you work there or if they can help you. You obviously know what you're doing, and they know how to give you what you want.

Playing Dumb

While the old saying about how ignorance of the law is no excuse is completely ludicrous, considering how many thousands of irrational and non-intuitive laws there are and how frequently and arbitrarily they're changed, cops and security guards really, really take that saying to heart. They don't always know the laws that well themselves, but they sure as heck expect you to have them memorized — at least, all the ones that work against you. They don't mind if you don't know the ones about your rights and stuff. They usually don't know those ones, either.

While playing dumb is hard to do, it often beats the alternatives. You would usually be much better off saying you didn't realize you were breaking a rule or a law than you would be saying you knew what you were doing was technically against policy but didn't think you'd be hurting anyone. Most cops and security guards, at least those who take their positions seriously, *hate* the idea of people making a conscious and deliberate decision to ignore the rules, since such decisions challenge their conception of society's basic framework. A mere idiot, on the other hand, doesn't challenge their worldview at all, so they'd generally prefer to catch someone being stupid than catch someone being disobedient. Thus, you're probably better off saying that you didn't realize that taking a few quick pictures just inside the employees-only area would be considered trespassing, or that you didn't know that abandoned buildings were considered private property, or that you had no idea storm drains were off-limits to the general public, or that it never occurred to you that roof access might be restricted and so on.

You may have inadvertently passed a few warning signs in your travels, and the person questioning you may have noticed this. If they point out that you passed a "no trespassing" sign, you should simply respond that you weren't *trespassing*, you were just here looking for the washroom, or the payphone, or your friend, being careful to stick to the main hallway and not actually going into any of the rooms. If the sign in question reads "authorized personnel only", "unauthorized entry prohibited" or something of that sort, just explain that you thought since you were here to meet your friend (or had a ticket to the event, or had an appointment here, or paid for parking here, etc.) that you *were* authorized. You thought the sign was just to keep loiterers, bums and troublemakers out. Alternately, say that your authorization came from a guy who was in the area who said it would be okay, and you assumed he was an employee... you think maybe he had brown hair and sideburns.

Occasionally you can get away with playing dumb even when you're caught somewhere obviously off-limits, like a subbasement or a steam tunnel, as long as there is at least one way to get there without passing a bunch of clear, obvious "do not enter" signs. And there usually is at least one such route. I often pass "authorized personnel only" or "no trespassing" signs but, once I'm on the other side of the signs, three out of four times I find another way that I could have come which wouldn't have involved passing any signs at all. I always keep careful track of these things in case I'm caught and need to explain how I got in. (They're almost like "save points" in videogames.) If you are reluctant to admit that you spent half an hour climbing and crawling around to get where you are, you can also claim that some nearby locked door was slightly ajar when you found it and you had just wandered through. This usually works, as long as what you suggest is physically possible and there's nothing on videotape to contradict you.

Pleading that you are lost also works, since many people — even those who aren't exploring — do get lost surprisingly easily. Looking flustered but grateful, you can claim you missed or misread a sign, or that some other person gave you bad directions to a shortcut, and that you were just trying to find your way out of the building or to the washrooms or back to the public area. Be polite. Apologize for your ignorance and the hassle and thank the employee or guard for his or her help in getting you back on track. Ask about how to do things the right way in the future.

Attempting to portray yourself as an irrational or deranged person is unlikely to work even if you're not really exaggerating the case that much, since security guards tend to be less sympathetic than the average person and few will take pity on you just because you're deranged. Mentally stable or not, you're still annoying them, and that's what really counts. Acting like you don't speak English or whatever language the guards are using isn't a very good idea either, since it's quite possible that this will just make them more determined to make your life unpleasant. Nor should you think that threatening to make a scene is likely to help you out — guards generally have boring jobs and would welcome a scene. Furthermore, the more people who notice the incident, the less likely it is that the guard will decide to forget the whole thing.

Fast-talking

Those who occasionally fib their way out of a tight situation — or into one — generally refer to the practice as "fast-talking", which certainly sounds much nicer than lying. While I don't like the idea of using euphemisms to cover up the act of abusing people's trust, I like the term fast-talking because whereas "lying" sounds like it requires nothing more than a willingness to deceive, "fast-talking" quite rightly sounds like a skill that needs to be developed, and like something that shouldn't be attempted by those who don't know what they're doing. And fast-talking is usually more about misleading, misdirecting, confusing and exhausting people's patience than about exploiting people's trust.

Some people have a natural talent for fast-talking, whereas others must develop it through practice or by watching people who are good at it. You probably have a rough idea of whether or not you'd be any good at fast-talking your way out of a delicate situation from your past attempts to squirm out of sticky situations with your parents, teachers, bosses and so on. If you know you're good at sounding earnest, sincere and convincing, and that you're good at thinking on your feet, you may have what it takes. If you turn red, stutter and say "umm" a lot when you're trying to make up excuses, you shouldn't try your skills out for real until you've practiced a while with a mirror or a video camera, or with friends — preferably with friends who *know* you're practicing on them.

When you're fast-talking in the field, don't make your story any more elaborate than it needs to be. A lot of amateurs seem to think that fast-talkers communicate a lot. This is wrong. They communicate very little, they just use a lot of words to do it. Don't concoct an epic tale, just reiterate the same four or five ideas over and over again, sounding more earnest and sincere each time, until the person gets sick of hearing your routine and sends you on your way. If you instead make up a long and complicated story, you're likely to paint yourself into a corner with inconsistent details. There's just no need for you to fashion a completely functional alternate reality. A total non-story will often work better than an interesting and creative tale, so feel free to be boring. "An older woman with brown hair and glasses said this was the way to the parking garage, or at least I thought she did" is much more likely to get you the results you want than "These three big Hispanic guys tried to mug me, and then started to chase me, so I ran in here to look for a place to hide". If you were the guard who heard these two unlikely excuses, which person would you want to dismiss and which would you want to question in detail? In this case, the suggestion of violence in the second story would likely require that the excuse be taken seriously and the appropriate reports filled out whether the guard bought it or not.

While it's important not to make up a bigger story than necessary, it's true that throwing in small, irrelevant details can help make a story seem more realistic. Quickly creating believable scenarios and characters is a lot easier if you base them on real situations and real people — your tongue is probably going to be working faster than your imagination, so tell a real anecdote you're heard before, or describe a friend or co-worker rather than trying to invent a fictitious story or character on the spot. Whenever possible, use misdirection to change the subject, or stress the points that are least important. Act like you're defending yourself against an accusation of being stupid, or vandalizing, or stealing, or having done something embarrassing, rather than an accusation of having trespassed. If the person you're speaking with clarifies that they're actually accusing you of having trespassed, act baffled.

One key to fast-talking, as with all excuse-making, is to never admit to having broken any rules knowingly. You can certainly admit that you inadvertently did something wrong or something careless, having missed the "authorized personnel only" sign or not having understood the policies about rooftop access, but you should treat any suggestion that you deliberately ignored a sign or disobeyed a rule with shock, confusion and indignation. Your reaction should be along the lines of "But why on earth would anyone ever do such a thing, except by accident?! It wouldn't make any sense!" Refuse to comprehend any suggestion that your story could somehow be considered questionable.

The other key to fast-talking, and to much interaction with other people, is to make good eye contact. Most people, even most explorers, are terrible at this. You don't want to stare at the person, but neither do you want to avoid their stare or lower or avert your eyes when you're embarrassed. This is a really important social engineering skill — right up there with smiling, really. Practice in the mirror and practice with friends. As you speak, focus on trying to read the other person, not on making sure they don't get a good, straight-on look at you. Let them look. You've done nothing wrong, damn it!

If you are a girl, and the person who catches you is a guy, a little flirting will not hurt. In fact, it will probably get you out of a bad situation nine times out of ten. Unfortunately, the same is probably not true if the genders are reversed, unless you're an unusually easy-on-the-eye fellow. Girls also have the option of starting to cry to garner sympathy. Guys do not. The world is full of double standards.

Being Straightforward

Just as it doesn't make sense to sneak around a building when hiding in plain sight will work best, it doesn't make sense to deceive or make up excuses when being straightforward will get you where you want to go just as well.

Sometimes you'll arrive at a place and find the area you're interested in is off-limits and guarded or supervised and that there doesn't seem to be any way to sneak past. If you get the impression that the person barring your progress just might have a drop of compassion, try approaching them and telling them that you've come a long way and that you'd be really grateful if they'd just let you take a quick look and grab a few pictures. Occasionally it works, if you're friendly and enthusiastic enough — indeed, occasionally it *really* works, and they'll give you the grand tour or even let you show yourself around. Other times they'll tell you who to talk to about getting a tour, or tell you when you might come back and try again. And still other times they'll just tell you to get lost.

Some explorers think exploring with legitimately gained permission somehow "doesn't count" (count towards what, I don't know). It's true that getting permission does remove some degree of danger and excitement, but you can still discover and document a spot's little-known and neglected areas and enjoy its architecture and infrastructure, as long as it isn't one of those very closely guided tours that focus solely on those uninteresting parts of the building that have been deemed suitable for public consumption (such as the gallery of paintings of old, dead white guys). A loosely guided or do-it-yourself tour with permission can be a wonderful thing.

In my opinion it's ridiculous to think that you're exploring "for real" if you deceive your way in but not if you ask nicely. Urban exploration isn't about putting one over on The Man so much as it's about going beyond the safe, sanitized and commercial spaces that are generally the only areas open to the public. It doesn't become a "real" exploration because you threw yourself on someone's mercy and asked if you could use the washroom and then took off into the basement — that's just abusing someone's goodwill and making him or her likely to be less trusting in the future. I won't suggest that taking advantage of people is always wrong — it's fine and dandy to take harmless advantage of someone's stupidity, carelessness, incuriosity, laziness or forgetfulness — but no one is going to award you extra points because you took advantage of someone's trust. There's no cunning in that, just abuse. Trust is a pretty precious and easily damaged thing and you should play nicely with it.

Naturally, there are reasonable and unreasonable approaches to this whole straightforwardness business. Lines like "I was wondering if you could tell me how to sneak down to your steam tunnels" or "I'm hoping to trespass here, can you give me some tips?" are not likely to get you anywhere. On the other hand, equally truthful but more carefully phrased explanations like "I'm interested in church architecture and wondered if there was any way I could take a look at the bell tower" or "I've read a lot about your abandoned observation deck and I'd love to see it" are reasonable and good and may occasionally open a few doors for you.

In some circumstances, being straightforward can also be a good strategy when you're caught. If an employee or a guard spots you casually checking behind a door in a public area and asks what you're doing, you don't really need to expend any energy coming up with some long, convoluted excuse, unless you feel like it or think you could use the practice. You haven't done anything wrong, and honestly explaining that you're "just curious" should do the job nicely. "I just wanted a picture" is another totally honest and usually totally sufficient excuse, provided you have a camera. People understand the hobby of photography a lot more easily than they comprehend urban exploration, even though a lot of people have trouble understanding why anyone would ever want pictures of tunnels or machinery. The guard or employee might direct you back to a more public area, but unless you've passed warning signs or are somewhere very obviously off-limits, you shouldn't put up with a lecture or anything of that sort.

While I usually recommend avoiding any admission of wrongdoing, it's okay to deviate from this slightly if you're caught somewhere that's only a *little bit* off-limits and you judge that the person who has caught you isn't on a power trip. Sometimes a simple "I'm sorry, I thought maybe I wasn't supposed to come down here, I was just curious, I'll take off" will get you further than a string of excuses. Try to read the person you're dealing with to determine if they're likely to reward or punish you for being straight with them. While a lot of security guards are frustrated bullies who live for the moments when they can inconvenience and intimidate people, others are real people who just needed some money and accidentally wound up being security guards. Some people will pounce on any admission of wrongdoing, but others will appreciate being taken into your confidence and treated with respect. In guessing which type of guard you're dealing with, your gut instinct is your best guide.

Sentence Yourself

My favourite bit of the story "The Song of the South" is the bit where Brer Fox catches Brer Rabbit. Brer Fox isn't exactly sure what to do with his captive, so Brer Rabbit repeatedly cries, "Whatever you do, please just don't throw me into the briar patch!" until at last Brer Fox decides to make Brer Rabbit's nightmare a reality by throwing Brer Rabbit into the briar patch. This, of course, is what Brer Rabbit had wanted all along, because he knows how to navigate the briar patch without any problem at all. That is one smooth rabbit.

Like Brer Fox, many police officers, guards and nosy employees have no real idea what to do when they catch someone whose only crime is curiosity. They're trained to spot and deal with thieves, vandals, troublemakers, terrorists and other bad people — not people who desire nothing more than to see the basement or take a photo from the roof. There is nothing in their manual to tell them how to deal with someone who is just curious, or who just wants a picture and who doesn't seem to be harming any people or endangering any property or even invading anyone's privacy. This gives you an advantage in a situation where you're caught and your opponent has no real idea what to do with you.

Although few people you'll encounter will ever actually *ask* you to suggest your own punishment — that's more of a dad thing — if you have an idea and they don't, they're likely to take your suggestion. This is especially true if you can avoid drawing attention to the fact that it's your suggestion and make them think that it's their idea or their organization's policy. People are lazy and slow so, in most cases, lines like "Sorry, well, I guess I have to go now... I know the way out" or "I guess you have to ask me to leave now" work wonders. (Start nodding yes as you make your suggestion. Nodding, like yawning, is subconsciously catching.) Such sentiments aren't an admission of guilt, of course, just an expression of your willingness to avoid making things stressful for the other person. Since your presence is the only problem, your volunteering to leave should solve the whole thing. Volunteering this solution at the right time and in the right tone will almost always help keep the situation from being passed along to a supervisor, or otherwise becoming awkward or unpleasant.

EQUIPPING

A lot of people watch James Bond or Batman movies not so much for the intense sex appeal of Roger Moore or Michael Keaton as for the treasure trove of cool gadgets. We love the pen that turns into a gun, the watch that turns into a hovercraft and the belt-buckle that turns into a refrigerator, and we dream of the day when we will have it all hanging from our own personal utility belt, preferably after a long, loud, Dolby-enhanced equipping sequence.

Gadgets are indeed neat, and when a lot of people first get into urban exploration they begin a mad scramble to equip themselves with as much secret agent swag as possible. In some cases, a team of explorers will divvy up their joint wish list and collect a communal stockpile of gadgetry, not resting until they have a veritable arsenal of flashlights and other battery-powered whatsits.

This is fun stuff, and there's absolutely nothing wrong with it if you can afford it, but please don't get the impression that it's necessary, or that the more gadgets you get the more of an explorer you will be. Most gadgetry is not only unnecessary but worse than useless outside of a few rare special instances. Often toys will just weigh you down, bulk you up and slow your progress on excursions that don't require any special equipment. Some equipment — night vision goggles, say — can cause you to look more suspicious and make it more difficult for you to convincingly plead your innocence if you are caught. Besides that, the less equipment you have, the more fun you'll have improvising and following in the proud traditions of the A-Team and MacGyver (the TV character, not the explorer of the same name, though he's good too). I normally recommend travelling with only the real basics, though I concede that a few more specialized supplies and tools have their uses in certain circumstances.

The Basics

While no equipment is actually essential, there are three pieces of basic equipment that I regard as the explorer's best friends: the flashlight, the camera and the moist towellette. Because exploration opportunities can arise suddenly and at any time, I recommend having these three essentials on you not just when you go exploring but *at all times*.

Since its invention in 1898, the battery-powered flashlight has virtually put the kerosene-soaked-torch industry out of business. As you get into urban exploration, it's likely that you'll come to think of your flashlight not so much as a piece of equipment but as a part of your body that you remove in order to shower. Flashlights are all-but-essential equipment for explorers who are interested in touring storm drains or unlit tunnels or visiting abandoned buildings at night, but they're also pretty important even if you're exploring somewhere more populated, like an open-for-business school or a hotel, because the most interesting areas are often unlit.

There are many types of flashlights out there. Some people like big, heavy, six-D-cell Maglites that can be used as baseball bats in an emergency (you never know when an impromptu baseball game is going to break out); other people, with a different set of unresolved childhood issues, prefer two-million-candlepower halogen spotlights that act as portable suns. Those who fancy themselves secret agents tend to favour tiny, slim penlights or key chain lights powered by long-lasting light-emitting diodes (LEDs) that are light and easy to conceal, while those more in the survivalist vein tend to prefer sturdy, waterproof flashlights that won't be damaged if you accidentally drop them in a storm drain and then run back and forth over them with a truck. Some, like me, like a few of each. Whatever you prefer, it's a good idea to keep at least one flashlight with trustworthy alkaline batteries (never rechargeables, as they die much too suddenly) on you at all times, just in case an opportunity arises unexpectedly, which is generally how opportunities work.

Take at least two flashlights with trustworthy batteries with you when you're touring storm drains or other locations where you could be stranded in the darkness if your primary flashlight breaks (and no, taking backup batteries isn't just as good as taking a second flashlight — sometime the batteries are fine but the flashlight isn't). Don't use a glow-in-the-dark flashlight for exploring. Oh, and definitely don't use one of those crank-powered survivalist flashlights. Sure, they'll be fun after the apocalypse, but in the meantime they're just noisy.

After a flashlight, the second most desirable piece of equipment you can take along is a camera of some sort. Cameras help capture vivid memories of a place and time and allow you to share your findings with others. Expedition photographs are not only enjoyable to reminisce upon or appreciate as works of art or slices of history, but can be useful aids to your future explorations or to the explorations of others, as someone will often see something in the pictures that you missed while you were there or will see the picture and be reminded of some useful fact. Photos can also be a useful method of recording blueprints, maps and manuals you find on-site for later analysis at home. Even more importantly, explorer photos may also provide some of the only remnants of a place after it is destroyed. While taking a pen or pencil and some paper along is often a good idea as well, since these allow you to capture details a camera misses, photographs provide an excellent aid to later constructing written accounts of an expedition, and taking a photograph takes a lot less time than writing down a full description of a scene. Can you imagine if you had to write a thousand words every time you wanted to describe something? Your hand would get totally cramped. As mentioned, cameras are also useful as credibility props, since many people consider the hobby of photography to be more socially acceptable than the hobby of urban exploration, and tend to prefer the explanation "I was just taking pictures" to "I was just looking around". People's tastes in cameras differ even more radically than people's tastes in flashlights, with some preferring large, heavy, single-lens reflex film cameras with special lenses and tripods, cable releases, flashguns, flash reflectors and so on; others preferring tiny digital spy cameras with no features other than fitting comfortably in one's pocket (or cell phone); and still others preferring disposable cardboard cameras that they don't have to worry about dropping in sewer water.

My general advice on this front would be to scout with a smallish camera and, if you find that you're not satisfied with your snapshots and you feel that security won't be a problem, try to come back with a camera that will allow you to do justice to the location. Digital cameras are very well suited to urban exploration, since explorers will frequently take several dozen underexposed shots a month, and it's frustrating to pay to develop those. That said, most accomplished photographers agree that film still has an edge over digital, and that truly breathtaking shots deserve to be captured on film rather than in pixels.

Finally we come to the last piece of basic equipment, the moist towellette. Moist towellettes, sometimes known as Wet Naps, can be purchased at some pharmacies, or you can simply grab large handfuls of them at restaurants that sell fried chicken or other greasy food. They offer an extremely compact and portable method for transporting backup cleanliness. Moist towellettes are handy for washing dirt, soot, pigeon droppings, bacteria, sewage, blood or what-have-you off your face and hands and, although they're no substitute for soap, water and disinfectant, they're useful for getting dirt and germs out of cuts. They're also good for tidying up clothing and polishing shoes, in those common situations where you need to pass through civilized, populated areas on your way back from tunnels, basements, mechanical rooms, rooftops and other dirty areas without looking suspicious. Moist towellettes allow you to instantly switch from a grime-and-mud-coated thug to a respectable-looking citizen incapable of naughtiness. For the explorer who likes to climb down from the attic and go back to the wedding reception, or to end a long night of tunnel running with a relaxing swim in the pool of a luxury hotel, moist towellettes are indispensable.

Clothing
To the outsider, most explorers probably seem quite casual in matters of fashion, but in reality explorers need to pay a great deal of attention to how they dress. On top of worrying about how good-lookin' they are, explorers must consider the utility, warmth, protection, durability, manoeuvrability, stealth, waterproofing and disposability of their wardrobe, as well as its appropriateness to their chosen setting.

Utility. The purpose of clothing is to hold pockets. This is clothing's function; it does not make sense to wear clothing that does not have pockets. If you're wearing a jacket, it's really not pulling its weight unless it has at least eight pockets. Vests filled with pockets are your friends. Wear pants with lots of pockets — in locations where you don't need to look businessy, cargo pants are great, since they can hold a regular-sized camera or a drink without too much discomfort. You may as well have pockets in your shirt. If you can get some pockets in your underwear or bra, go for it. If you have sufficient pockets, you can get away with carrying your flashlights, your camera, your moist towellettes, your cell phone, your pen and paper and your what-have-you, all without burdening yourself with a cumbersome and potentially suspicious backpack, purse or (*shudder*) fanny-pack.

Warmth. For those of us north of the south, warm clothes are essential for late-night expeditions in the chill of winter where you may wind up spending a lot of time outside, or in buildings so drafty that you may as well be outside. The best sorts of clothes are those that provide a lot of heat without adding a lot of encumbrance in the form of weight or bulkiness. Dressing in layers, as you may have heard before, is a very good idea. Long underwear, gloves and a toque can make you very happy; scarves not only keep you warm, they can even be used as a rope substitute in some situations. If there's a chance you might get wet on a cold night, be sure to bring a change of clothes, since in cold weather wet clothing is worse than useless.

Of course, most explorers probably worry about being too hot more often than they worry about being too cold. Running around stairwells and steam tunnels and climbing buildings and ladders can be sweaty work. These problems are made worse when you visit someplace hot in the middle of winter and find yourself saddled with a heavy jacket you don't want. In these situations, it's often good to see if you can find a locker or a hidden cubby-hole somewhere you can stash your jacket and grab it later, since overheating is bad for your body and your brain, and greatly increases your chances of injuring yourself.

Protection. On hot summer days you may be tempted to go visit your local abandoned factory in nothing but shorts and a t-shirt, but that really isn't smart, as the place may be swarming with tetanus and other germs that would love to make your acquaintance. Wear jeans or durable pants and a lightweight long-sleeved shirt, take a lot of water and try to stay in the shade. In all situations where the temperatures you'll be encountering will allow it, it makes sense to wear long pants and long sleeves, as these will provide you with extra protection against cuts, scrapes, burns, bug bites, train derailments and the like.

Durability. While it makes sense for you to wear clothing that you can bear to see damaged, it's a bad idea to head out in cheap, flimsy rags. If you start out with jeans with big holes in the knees, you're going to be frustrated down the line when you find a really tempting crawl tunnel and can't see where it goes. In potentially scrapey situations, think thick. Denim is good; thin cotton or polyester clothes are bad. Leather pants are a bit much, but a leather jacket isn't a bad idea. Thick leather work gloves are ideal for crawling through tunnels or climbing slightly rusty ladders. Sturdy shoes or boots are so important that it's worth devoting not only extra time but even extra money to finding an ideal pair. Caterpillars and Terra Wildsiders are popular sturdy shoes with good grips. With boots, a steel toe is nice if you can afford it, but at the very least try to get ones with thick rubber soles, of the sort that won't allow rusty nails, bits of broken glass, crack pipes or used syringes to protrude into the soles of your feet. That can suck.

Manoeuvrability. While you have to dress for warmth and protection from the elements, it's also important to dress for manoeuvrability. In many locales, you'll need to make some pretty awkward climbs and crawls and shove yourself through some pretty narrow holes if you want to see everything. You're not going to be able to do that if you're wearing overly bulky snow gear, a trench coat or tight jeans, or if you're one of those demented people who thinks it's a good idea to pretend your crotch begins at your knees. Wear clothing that fits snugly but comfortably, and that doesn't weigh you down more than necessary. Don't wear track pants, as they're baggy and offer heat but no protection. If you're likely to get wet, try to wear clothing that will dry off relatively quickly, as wet clothing can slow you down a lot. If you choose to wear a hat, get a tight-fitting one. Don't wear anything that's likely to fall off.

Stealth. Some people think of dressing for stealth and immediately conjure up images of black clothes, balaclavas and camouflage. While those things have their place (in movies, mostly, but also occasionally for sneaking into all-but-unpopulated areas), they have some significant drawbacks when one is exploring even sparsely populated areas. People dressed all in black tend to arouse suspicion, since thieves, vampires and other bad guys tend to favour dressing entirely in black. You do not want to be found in a utility tunnel wearing a black trench coat, as black trench coats have certain lingering connotations of deep psychological notgoodness. Similarly, people dressed in combat fatigues or military camouflage often earn themselves extra attention, since delusional, unstable people who think they're paramilitaries and the last true defenders of freedom often sport such attire. This is extra attention you don't need. Furthermore, should you happen to be caught on a rooftop while enrobed entirely in black or in camouflage, you're going to have a much harder time convincing someone you were just casually looking or just grabbing a quick breath of fresh air than you would have if you were wearing, say, a Charlotte Hornets jacket.

This isn't to say that I think you should go exploring in a Charlotte Hornets jacket — they're tacky, and besides, dressing in dark clothes when you're exploring dark areas makes a lot of sense. There's nothing suspicious about wearing black pants, black shoes and black socks, but with shirts and coats, you should favour dark blue, dark green or dark brown over black. Dark colours look black in the dark, but don't arouse suspicion in the light. Besides, they really bring out the colours in your eyes. I mean that.

When you're picking out jackets (or backpacks), make sure you don't accidentally get anything with a reflective strip, or if you do, make sure you remove it. You don't want to be reflectin' nothin'.

Another part of dressing stealthily is dressing in quiet clothing. While you probably don't need to worry about the tiny creaks from your leather jacket that has not yet been fully broken in — unless you take a lot of pleasure in being anal retentive — you don't want there to be loud rustling, swishing or jingling noises while you're walking down a darkened hallway late at night. Don't wear vinyl clothing, or jackets or pants with jangly zippers or Velcro pockets. Don't wear shoes that squeak. Don't accessorize with clinking jewellery or chains.

Waterproofing. Guarding your lower body against *l'eau* is primarily an issue in drains and sewers, but it's a concern in flooded tunnels and basements as well. Don't bother picking up the $15 eight-inch-tall boots they sell at Wal-mart or Zellers — you'll flood those almost immediately in almost any drain and quickly find yourself out $15 for nothing. If you think you're going to spend any time at all in water tunnels or flooded sites, you may as well go straight for what my colleagues in Alberta call *uberboots*, thick rubber boots that come up to the knee or higher. The next step after this is to get a pair of hip waders, which some explorers actually do use. Those who spend time in wet and misty drains and sewers may even go a step further and sport raincoats as well, but usually the boots or hip waders will do the trick. A hat is also a good idea when looking at drains with icky stuff hanging from the ceiling.

Disposability. In many exploratory locales, including drains, tunnels, abandoned buildings, construction sites and basically any other site where one need not dress to impress, it makes sense to dress disposably, or at least to wear clothing that can get dirty or ripped. If you don't have anything like this handy, thrift stores like Goodwill can hook you up. In some exploratory situations, it makes sense to bring along some extra clothes to change into; after visiting a sewer or somewhere with a hearty helping of asbestos, if you spent less than $10 putting the ensemble together, you may want to just throw your whole exploring outfit away. But don't do this unless you remembered to bring something else to change into. Wearing disposable clothing can also be helpful as an element of subtle disguise — if you're spotted on the roof in a dark brown shirt you bought for $2 at a garage sale, just get rid of it and walk around in the Day-Glo orange shirt you had on underneath. No one will recognize you.

Appropriateness. Since explorers are normally eager to avoid sticking out or creating an impression, we tend to dress the same way most other people at a location will be dressed. In some cases, certain clothing will be chosen not so much for its utility as for its value as a credibility prop — as when you wear a suit to a fancy soiree, for example. In most situations involving live buildings, it's hard to overdress, short of wearing a tuxedo to a ball game. Employees simply don't have time to get to know you and determine if you're trustworthy, and so tend to assess you quickly based on what you're wearing. Explore the exact same office tower, once in jeans and a t-shirt and once in a suit, and see how much further the suit takes you. If you dirty and scuff your dress shoes a lot, like me, make sure your home Batcave is well stocked with shoe polish. In most businesses and institutions, nothing cries "I'm a harmless drone, ignore me" like a well-knotted necktie. When dealing with construction sites, on the other hand, it's important to think casual. Basically, you should try to dress like the people that *should* be visiting the site in question, or like a harmless and forgettable person in situations where this doesn't apply. When you're trying to blend in, don't wear a hat or sunglasses. Avoid wearing bright colours or shirts featuring words or distinctive logos. If you must bring along a bag, make sure it's indistinct and appropriate to the site.

Supplies and Tools
What follows is neither a list of everything you should bring on every trip nor a list of everything you'll ever need. Rather, these are a few basic items — beyond the aforementioned flashlight, camera and moist towellettes — that you should considering packing if they seem appropriate to the site you're visiting and you don't think they'll weigh you down or bulk you up too much. Unlike gadgets, which people just like to buy and tend to justify their expenditures by pretending there is a need, the following items are often of actual use.

Antihistamines. If you have allergies or asthma, don't forget your pills, spray, inhaler, epi-pen or what-have-you. Many places you'll visit are dusty and full of allergens.

Cell phone. A cell phone is not only a great credibility prop but also a communication tool useful for calling friends and loved ones and telling them that you're trapped in a pit and you think your leg is broken. You may want to keep the numbers of some fellow explorers on hand in case you get into a situation that requires another explorer's help. Of course, you can't count on having reception when you're in the middle of nowhere or deep underground, but hey, cell phones aren't really that heavy these days, so why not bring one along? Cell phone cameras, while they typically have pitiful resolution, can also provide a convenient means of taking pictures stealthily. Obviously, when you bring your phone, make sure you remember to turn the ringer off. And remember to charge your battery beforehand!

Compass. One of the primary tools of explorers since the late Middle Ages, the compass remains a useful navigational aid for explorers today. Knowing which way is north is invaluable when one is working from a map or creating a new one. The only problem with using compasses when exploring is that they may not be completely trustworthy in the presence of electricity and large quantities of metal, so take compass readings in utility tunnels with a grain of salt.

Drinks. Bringing along a bottle or two of water is a good idea on long trips, especially if you're visiting hot areas where you're likely to do some sweating. Gatorade and similar drinks serve basically the same needs as water, but have some salt, sugar and electrolytes to help out. Providing you don't have a problem with nervousness or shakiness, you may also want to bring along some caffeinated drinks to give you a little more energy and alertness. Bear in mind that caffeine is a diuretic, and thus might make you need to pee at an inconvenient time or in an inconvenient place. Save those empty bottles! Women will need to find other solutions. Sorry.

Duct tape. You certainly don't need duct tape on every trip, but you may find it figures into your planning every now and then, especially on longer and more complex trips where you're packing for many contingencies. Duct tape is not only handy for repairing anything that might ever break, it's also quite helpful for subtly keeping doors from latching, holding down buttons, blocking motion detector sensors and hundreds of other minor feats of creative engineering.

First aid kit. If you're visiting somewhere dangerous and slightly removed from civilization, such as an abandoned building, it's a good idea to have access to a stocked first aid kit. You don't necessarily need to bring this into the site with you; just store it somewhere you or someone in your group will have access to it if something goes wrong. At a minimum, your kit should contain a burn pack, bandages, several rolls of gauze and gauze pads, adhesive tape, alcohol or antibiotic ointment and a pair of sterile scissors. Don't waste space by bringing supplies you don't know how to use or will be too grossed out to use, like bone saws. Ideally, you should obtain basic first aid training. Colleges, the Y and other places offer cheap courses.

Gloves. Gloves are handy in any location where you're likely to be climbing, crawling or handling gross stuff. They protect you from sharp objects and rope burns, keep wood slivers and shards of rusty metal out of your skin and provide a handy reminder that you shouldn't touch your face when your hands are coated with dirt and slime. They're very helpful for crawling along on rocks or climbing up rusty or hot pipes. The best gloves for the job are proper, sturdy work gloves, which sell in hardware and army surplus stores for about $10–20, though the kind of gloves that are just designed to keep your hands warm are better than nothing.

Grappling hook. I'm almost embarrassed to add this one to the list of legitimate supplies, just because it sounds so spy-wannabe, but the fact is that at least a handful of explorers use grappling hooks to good effect when the only route into a building requires them to start one or more storeys above ground. These can't be purchased in most hardware stores, but some online retailers sell them. Obviously, grappling hooks are extremely suspicious, so only use these when there really appears to be no other way, and then don't keep them with you any longer than necessary.

Hat. Remember to bring a non-mesh hat when you go draining or sewering. It will help keep nastiness out of your hair.

Headlamp. While many explorers purchase LED or incandescent light headlamps mainly because they're cool, headlamps can also be practical tools in a few situations, since they let you keep your hands free for climbing, photography or what have you. In general, however, a long-lasting, bright, durable, easy-to-aim, easy-to-conceal flashlight will serve you better than a headlamp, especially in situations where it's possible you might encounter people. Hands and wrists swivel much more freely than heads and necks, so a handheld flashlight has much more manoeuvrability than a headlamp. You're much more likely to shine a light right into your fellow explorers' eyes while using a headlamp than while using a handheld flashlight. Finally, if someone suddenly shows up, it's much easier to quickly and subtly slide a flashlight into a pocket or up a sleeve than it is to peel off a headlamp unnoticed. In almost all situations, you're better off planning to use a flashlight as your main light source, though a headlamp can be a handy specialized tool in certain situations.

Identification. You may have heard rumours that you'll be better off if you don't have ID with you when you are caught by security guards or police, but nothing could be further from the truth. Not having ID is considered extremely suspicious behaviour, and is likely to encourage them to pay much closer attention to your case than they would have otherwise. In most cases, presenting your valid photo ID to the powers that be* has a very powerful calming effect. They are reassured to see that you are a registered citizen in good standing, and they feel safe knowing they know how to get in touch with you if it turns out that the crown jewels have gone missing or anything like that. Assuming you were doing nothing more than trespassing, it is likely that your information will be discarded, misplaced or simply filed away and forgotten. Presenting fake ID is asking for a whole other crop of problems — don't do it.

Insect repellent. Abandoned buildings and drains are often filled with stagnant or slow-moving water, and this naturally means they're full of mosquitoes and related pests during the warmer months. If you don't like the idea of being itchy, or the idea of catching West Nile virus or something similar, you may want to bathe thoroughly in insect repellent. The non-aerosol kind is better suited to application in semi-confined spaces.

Knee pads. While knee pads are not something you want to pack for every trip, when you know you're going to be spending some time in crawl tunnels or undersized storm drains, and you think you might enjoy being able to walk afterwards, do yourself a favour and at least invest in some cheap knee pads. If you forget, you can improvise knee pads with towels or other similarly thick fabric. In cases where subtlety might be handy, consider wearing your knee pads under your pants or jeans.

Pen or *pencil.* While it's almost always easy to find some scrap paper (or scrap skin), it's often trickier to find something to write with, and it's likely that you'll want to take some notes about room numbers, building navigation and the like, or sketch out a quick map or two. Pens and pencils are also quite useful for temporarily propping open doors that might otherwise be inclined to lock behind you.

---

* Note on terminology: I don't like the term "official" because it is meaningless (anyone with an office can honestly call themselves official, and a bathroom stall can be an office), and I don't like the term "authority", because explorers and other enthusiasts are often greater authorities on the buildings they explore than the legal owners and occupants. In this book, I usually refer to the people with the muscle and guns — or the people who pay the people with the muscle and guns — as "the powers that be".)

Pocket knife. A short-bladed pocket knife is a very handy tool for cutting rope, cutting clothing, turning screws, nudging deadbolts and more. Multi-function pocket knives, more commonly known as Swiss Army knives, have additional features, ranging from combs, clocks and corkscrews on the popular models to saws, magnifying glasses and lighters on the more advanced and sillier models. The main drawback to pocket knives is that if the powers that be take a real disliking to you and can't find any *real* crimes to charge you with, they may try to pretend that your pocket knife is actually a concealed weapon. It's a ridiculous position for them to take, of course, but that's not to say they won't get away with it.

Maps. Whether professional or explorer-made, maps are handy supplies to bring along even when you know where you're going. When you get lost, or get to a confusing area, it's handy to check it against the map and try to determine whether it's you or the original mapmaker who's confused. Amateur maps are likely to have some mistakes, and even professional maps often do a poor job with multi-level structures. You may be able to correct the map or add useful information that will help either you or other future explorers. In some situations, it may be helpful for you to maintain two different maps: at home, a full map with details about entrances, cameras, alarms, etc.; while exploring, a "travelling map" that shares no more information than you need it to, and doesn't stress potentially incriminating information or refers to it only in coded symbols. Transcribe your notes from the travelling map to the full map once you get home.

Multitool. Multitools, more commonly known by the trade names Leatherman and Gerber tools, are small-bladed pocket knives with bonus lightweight aluminum, stainless steel or tungsten carbide tools such as cross- and flat-headed screwdrivers, scissors, files, pliers, wire cutters and more. While multitools are considerably more expensive than regular pocket knives, they're also useful in many more situations. Some models fold up small enough to be carried on a key chain. Again, unfortunately, hostile police or guards may pretend that these short-bladed tools are actually concealed weapons.

Respirator. While dust masks or painter's masks are suitable for places where dust is the only concern, in a great many places you'll visit — particularly older steam tunnels and some abandoned buildings — you'll want to bring along a proper half face mask with a HEPA filter to guard against asbestos, fungi, lead dust and other airborne nastiness.

These half face masks only cost $40 or so, and you can buy them online or at most hardware stores that sell paint. Look for a marking indicating that the mask uses high efficiency particulate air (HEPA) filters, and then purchase filters that have either an N100, R100 or P100 rating (the "n" refers to "*n*o oil", the "r" refers to oil *r*esistant and the "p" refers to "oil *p*roof"; the 100 refers to the rounded-up percentage of protection from airborne hazards).

You can also safely employ masks and filters that specifically mention that they are rated for asbestos. Bear in mind that neither the 95- nor the 99-rated masks provide sufficient filtering against asbestos fibres. Only use filters with a 100 rating (nitpickers will note that even the 100 filters have a minimum efficiency of only 99.97 percent, but c'mon, that's even better than Ivory soap). Pick up some replacement filters while you're there, and remember to replace your filters after every eight hours of use or so. It's a good idea to practice wearing your respirator while you're not actively exploring, so you get an accurate sense of how it impairs your ability to communicate and to take in a lot of oxygen quickly. Also make sure your respirator fits correctly — if it doesn't form a proper seal, it won't do you much good.

Rope. Rope is not necessary on most expeditions, but it's often handy in situations where tricky climbs or descents are likely. You can pick up sturdy climbing rope at hardware stores or outdoor-adventure-type stores. Avoid brightly coloured rope if you can. If you can't afford proper climbing rope, at least be sure to buy thick rope that can hold twice your body weight. A rope that's less than three metres (12 feet) long will rarely be helpful; on the other hand, it doesn't make sense to haul around 20 pounds of thick rope "just in case". Only pack long coils of rope when you know or strongly suspect you'll need it. Be sure someone in your group knows how to tie proper knots before you ever trust anyone's weight to the rope. Rope can also be useful for hauling up equipment, or dragging it behind you down narrow tunnels.

Snacks. While not as important as drinks, taking along a few salty snacks is a good idea if you're going to be exerting yourself for a few hours. Take snacks that won't produce garbage, like a resealable bag of trail mix or shelled peanuts.

Survival gear. When you're visiting somewhere far from civilization and worry that you might wind up staying a little longer than you'd like, it's a good idea to bring along an extra pack filled with food, water, matches, candles, a blanket, extra batteries and signalling equipment.

If you need contact lens solution or medication, bring that along as well, just in case. You'll probably never wind up needing these things, but it's worth the extra 10 minutes to pack them up if you're heading somewhere remote.

Whistle. I've never used this myself, but some fellow explorers suggested it and I think it was brilliant advice. A whistle would be very handy in a situation where you were trapped somewhere, especially if you lack strong vocal chords. And whistles are light, small and cheap.

Wire ladder. These easily portable ladders, also sometimes called cable ladders, are the sturdier modern version of the rope ladders of old. They fold up fairly small and light, and can be handy in drains, at abandoned buildings and in a variety of sites where some tricky climbing is involved.

Gadgets

Tools and gadgets are both things you bring along in order to help you out while exploring; the difference between the two lies in your motivation for bringing them along. Whereas you bring along tools to help you overcome a particular hurdle, you bring along gadgets in the hope that you'll be able to find or engineer a way to use them, because you know it would be cool if you did. This isn't to dismiss or diminish gadgets — they *are* cool and fun — but simply to acknowledge that they're generally brought along *because* they are cool and fun, not because they're especially useful. In situations where extra gear might weigh you down, impede your movement or make you look suspicious, or in situations where you stand a decent chance of getting caught, you should be able to differentiate your gadgets from your actual supplies and tools, and leave your gadgets behind. All of the following are fun, but none of them are necessary.

Binoculars. Binoculars, as you've probably heard, let you see things clearly even though they're far away. While it's conceivable that this ability might actually be useful — if you were trying to see if there were workers on a distant rooftop, or tell whether or not a far-off door was ajar, for example — it's mostly just cool to be able to see things that are far away. A small pair of fold-up binoculars is an indulgence you might permit yourself, but don't waste a lot of weight on this one.

Computers. It's true, you *can* bring your palmtop or even laptop computers with you, and they can be handy places to store directions, maps, access codes and the like. But as thin and light as portable computing devices are getting these days, they still aren't as thin and light as good ol' fashioned paper. Paper is also less likely to have a technical glitch and requires less electricity. If the need arises, paper is also significantly easier to swallow.

Gels and filters. Coloured gels, and the more permanent coloured filters, are designed to colour and shade one's flashlight beam so as to make it less detectable from a distance, or less damaging to one's night vision. Some companies have also begun selling flashlights powered by red, green or blue LEDs rather than the brighter white LEDs. These coloured lights look cool and are extremely popular among explorers who fancy themselves secret agents or paramilitaries, or who like buying things, but I've yet to be convinced that there is any real need for them — shining your flashlight beam through your fingers or through a piece of cloth usually does the trick. (I freely admit that I love my red, green and blue LED flashlights — I just won't admit that they're necessary.)

GPS units. Handheld units that use orbiting satellites to pinpoint your location on the globe using the Global Positioning System (GPS) are ridiculously cool, and can be a lot of fun when used for geocaching. Some explorers, eager to convince themselves that their GPS receiver is useful for something other than geocaching, manage to convince themselves that knowing the precise coordinates of entrances and other key locations will make life easier for themselves and future explorers. That may be, but waiting for a GPS unit to find the requisite satellite signals can be tedious, and "look for a manhole in the middle of the field" should be directions enough for any explorer.

Night vision equipment. Whether it be scopes or goggles, night vision equipment is perhaps the ultimate example of something you'd bring along because it's cool, rather than because it's useful. I have a scope myself, and while it is definitely cool, I acknowledge that it would take some pretty creative thinking for me to come up with a scenario in which it was actually useful enough to justify bringing it along — it would be much easier to think of a situation where, say, an elastic band or a handheld mirror would be handy. Night vision equipment has also been demonstrated to be unusually suspicious when found by the powers that be (thank you, Landmark Six). Unless you're just fooling around, leave it at home.

Radios. Radios, whether two-way walkie-talkies, radios employing the 14-channel Family Radio Service (FRS) or units on the more powerful General Mobile Radio Service (GMRS) are totally fun. They can also be useful in certain specific situations, such as when one person is acting as a lookout for the rest of the group or when it is actually necessary for the group to temporarily break up and regroup. In the right hands and in the right situation, radios can also provide a decent credibility prop — though it is equally true that in the wrong hands or the wrong situation they can look suspicious and draw attention. Often people who use radios choose to use them with an earpiece or even a full headset, though in most circumstances a conventional pair of headphones would be much less conspicuous. Unfortunately, more often than not, radios do more harm than good, encouraging a group to break up unnecessarily in order to experience the joy of communicating by radio. In the wrong hands, radios breed noise, encouraging more and louder conversation than there would be if the group simply travelled together. Radios also often transmit or beep at inappropriate times, and their signals are not reliable. Legally, at least in the US, GMRS radios can only be used by people who hold licenses, and then only to communicate with immediate family members, so using them may compound the charges against you if you are caught. Overall, radios are a distraction, and should only be used when they offer real and obvious benefits.

Scanner. Scanners are entertaining devices that allow you to listen in on what police and various security forces are chatting about. A quick online search for your city name plus "scanner frequency lists" will probably turn up all sorts of interesting results, including lots of frequencies that might be especially interesting to explorers. Scanners are legal for home use in most places in North America (New York State being one significant exception), provided they aren't used "in furtherance of a crime". Unfortunately, in most places, using scanners in furtherance of simple trespassing counts, so it is not generally a bright idea to bring a scanner with you on an excursion. What might make more sense would be to have someone off-site listen to the relevant frequencies and warn the group by phone if there's a problem. There's no law against receiving useful advice over the phone.

Red-Flag Items
Finally, don't just stuff your bag with your desired gear and go: start your packing from scratch, so you're well aware of everything you're bringing along, especially anything that would be awkward to explain. Common sense is your friend here. If you're going to try to play it casu-

al if you get caught, then don't brand yourself as a hardcore explorer. If you're caught, it won't do you any good if you're wearing a balaclava, a Cave Clan t-shirt and camouflage pants, or if your backpack is filled with detailed and labelled maps of entrances to the site, a few copies of *Infiltration* and a six-D-cell Maglite.

While it's a real shame when an expedition ends at a locked door just when it was getting good, it is not a good idea to bring lock picks on a trip. This isn't for any ethical reason — there's nothing even vaguely unethical about opening up a long-disused door in a deep subterranean tunnel — but for a practical reason. Carrying lock picks instantly escalates your potential punishment from a stern warning to a prison stay, throwing your risk-to-reward ratio severely out of whack. In the eyes of the police, those tiny scraps of metal identify you as a burglar, whether there's any possibility of you actually burgling or not (usually there is not), and make it likely that you will be charged with possession of burglar's tools. If you are found to have used them, you will likely be charged with breaking and entering, even if you haven't broken a darn thing.

For the same reason, and also because you should do no harm to a site, you should also leave your crowbars, bolt cutters, welding torches and wrecking balls at home.

Don't bring spray paint or thick markers. Making artistic graffiti pieces that beautify plain wooden hoarding or boring cinder block walls can be a creative and worthwhile pursuit, but tagging is generally stupid, and people who tag while exploring give more benign explorers a bad name. If you have nothing to say beyond a messy scribble of your name or your group's name, don't say anything at all. If you really can't suppress your instinct to mark your territory, please just wait until you get home and then urinate on your furniture until you get that weird evolutionary misfire out of your system. When you're exploring, respect the site and your fellow explorers by not marking the place up. Not only does tagging a site increase your odds of getting punished if you're caught, it also damages the character of a place and makes it much more likely that the owners or the government will have it sealed. (If the ethical argument doesn't persuade you, restrain yourself for selfish reasons. Spray paint fumes are full of neurotoxins that can wreck your nervous and immune system, so it's really stupid to tag up inside an enclosed space like a basement, a storm drain or a utility tunnel.)

It's an even bigger mistake to bring weapons when you go exploring. While it's true that you're leaving the protected zone and may occasionally encounter people with an "off-the-grid" mentality, there are much friendlier ways to look out for yourself than with weapons. Defending yourself need not involve force: just being polite and respectful is almost always the right way to deal with squatters. (Note that I say "being respectful" rather than "acting respectful" — it's foolish to look down on someone just because they don't have a house.) On the extremely rare occasions when those tactics don't work, walking away or running and hiding is much more likely to keep you alive than brandishing a weapon. It's neither suspicious nor dangerous to carry a small pocket knife; just make sure you remember that it's a tool and not a weapon.

Finally, avoid overpacking. If you're heading into a situation where you're likely to wind up scaling fences, climbing ropes, squeezing through grates or trudging along for a few hours, do yourself a favour and pack lightly. Leave your enormous tripod at home and just try to find a flat surface for your long exposure shots. Forget the gadgets and stick with what you need.

PREPARING

While unexpectedly stumbling upon a cool exploration site and touring the whole thing in one go is always satisfying, in most cases urban exploration trips require some degree of advance planning. This can be anything from "Tomorrow let's go see what we can see at the cathedral" to hours of searching through archives, finding blueprints, preparing maps, making up cover stories, choosing a date when there will be minimal moonlight, establishing code words, synchronizing watches, running through the plan repeatedly and the whole spy-movie deal. While it's easy to take it too far, a reasonable amount of advance planning can increase your chances of getting in and finding what you're looking for, decrease your chances of getting caught or injured and add to your overall enjoyment of the exploratory experience.

Some people prefer to find out all about a place in advance and then go scout it out, while others prefer to stumble upon something cool, scope it out and then figure out what its story is later. Either approach is fine, but in my humble opinion you're really skipping steps — and possibly cheating yourself out of both useful clues and full enjoyment of a place — if you don't do some research and scouting before you stage an in-depth infiltration of a place. After researching and scouting, you're ready to sit down with your friends and formulate an intelligent plan of attack.

Legal Considerations

When people ask me if the zine *Infiltration* is about breaking into buildings, I say no, it isn't. I've never broken anything to get into a building and, whatever the law says, it's ridiculous to refer to walking through an open door as "breaking and entering". "Entering" just didn't sound sinister enough on its own, so they had to partner it up with "breaking" and hope it would come to sound evil by association. Personally, I don't think it's worked. To me, "entering" still sounds pretty damn harmless and natural and in keeping with the best human instincts.

Urban exploration revives an old and long-out-of-favour legal concept called *usufruct*, which basically means that someone has the right to use and enjoy the property of another, provided it is not changed or damaged in any way. Back in the day, before all property on earth came under the control of corporations, usufruct was a legal privilege that could be awarded or withdrawn by the powers that were. Today, urban explorers see nothing unreasonable or disrespectful about claiming the same privilege for themselves and applying it to their utterly benign explorations of other people's property.

Unfortunately, relatively few states and municipalities see things this way. None, actually. If you're caught while exploring, you could potentially face some fairly serious punishments, if you're unlucky enough to be caught by an unfriendly cop and sentenced by an unsympathetic judge. It's a good idea to familiarize yourself with your provincial or state laws and municipal by-laws regarding trespassing and related offences, so you know what specific bizarre anti-trespassing laws are enforced in your area. These are often available online; if not, you can probably look them up in the library. Don't make the mistake of assuming your local laws are based on common sense! Even assuming that you have taken nothing, damaged nothing and neither harmed nor risked harm to anyone but yourself, some of the different things your local police may decide to try to charge you with include:

Breaking and entering. As mentioned above, "breaking and entering" is an utter joke of a name in that this crime requires no breaking, not even the breaking of a seal. Realistically, the crime should simply be called "entering", since it requires only the most minor application of pressure. ("I'm in for murder. How about you?" "I entered.") Even if you just gently blow on an unlocked and slightly ajar door to permit entry to a site, you can technically be charged with B&E. Any judge that would actually charge you with this would obviously be doing so in utter disregard for the *spirit* of the law, which is clearly intended to punish people for forced entry, but that's not to say it wouldn't happen. In more enlightened jurisdictions, the breaking and entering charge is only levelled at those who enter with the intention of committing a crime, but most locales will charge you with breaking and entering for simply pushing open a door they didn't want you to push open. The best defence against this charge is to go in through an already-open door, window or hole in the wall, rather than opening something yourself, whenever possible.

Burglary. Burglary is very similar to breaking and entering, except that the person who does the entering must be deemed to have done so in the hopes of stealing or committing some other crime, and the charge is normally only applied in situations involving active buildings. The easiest way to prove that someone entered with the intention of stealing something is if they did, in fact, steal something, but that's not to say you won't be charged with burglary unless you take something, since confused cops and judges often attribute false motives to explorers. A burglary charge normally requires a demonstration that the person being charged either (a) intended to steal or commit some other crime on the premises or (b) brought a dangerous weapon onto the premises. Punishments can be more severe if the building is actually occupied at the time of entry. Identifying yourself as an explorer and demonstrating this to be true might provide you with a defence against a charge of burglary.

Forgery. Legally speaking, lying to people verbally is one thing; misrepresenting yourself via documents is another. Explorers who use fake IDs or register or sign in with phoney names render themselves vulnerable to a charge of forgery or the related charge of impersonation. The best defence against these charges is to simply avoid situations where you must identify yourself on paper. If you wish to make yourself business cards or something along those lines, use a generic title such as "photographer" rather than an obviously misleading and easily disprovable title such as "health inspector". And feel free to take advantage of the fact that people in certain occupations, such as actors and writers, frequently operate under professional pseudonyms without being guilty of misrepresentation.

Mischief. Mischief is a sort of grab-bag crime, a miscellaneous category just in case someone does something naughty that the powers that be forgot to outlaw. In many situations where the powers that be feel that punishing you with trespassing alone isn't serious enough, they may figure out a way to tack on an additional charge of mischief — rather than the more traditional "assorted wrongdoing and mucking about". Many definitions of mischief require that the person charged be responsible for some damage to property, but other broader definitions require only that one obstruct others from using property. For example, you might be charged with mischief if you were caught on the subway tracks — thereby potentially delaying the travel of a subway train and inconveniencing all its passengers. It's tough to keep yourself completely safe from a charge of mischief, but your odds of avoiding the charge are better if you avoid fiddling or tampering with anything.

Possession of burglar's tools. You can be charged with this crime if you are deemed to have been in the possession of any tool or instrument designed or commonly used to aid in forcible entry into a site. Some jurisdictions quite reasonably add that the person must also have intended to steal or commit another crime on the premises in order to be charged; others, less reasonably, do not. Obviously, the best defence against this charge is to never get caught with lock picks on your person; the easiest way to do that is to not carry them.

Trespassing. Trespassing, as you might guess, is deemed to have occurred when one knowingly enters a property without the expressed or implied permission of the owner, or when one refuses to leave a property after having been asked to do so by the owner or one of his or her representatives. "Implied permission" is a tough thing to define, but it's generally tough to claim there was "implied permission" if there were a lot of "keep out" signs or if you had to climb a fence to get in. It's easier if you're at the mall or a train station. (Some jurisdictions — far too few, alas — add that a person must have caused at least a very slight bit of damage to the property to be guilty of trespassing. In most cases, unfortunately, this isn't necessary.) In most Canadian jurisdictions, a ticket for trespassing will set you back under $100 and won't go on your permanent record as long as you pay it promptly. These tickets are roughly as serious as parking tickets. Penalties can be much more severe in parts of the US — research the current laws for your state and municipality online.

I won't mention anything about the penalties you face for vandalism or theft, except to say that they're appropriately harsh, and that often stealing something worth four and a half cents is punished exactly the same way as stealing something worth $1,999. And while the powers that be are occasionally willing to give you a break if all you're guilty of is trespassing, this becomes far, far less likely if even minor theft or vandalism is involved. You really are better off if you just resolve here and now never to take any souvenirs, tag any walls or cause any damage while exploring.

The way citizen's arrest works varies dramatically from place to place. According to section 494 of the Canadian Criminal Code, any citizen can arrest anyone they see committing an indictable offence, or if they have reasonable ground to believe they were committing an indictable offence, or if they see someone being chased by someone with the authority to arrest that person. The laws on citizen's arrest in the US vary more widely from state to state — for detailed information on how it works in your area, try doing an Internet search.

Normally, citizen's arrest will only come into play when security guards try to stop you. As much as they like to pretend otherwise, security guards do not have the same powers as cops. Legally speaking, in most jurisdictions, they can't arrest you unless they catch you red-handed, can't confiscate your property and can't detain you unless they place you under arrest. If the guards don't place you under arrest, it's probably because they realize they aren't legally able to do so. Be sure to ask them if you are able to leave — if they know and care about the law, they will likely be reluctant to say no, since they can face serious consequences for illegally detaining you. If they do place you under arrest, they're legally required to turn you over to the police immediately.

So, those are your legal rights with regard to security guards. While they're interesting as a matter of trivia, they won't necessarily make that much difference in the real world unless you're lucky enough to have some witnesses when you're caught. In reality, security guards can do whatever they can get away with, including driving you down to the beach, beating the crap out of you and leaving you there in a pile overnight. Don't be so naïve as to assume that knowing your rights will keep you safe, and if detained by security aim to stay in the public eye as much as possible. When they ask you to accompany them back to the office, just politely refuse and say you'd prefer to stay in public. While it's certainly unfair and inaccurate to say that all guards are overgrown bullies, unfortunately, it is a profession that appeals to a lot of people who like the idea of intimidating and inconveniencing others for their own amusement.

As for the police themselves, their powers are a little more extensive. Police powers vary greatly from jurisdiction to jurisdiction, so this is only a very rough outline. In any police encounter, be polite, respectful and cooperative, while still being aware of your rights and invoking them whenever it is in your best interest to do so. A police encounter will often begin with the officer asking you for your name, address and identification; you should probably provide these whether you are legally compelled to or not. Officers can search you and your vehicle if they suspect you may have weapons (or drugs, in some areas), or if they are willing to claim they harbour such a suspicion, but you can and probably should refuse their search request otherwise. Make your refusal very polite — "I understand that you want to do your job, officer, but I do not consent to a search of my private property" — but do refuse. Don't listen if they say that you'll make things easier for everyone if you just consent to a warrantless search; you'll really only make things easier for them. Refusing to consent to a warrantless search is not only in the best long-term interests of society as a whole, but it can also benefit you in the short term, since any potential evidence the officers subsequently turn up on you or in your vehicle may be legally inadmissible. While still being polite and respectful, determine whether or not you are being officially detained — officers sometimes like to be vague about this until they're asked directly. If you are not, you can be on your way. If you are, be careful about what you say without a lawyer present.

If you are ticketed for trespassing, accept the ticket and leave. If it seems unfair, or you think the fine is too high, you can think about appealing the charge later. If you are arrested, you have a right to know why you're being arrested and a right to see a lawyer as soon as possible. Despite any suggestions they may make to the contrary, you shouldn't speak to the police about your alleged crime until you've spoken with a lawyer. Be especially certain to refrain from signing anything until you speak with a lawyer.

Being arrested isn't the same as being charged, so being arrested isn't necessarily anything to panic about. They may just be double-checking some details before letting you go with a warning or a ticket. Some less-than-decent police forces will arrest you and hold you without charging you for a time as a method of punishing you without ever having you appear before a judge.

Finding Sites

While some people are content to follow in other explorers' footsteps and revisit sites that have previously been deemed interesting and photogenic, others take more pleasure in discovering uncharted realms, or at least discovering previously charted realms on their own. Of course there's nothing wrong with visiting sites revealed to you by other people, since a large part of this hobby is about aesthetic appreciation and sharing interesting finds, but I think your greatest exploratory joys will come from finding new areas yourself.

A big part of finding new sites lies in acquiring the sensibility that potential places to explore are everywhere. With experience, you will realize that our urban environments are ripe, juicy melons, waiting to be squeezed and suckled, and that you just have to get through a tiny bit of flavourless rind to get to the good stuff. And what good stuff it is.

When someone in Toronto says they're at the northeast corner of Yonge and Bloor, they're being imprecise. There are lots of places to be at that corner, including 35 storeys up on the roof of the Hudson's Bay Centre; at various abandoned floors or mechanical rooms within the tower; inside the tower's elevator shafts; in the pedestrian walkway under the street; at the abandoned movie theatres or the abandoned nightclub in the building's basement; in the mazes of service corridors, steam tunnels and storage rooms in the various subbasements; inside the small man-made cave accessed through those service corridors; in the subway tunnels, mechanical rooms and ventilation shafts under that; or in the storm drains, sewers and water tunnels under that. Oh, I suppose being at street level is also a possibility, though certainly the least interesting one.

If all that can be found at one dull-looking corner of one dull-looking intersection, you can just imagine how much more is out there waiting to be found by those who pull back the curtains and take a peek. It's true that finding out about all this three-dimensional potential in the first place can require a fair bit of effort, but really this is a good thing, as it keeps lazy, careless and uncreative people from dabbling in our hobby too much and spoiling it for those of us who are more determined. While any idiot can find an abandoned building to visit by searching an online database, only devoted explorers can experience the joy of discovering, forging their way into and ultimately unveiling fresh, new sites.

Part of finding exploration sites involves casting off a certain restrained mindset, in the manner of the protagonists of movies like *They Live*, *The Matrix* and *Fight Club*, and realizing that many of your boundaries are self-imposed, voluntary and, ultimately, illusory. Fish farmers — who, incidentally, have not yet been the focus of a single major motion picture — occasionally employ a clever trick to keep their stock penned up. They corral their fish into a certain section of the ocean and then surround the area with a curtain of air bubbles being released in a steady stream from a perforated tube or hose at the bottom of the corral. The fish perceive the air bubbles as a solid wall and believe they are helplessly penned in, though in reality no barrier stands in their way except a thin strand of colourless gas. The only thing stopping the fish from swimming to freedom and exploring all the infinite wonders of the ocean is a simple problem of limited perception.

It's the same with people. Many people think urban exploration is about bravely or foolishly defying "do not enter" and "no trespassing" signs, but in actuality most of the signs that keep people away from interesting places are much more subtle — a door that just *looks* like it's for employees only, for example, or a hole that you're *probably not* supposed to climb down into. A lot of people equate the absence of a sign saying "sale" or "admission prices" with the presence of a sign saying "keep out". But these aren't real barricades — they're just air bubbles. (Incidentally, this is an important lesson in perception that you can take from urban exploration and apply to all of your everyday affairs: you set your own boundaries, and can expand them as you see fit.)

Once you're constantly on the lookout for places to explore, you'll find them. I've seen it happen to people — they go from having no idea that a secret world exists to having no time to check out all their leads. Basically, once enlightenment occurs, the blinders fall off and you re-learn how to pay attention to your surroundings, at least temporarily.

Once you get the right mindset, you'll see countless opportunities every time you walk down the street. You'll see intriguing stories about new construction projects or factory closings every time you read the paper. You'll strike up friendly conversations with janitors, people poking theirs heads out of manholes, security guards and other employees and find out about the most interesting secret places they've found in their jobs. You'll talk to old people and hear about interesting areas that are no longer open to the public and how the city used to be laid out differently. You'll talk to squatters about interesting places they've found or heard about. You'll read local history books and pore over local topographic maps and come up with a checklist of dozens of different places you need to go check out. You'll visit your town archives and find boxes and boxes of delicious blueprints and maps and notes. You'll do web searches for your town name plus "tunnels" and "abandoned" and "underground" and "no longer in use" and turn up dozens of hits. You'll read minutes from municipal government meetings, paying special attention to the zoning, planning and transportation sections and get advance notice about all sorts of upcoming opportunities. You will seek and you will find. Your greatest challenge, as you get into the hobby for the first time, may be making sure it doesn't become your whole life. A lot of urban explorers are total geeks.

Research
Knowing is at least half the battle, so learn all that you can in advance, especially if you're going somewhere dangerous or difficult. Ask people who've been to the site before for advice and warnings. Read any histories or descriptions of the area you can get your hands on. Track down whatever relevant maps you can find to locate as many potential

opportunities and threats as possible. Search online for satellite images of the area. If you can find pictures, maps or blueprints of the site in question, study them. Try to gather an idea of how well you'll be able to blend in. It's usually easy to go unnoticed at a large institution, but it can be more of a trick at smaller establishments — such as community churches or small schools — where everyone knows each other. Be aware of any special events or construction projects in the area you'll be visiting.

If you can, get a rough idea of what sort of security you're likely to face. If the site you're interested in features expensive equipment, or is populated with children, or is a potential terrorist target, expect a higher level of security. Also expect better security if the building was built or extensively remodelled within the past 15 years. If you can, find out what security company serves the building you're interested in and research that company's policies on arrests, carrying weapons and the like. If not, maybe you can pick up a few ideas about what you're up against.

Scouting

It's a mistake to go somewhere risky if you don't have any idea what you're getting into, and it is for this reason that many explorers will devote at least one trip — and often several — to scouting out a tricky location before trying to infiltrate it.

Casing the joint is part of the fun of exploring, particularly for those with a bit of a private investigator or investigative journalist streak. Generally, you needn't make much of an effort to be stealthy on a scouting trip, since hiding in plain sight will work better. Because the scout doesn't do anything but look, he or she can usually take lots of pictures and notes or film lots of footage without worrying much about drawing attention. Subtlety is still useful, of course: obviously, you should attempt to seem more interested in the spectacular views and fancy decorations than in the elevator banks, security keypads or apparent trap doors in the floor. Taking along an opposite-sex friend and having the "couple" pretend to take pictures of each other, while actually taking pictures of various doors and signs and security measures, is one good trick; another is to bring along a video camera and leave it running after you pretend to turn it off. Of course, these tricks only work in those places where photography or filming are allowed; in more shy buildings, the scout has to find ways to do the job more subtly. Pictures taken on such scouting trips can usually be forgiven for occasional blurriness or for being partially obstructed by a part of a hand or shirt.

On your scouting trips, you should determine, at least, the size and shape of the structure you're dealing with, where its entrances and exits are and whether any portions of it are alarmed, watched by closed circuit cameras, surveyed by motion detectors or guarded by any other sort of electronic access control. If you're dealing with an abandoned building or a construction site, note whether or not the perimeter is completely fenced in, and try to get an idea of what the lighting is like at night. If you're dealing with an occupied location, a construction site or an abandoned building near a populated area, it's also useful to note just how populated the area is at various times and by whom.

On top of these bare essentials, it's helpful to know roughly how many on-site security guards the place has, if any, and what their stations or circuits are, and any security checkpoints you find. If you can, note how they're equipped, so you know whether or not running away is a good option and have an idea how they'll communicate with others. Knowledge of any sensitive areas may be useful, as you'll know to avoid those areas or at least visit them only with great care. If you're just trying to determine whether security ever visits a particular portion of a site, leaving a few quarters on the ground and casually checking on them every now and then is a good way to find out. Similar tricks involve lightly dusting a floor with dirt and later checking for footprints, or putting a small marker such as a toothpick or a piece of tape in front of a door to see if and when it gets opened. But enough spy games. In reality, a scouting trip only requires the scouts to map the buildings, know the exits and get a pretty good idea of the hazards and opportunities. The information collected on the scouting trip or trips should be shared with everyone who intends to join in the actual exploration.

If you're too picky, or your town is too small, and you find you can't easily turn up places to explore, spend some time at your local library and town archives (if your town doesn't have a separate archives building, the archives will likely be located inside the town hall or courthouse). Look for material on local history or histories of construction, industry, transportation and health care in the area. Look for detailed maps from different time periods and look for puzzling changes like disappearing rivers or rail lines. Every time you find something hard to explain, look into it. If you aren't totally creepy and suspicious, feel free to ask the librarian or archivist for help. They usually love to talk about this stuff, or at least will know where you can find someone who does.

Looking Online

While it's a huge mistake to rely entirely on the web, online resources can be pretty handy aids to your research. As mentioned, a search for your town name plus the type of site you're interested in can often give you a few useful starting points for further research. Aside from Google, some of the other big general-use sites can be helpful, especially if you happen to be part of the American audience that most of them target.

The Emporis Building Database (*http://www.emporis.com/en/bu/*) provides useful statistics about buildings and structures in more than 7,000 cities worldwide and is a great place to look for interesting buildings or construction projects near you, and to find out more about places that have already caught your eye.

The Center for Land Use Interpretation's Land Use Database (*http://www.clui.org/clui_4_1/ludb/*) is a free site that bills itself as a guide to "unusual and exemplary sites throughout the United States". CLUI's database provides relevant links and information about noteworthy mining sites, features of transportation systems and field test facilities for a variety of high-impact technologies. The Environmental Protection Agency's Superfund site (*http://www.epa.gov/superfund/*) provides similar information, including maps and addresses, for those who don't mind a little toxic waste with their abandoned factories. Seriously, you may want to search your area — sometimes the Superfund sites aren't *that* contaminated.

TopoZone (*http://www.topozone.com*) and Terra Server (*terraserver.microsoft.com*) are commercial services with some free features. They can display maps of almost any location in the US by a variety of methods, including some that are extremely useful to explorers, such as one-metre-scale aerial photo maps. The excellent Google Maps site (*http://maps.google.com*) now features up-close satellite images of addresses in the US and some of southern Canada. These scrollable images make it very easy to find storm drains and other potential exploration sites. Plus, you can look at your own house.

The National Register of Historic Places (*http://www.nationalreg-*

isterofhistoricplaces.com) is another site primarily useful to Americans — it lists districts, sites, buildings and structures deemed historically important, many of which would be cool places to explore. The "vacant/not in use" section is of particular interest.

You may also find some major location urban exploration databases, such as those featured on Urbanexplorers.net *(http://www.urbanexplorers.net)*, Urban Exploration Resource *(http://www.uer.ca)* or the Virtual Museum of Dead Places *(http://www.vimudeap.de)* to be of use, though their fill-in-the-blanks approach tends to lead to results that are less than moving. (There's never an "Emotions Experienced During Trip:" field in these databases.) If you, like me, enjoy a little local colour and personality along with your raw data, go directly to the source and visit the local websites themselves. Many of these can be accessed through the links section on Infiltration *(http://www.infiltration.org)* or through the Urban Exploration Webring *(http://e.webring.com/hub?ring=draining)*.

Urban Exploration Resource has a very large and active message board that can be a good place to ask questions and share information on both localized and general subjects, especially for North Americans; many of the more local sites have fairly active and useful message boards as well. It's always a good idea to search the archives for keywords before you start a new conversation.

A variety of non-urban-exploration sites dedicated to mapping out places like historic sites, ghost towns, mines, "haunted" sites or airplane graveyards can also be useful.

Communications
If you and your friends want to develop a complex system of code words and hand signals, have fun with that, but make sure everyone in your group really has your system down. You don't want to be hunched down around the corner from the guard trying to remember if your friend's clenched fist means he wants you to hold still or back off. For the same reason, if you go exploring with people outside of your regular group, don't assume that the strangers will intuitively pick up the bizarre gestures you and your friends have concocted. Give them a proper tutorial and quiz them before you go out. (Incidentally, as useful as practice is, don't communicate silently while you're walking around in the public areas of an active building. People walking along silently while occasionally gesticulating are

much more suspicious than people walking along talking, especially on camera.)

As fun as it is to play spy and make up code gestures, I've found that the universal gestures that almost everyone understands — nodding, shaking your head, shrugging your shoulders, putting your finger to your lips, pointing, holding up your hand in a blocking gesture — can be combined with a little basic miming and lip-reading to communicate almost everything when it's necessary to be silent. It may not be the most elegant or the most efficient method of communication, but it's the most universal and least likely to lead to misunderstandings.

In most situations where other people are around, you're better off avoiding whispering, since even if the other people can't make out your words, nothing attracts attention like the hissed "s" sounds of whispering. Speaking in a low but regular voice and phrasing things in a slightly roundabout way — saying "I'm gonna grab some fresh air; join me in couple minutes if you're free" rather than "Watch my back while I try to sneak away and climb out to the roof, and then if I haven't come back in a few minutes and the coast is still clear, follow me up" — will usually work much better than using hushed tones. If you're not whispering, people will just assume what you're saying is dull.

Radios, such as FRS radios and CBs, can be useful in certain situations, provided everyone knows how and when to use them and provided they work properly, but they can also be more trouble than they're worth. Unless you're exploring just the above-ground areas of a wooden building, you can pretty much count on the fact that there will be times when they don't work, because radios can have a great deal of difficulty with cement and metal, and don't work reliably underground. Sometimes slightly different systems don't synch up properly. Sometimes batteries fail. Sometimes people accidentally hit the "page" button or ask "are you there?" at exactly the wrong time. Many things can go wrong, so radio communication should be regarded as a potential aid rather than an integral part of your plan. In most situations, you're better off if your group just sticks together, or if you employ cell phones set to vibrate rather than ring.

Of course, there's more to communicating with your fellow explorers than just knowing your hand signals and having your radios set to the same channel. You and everyone you're with must be willing to put aside any macho posturing and actually behave as if you're concerned for your own safety and for theirs. I realize this is a pretty radical thing to ask of some people who have made the appearance of apathy and toughness an art form, but you really should give it a whirl if you're in some place where there's a real chance someone could be hurt. This means warning people behind you if there's something to step over or duck under, rather than just dodging the hurdle silently and figuring they'll spot it too. It means assuming a pace that works for everyone, instead of racing ahead quickly to show how familiar you are with the location. It means telling your fellow explorers if you've ever had a problem with fainting or vertigo. It means asking people if they're okay if they trip, and making sure they mean it when they automatically say yes. It means checking on people to make sure they aren't exhausted before doing something physically demanding and checking that they aren't freaking out before doing something dangerous. It means sharing water and making sure no one is getting dehydrated. It also means admitting when you hit your head and it really hurts, or you're dizzy, or when you're feeling claustrophobic — it may be tough to admit your weaknesses, but the people you're with *have* to know that kind of thing to make informed decisions about what your group is capable of. You can put everyone at risk if you conceal these things until it's too late.

The Plan
In many cases, you or your group will have a specific goal, like "get to the top of the tallest roof" or "find the entrance to the steam tunnels". Such goals are handy, since clearly visualizing what you want to accomplish will generally help you achieve it, but try not to be too result-oriented. One of the main beauties of the hobby of urban exploration is that the main goal is just to see what you can see. It's frustrating when, after a fun afternoon of dodging cameras, climbing ladders and hiding from employees with some fellow explorers, someone acts as if an excursion was a failure because your group didn't get to the roof or the pool or whatever specific target you had in mind, when you thought it was a huge success because you had fun. While having specific goals is useful, you're more likely to feel contented and successful if your broader goal is simply to explore and maybe gather useful information for your next attempt. Often, exploring is what happens while you're busy looking for other tunnels.

Other aspects of your planning should be more detailed. You should pre-arrange a meeting place that everyone will be able to get to in case your group gets split up at any point, such as when you're running away from security. Based on where you're going and what your group is like, decide in advance if you're going to run, hide or try to talk your way out of the situation if you're caught — it's best that everyone in your group agrees on one solution. You may want to modify the game plan at various points during the expedition — for example, you may decide that in the basement you're better off trying to talk you way out of it, but once you get into the tunnels, you may decide that you're better off running for it if you encounter anyone. Again, make sure everyone is fully up-to-date on what the plan is every time you alter it.

If someone in your group wants to bail out, you should all bail out. It doesn't really matter how hard it was to get in, or even how once-in-a-lifetime this particular opportunity seems: the other people you're exploring with should always come first if you want to develop an enthusiastic team of explorers who trust each other. If someone really, truly doesn't want to go on (or wait somewhere safe), it shouldn't be put to a vote: they should just have veto power. Maybe knowing that they're able to bail out at any time if things get too strenuous or too scary will make them more confident on the next mission. Of course if the same person is always bailing out you may want to stop inviting that person along, but the time to discuss this is after you've left the dangerous situation, not while you're in the middle of it. Obviously it's frustrating to turn back in the middle of an expedition, but the potential long-term benefits of having a group that really trusts one another outweigh the short-term thrills of a cool trip.

Before going on any sort of dangerous expedition, always inform at least one other person who isn't coming along where you will be and when you expect to be back. If you're able, bring a cell phone so you can communicate with people outside the site if you should somehow become delayed or encounter other problems, if the reception gods are with you.

Getting There
In all situations where you're able, it's best to walk, ride a bike or take public transit to the site, as cars and their associated license plates are headaches that often play a significant role in explorers getting busted. Cars can be easily traced to people, so if your car is parked outside of the place you're exploring, there's really not much point in you trying to make a break for it. Cars can also be stolen, vandalized, disabled, blocked-in or searched by the police or other gangs. While bikes are

also vulnerable to theft or vandalism, you can usually recover from the loss of a bike more easily than the loss of a car, especially if you invest in a junk bike for use in expeditions to questionable areas. Bikes are also quieter and easier to hide than cars. Public transit, while sometimes slow and unreliable, doesn't have any of these problems. A subway train is the ultimate getaway vehicle.

That said, a lot of places, particularly semi-rural abandonments, can only be accessed by car. In such cases, unless you want to take a cab (not unthinkable, if you're able to split the cost three or four ways), the best you can do is to park your car somewhere inconspicuous but in the public eye, even if the place you're visiting is kind of in the middle of nowhere. Not only is it worth a 20-minute walk from your car to the site in order to have some peace of mind about your car, it also avoids the problem of your suspiciously parked car alerting police or security guards to your presence. Please don't do anything silly like trying to cover your car with leaves and branches.

Okay. We're there. Everybody got their tetanus shots? Let's go!

THE MOLSON BREWERY

The old Molson Brewery, like all other buildings in the Greater Toronto Area, was in the midst of being redeveloped into condos. After several scouting and exploring expeditions with Liz (during which we went in a few different entrances and established that claims that the complex was patrolled by packs of free-range guard dogs were greatly exaggerated), I eventually partnered up with Gilligan in order to explore the complex in more depth. We arrived on the property in the early afternoon and briskly strolled past the busy parking lot and security trailer to one of the entrances Liz and I had discovered earlier. We hoisted ourselves up and in.

The first four storeys, formerly devoted to storage, were just hallways suspended in the air. Not only do scarcely any interesting artefacts remain, most of the walls and floors have been stripped away as well, which makes for some interesting pictures but not a lot to explore. Fortunately, a partially flooded stairwell leads up to more interesting levels.

Closer to the top of the building, the "fermentation" levels are more interesting, mainly because they're still fully (or almost fully) in possession of floors. Additionally, each of the upper levels has a fantastic pinhole camera effect going on: a small, sunlit hole on the wall facing the expressway projects the images of passing cars across the whole room onto the opposite wall, so it's like watching a film of suspended cars driving along upside-down beneath an elevated roadway.

We would've missed that if we'd come at night; and we might have missed something else too. On the seventh floor we found a portable metal staircase lying on its side in the middle of the floor, and Gilligan propped this up so he could climb up onto an I-beam for a picture. While I was getting ready to take his picture, Gilligan pointed at the floor and mentioned I might want to look out. In the spot where the staircase had been, there was a two-foot by two-foot square hole in the floor leading to a 30-foot drop. We carefully lowered the metal staircase back atop this hole, and then headed up in search of the roof.

At the top of the stairwell, we were delighted to find a ladder leading up to an unlocked hatch. Gill climbed up and out first. When I popped my head up through the hatch, I saw that Gilligan was lying flat on his front in the gravel with a big smile on his face. As I climbed up, I looked up at the lightbulb-filled Molson billboard, and out at the city. My god were we exposed! There was no ledge at

Gilligan pressed face down into the mushy gravel and glass atop the Molson Brewery.

all around the sides of the roof, so we were just a couple of feet away from a nine-storey drop. And we were in plain sight of everyone on the elevated Gardiner Expressway: the reason the brewery is wrapped in three of the biggest billboards in Canada is that 200,000 cars drive past the building each day, probably making it one of the most visible places in the country. I flopped down in the gravel beside Gilligan, and we laughed out of happiness, excitement and nervousness.

Eager to get away from the edges of the roof, we made our way towards the billboard; Gilligan simply rolled through the gravel and broken lightbulbs scattered around the roof, while I tried to stay low as I crawled toward it. I noticed that the roof felt more like firm pudding than solid cement, though this was pudding with a lot of broken lightbulbs in it.

"This roof has a lot of give," I called over to Gilligan, as he rolled along behind me. "A LOT of give. Like maybe too much."

"It's probably good that I'm rolling, then," Gill replied.

We proceeded to the centre of the roof very cautiously, and climbed up onto the metal framework supporting the huge Molson billboard. We crawled along this into some much-needed shadow and took the best pictures we could manage from this shielded vantage point. We also noticed that the part of the roof in the shade seemed quite solid, and concluded that it was just warm tar that was making the rest of the roof seem, in my words, "like walking on a trampoline."

"It's more like being on a waterbed," Gill offered. "Might be a nice place to take a girl."

After only a few minutes of poking about under the billboard, I pointed out that a few thousand people had probably seen us now, and suggested that we get back inside. As we were making our way back through the hatch, a helicopter soared overhead, prompting us to hasten our departure. I'd forgotten that we were only a block or two away from the island airport.

Returning to a lower level, we made our way over to stairwell six and the southern half of the complex, and toured a variety of old mechanical rooms and distilling rooms still filled with a variety of photogenic artefacts before making our way back down to the ground floor and returning to the outside.

After a short rest, we headed on to examine the second building in the complex. We had begun discussing how pathetic the site's security was, and I was just explaining how ridiculous the claim about the guard dogs was, when a guard and a dog on a leash appeared a few feet away from us, behind a fence, and stared at us meanly.

"What were you saying?" Gill asked, as we strolled away.

"All right, fine. One guard dog, on a leash. He looked friendly."

ABANDONED SITES

Among the most delightful targets you'll find are abandoned sites, probably the most popular locales among urban explorers. Explorers tend to use the term "abandoned" in connection with anything currently uninhabited and out of use, whether or not the owners have actually abandoned their legal interest in the site. In common use, the term "abandoned" is applied to places ranging from long-forgotten, overgrown and barely standing ruins to merely depopulated sites that have been boarded up while they are gutted in preparation for their conversion into condos, even if they have active on-site security.

Half castle and half playground, the abandoned factory or hospital or theatre or train station that looms darkly on the edge of the skyline is virtually irresistible to those with a passion for seeking out and discovering the unknown and forgotten. Abandoned buildings can be incredibly moving and beautiful places; the whole tragic process of decay and entropy is both sad and breathtaking to behold. The silence and stillness of an abandoned building allow you to really take the time to pay attention to and reflect on the place and its impermanence, and to capture some aspects of the experience through photographs.

In addition, abandoned sites provide the best and most interactive museums of industrial archaeology and local history you'll ever find. Those buildings that haven't been stripped bare often house incredible old machines or technology we've all but forgotten today. And it's one thing to read about how psychiatric patients were treated, but quite another to find the records of their electroshock therapy sessions and read their reactions and see their drawings on the walls. Whereas in most parts of the city it's easy to forget that the past ever happened, in abandoned buildings you're surrounded by the past and can't help but feel connected to it and a part of it.

Along with their decay, their emptiness and their history, abandoned buildings offer city and suburb dwellers an all-too-rare taste of authenticity. Unlike much of the modern urban environment, which uses superficial tricks like simulated stone, decorative brick façades and ornamental arches to fool us into thinking the places around us are less disposable than they are, abandoned buildings are comfortable just being themselves. They're the real deal, beautiful without any make up. People who live in towns made of sloppy junk buildings constructed with a few silly architectural gimmicks to disguise their overall banality can't help but notice the amount of authentic beauty and character that these old abandoned buildings exude, even beneath all the dirt and decay. They capture our attention because they weren't just carelessly snapped together with mass-manufactured, pre-built doors, windows and walls like buildings today; they were fashioned by artisans who designed for specific sites and specific needs, and who cared about what they were creating. It's worth seeing every area because every area was individually planned and constructed, and all are glorious in their own way.

There's also something of a moral duty to explore abandoned sites. If you don't go and appreciate these beautiful palaces of decay, it's possible no one will, and that would be a terrible shame.

Safety Issues

Unfortunately there's a good possibility of getting injured at abandoned sites, if you aren't careful (and sometimes even if you think you are). Getting a tetanus shot in advance is both fun and practical. When you're visiting an abandoned site, bear in mind that the building is not meant for use by the general public, and that it's entirely up to you to keep yourself alive. Explore abandoned sites slowly, dress sensibly and don't go alone. (I admit, other explorers and I have occasionally gone into abandoned sites alone and so far we've generally come back alive. But common sense says that it's a bad idea.)

When navigating an abandoned building, don't place too much confidence in floors and ceilings. In many old buildings, there are large holes in the floors, or the floors are so old and flooded that they're on the verge of collapse. Stay away from sagging floors. Test the floors in buildings the same way you would test thin ice and remember that sections of abandoned buildings do occasionally just topple, even when there's no one in them. This is particularly true of buildings made out of wood and of buildings that have been damaged by floods and fires. It's a no-brainer that you should avoid any areas in which there is evidence of a past fire even if the floor still looks solid, since the high temperatures of fires not only consume wood but also melt and distort metal. Even in areas that have never faced a fire, it's a bad idea to venture above the first storey if the stairs and upper storeys are constructed out of wooden planks. Very few wooden buildings stay watertight after being abandoned for a few years, and water damage can seriously undermine a building's structural integrity. Soggy, old, wooden buildings will eventually collapse, and they're more likely to do it when someone is inside. Buildings made of metal, stone, brick or concrete are certainly safer than buildings made out of wood, but it's still a good idea to be careful when climbing stairs or using ladders.

Keep your eyes open for the possibility of portions of the building collapsing. Watch out for bits of sharp metal and glass. Avoid slippery surfaces (like puddles, moss and pigeon droppings), and don't trust wooden handrails to be of much use. Stay away from areas completely filled with clouds of dust or any areas where you can't clearly see where you're going. Don't squeeze yourself into any tight situations unless you're quite certain you can get yourself back out.

In addition to the risk of injury, there is also a significant chance of getting sick, as abandoned sites may be filled with nasty bacteria, particularly if they've become outhouses or cemeteries for birds, rodents and other animals. Swarms of bugs, including mosquitoes, also enjoy hanging around in damp areas inside abandoned buildings, and sometimes decent-sized spiders move in to take advantage of these opportunities. In some abandoned areas, there may be a risk of exposure to asbestos. The hazards posed by asbestos are covered in the utility tunnels section.

Finally, some people — not all of whom are necessarily connected to the mafia — think of abandoned buildings as handy places to dump their leftover garbage, hazardous materials and toxic waste. Stay well away from bags or piles of refuse and avoid barrels and drums, regardless of whether or not they're labelled with festive warnings like "toxic", "caustic", "corrosive", "poisonous", "radioactive", "biohazard" and the like. The sort of people who drop their waste in an abandoned building are not the sort of people who are concerned about compliance with the latest Occupational Safety and Health Administration (OSHA) standards, and it only takes a little bit of the wrong kind of acid to burn your hands off. Face it, you're never going to find anything really cool in a barrel, anyhow, so you're better off just avoiding them altogether. If you do find toxic waste at an abandoned site, do the world a favour and make an anonymous call to report it.

Residents
We refer to them as abandoned buildings as shorthand, but in reality a fair number of the underused buildings and sites explorers visit are still populated from time to time, and may even have one or more perma-

The homeless should be treated respectfully and as though they're on your side. Liz and I encountered a few transients in the tunnels of the Rochester subway and exchanged friendly small talk with them about the tunnels before going our separate ways.

nent residents.

While those who think of abandoned sites as good places to get drunk or smoke pot or engage in intimate encounters are unlikely to do you any harm, those who see them as an ideal spot to sell and smoke crack are more likely to have issues with casual visitors, and those who use them as labs for making or processing crystal meth or other drugs are likely to be downright unsociable. Avoid such types to whatever extent possible. If you hear a rumour that an abandoned building might be home to a drug lab, or if you hear or see evidence of dogs inside an abandoned building, just avoid it entirely. If you ever accidentally stumble upon something or someone that seems connected to the drug trade, hide your camera and just try to seem apathetic and non-threatening as you get the hell out of there as quickly as possible. People connected to the drug trade can be pretty bad dudes.

As mentioned previously, the best way to deal with most houseless people is just to treat them with respect and go along with their wishes. You can take pictures of the building or site in a general way, but don't take pictures of them, their personal space or their belongings unless they specifically invite you to do so. Try to treat the person like a curator and behave like a guest. If you're indulging yourself and happen to have extra drinks, snacks or cigarettes, offer them some. If they don't seem antisocial, make it clear that you defer to their authority by asking them for information and advice about their building or other buildings in the area. Occasionally you'll run into someone agitated, angry and nervous who behaves threateningly or insists that you leave, and in these cases you probably should. Even though squatters don't really have any *legal* right to ask you to leave, they do kind of have the *moral* right, since they actually live there, whereas you're just visiting for kicks. But in most cases squatters understand that they and explorers occupy roughly the same grey area, and they probably won't be too upset about you visiting as long as you treat them decently and make it clear that you don't intend to bother them or damage their place in any way.

Security Issues
Unless they have specific orders to the contrary (or are temporarily consumed with orange alert fever), the police don't care much about people entering abandoned buildings. They'll certainly be happy to charge you or at least give you a stern talking-to if they happen to catch you going in or coming out, but it's not something most cops get very worked up about. They don't have a task force on the problem, and they're not likely to bother chasing you inside unless they have reason to think you're up to something like stealing, arson or planning a rave. Of course, if you leave a car parked somewhere obvious outside the building, you make yourself more vulnerable to punishment. It's much easier for them to look up your plates than to chase you inside, and having access to your car also provides them with exciting new opportunities to figure out something amusing to charge you with.

Sometimes an owner of a property who is particularly concerned about trespassing, perhaps because of concern for the building itself or for valuables within the building, or fear of lawsuits if anyone is hurt inside, will hire a security company to take an occasional drive by his or her building. Such guards are not at all likely to follow you inside a building, and often have specific orders not to do so, but they may call the cops or hang around and try their best to catch you on your way out if they're bored.

Some abandoned buildings (and I'm using the term "abandoned" loosely here) perceived as being particularly important or vulnerable are connected to alarms, usually door alarms or alarms triggered by motion detectors. These alarms are usually loud rather than silent; they're designed to scare you off the property rather than to help someone catch you in the act. Either the police or a private security company may respond to these alarms, but in many situations they'll have a policy against actually entering the property. If this is the case, you may simply need to find a comfortable place to wait them out. In fact, this may be true even if they *do* enter the building, if the place is big enough and filled with enough hiding places. Dogs usually aren't suited to tracking in an abandoned building environment, unless the place is just a large single-storey warehouse. I've set off an abandoned building alarm or two and heard stories from a fair number of other people who have as well, and I've never actually heard of anyone being caught inside an abandoned building as the result of an alarm.

Finding Abandoned Sites
Beyond asking around and listening for rumours, there are a few other basic tricks for discovering interesting abandoned buildings. Walking or riding a bike through your city's older industrial areas, generally either along the waterfront or along the railroad tracks, is an obvious place to start. A visit to the city archives or the local reference library can hook you up with useful city maps (both historical and current), topographical maps and aerial photos; sometimes you can find these goodies online too. It's fairly common for city maps to use different colours or shades for residential, commercial and industrial zones; the industrial zones are the best places to browse. A web search for "abandoned" or "derelict" and your city name might provide some leads. You can also just keep your eyes peeled for tall brick smokestacks, as there's often something quite wonderful at the bottom of those.

Keep in mind also that "abandoned sites" need not necessarily be limited to abandoned buildings. Abandoned subway stations, boats, trains and planes are often extremely interesting places to explore, as are a wide variety of abandoned tunnels and, in some parts of the world, subterranean military installations.

When to Go
Abandoned sites are open to the public year-round, 24 hours a day, so you can plan your visit for both the ideal time of the day and the ideal

time of the year. Just don't put it off too long.

Many explorers go out of their way to visit abandoned buildings during the day, both to avoid potential problems with flashlights and camera flashes at night and also because buildings tend to look and photograph a lot better in natural light. As an additional bonus, exploring during daylight hours makes you less likely to step into a hole you didn't notice. The main advantage of exploring at night is that darkness, when properly used, can provide a good deal of concealment while you're trying to get into a building, or while you're climbing about on its roof. Exploring an abandoned building at night can also be very pleasantly creepy.

Being unheated, abandoned buildings tend to get very cold during the winter. Since they frequently have broken windows and issues with flooding, they're also quite likely to be filled with snow and ice, which can actually make the inside of a building colder than the outside. On snowy days, your footprints may leave a trail for undesirables, including guards and other troublemakers, to follow you. Ice and chilled metal can make climbing more of a challenge than it would normally be; snowdrifts might conceal potential hazards and slippery floors and staircases can be dangerous.

On the other hand, there are some advantages to exploring in the winter. Other people's footprints in the snow can provide useful clues to entrances, and sometimes freezing temperatures provide the only possible route for exploring flooded basements and tunnels. Just make sure the ice is very thick and solid before trusting your weight to it. Buildings that are open to the elements are much less likely to be occupied, either in a long- or short-term sense, during the coldest months of winter, and you are also likely to face fewer issues with the insect and rodent communities.

Over the Barricade
The main purposes of fences and walls are to clearly delineate a property line and to deter those with very little motivation from entering a site. Perimeter fences mainly function as psychological barriers; according to US Army statistics, a skilled climber can get over a seven-foot-tall chain link fence in somewhere between two and five seconds. Stone and brick walls are rarely much trickier, especially since they're usually built with appearance rather than functionality in mind. Fences and walls also make life difficult for thieves, since they do a decent job of

Abandoned buildings and restoration sites often beg to be climbed. This abandoned wing of Toronto General Hospital features walls with many handholds and footholds as well as a wide variety of potential climbing aids.

keeping out cars and preventing loot-laden burglars from escaping.

When you encounter a fence or wall surrounding a site, a reasonable first step is to stroll its circumference and look for gaps, holes under the fence or other means of getting in without climbing over, since such methods are usually easier and less conspicuous. Most freshly unrolled chain link fences will have some person-sized gaps at the bottom, unless the site is on perfectly level ground.

In situations where it's impossible to roll under, climb through or go around a fence or wall, there's little choice but to go over it. The idea of climbing barricades makes a lot of people nervous, but it really isn't very hard as long as you're reasonably fit and in a reasonably well concealed area. (Trying to scale and hop down from a barricade alone very quickly in the middle of the afternoon is certainly a trickier proposition than trying to do the same thing with help from three friends in a secluded area at night.)

Often the biggest trick with climbing a chain link fence is trying to get a proper toehold since, unless you have unusually small feet or unusually pointy shoes, your footwear will probably be a little too big

Loose barbed wire poses less of a threat than tightly stretched barbed wire.

to catch in the gaps in the fence. In such a situation, you can try a few different things. Sometimes just throwing yourself up on the fence and quickly scrambling for the top will work, especially if the fence isn't that tall and you have decent upper body strength. In other cases, you might find it easier to take off your shoes and climb up in your socks — but don't forget to arrange some way to retrieve your shoes on the other side. Don't be shy about looking for shortcuts to make the climb easier. Gates and corners are often easier to climb than plain patches of fence, since they tend to have more potential hand- and foot-holds. A variety of nearby junk — from boards to tires to broken furniture to milk crates — can be commandeered to give you a boost. Bicycle racks propped up against a wall or fence make such perfect ladders you can't help but wonder if that was an intentional part of their design. On construction sites, leftover wooden skids or pallets serve the same purpose. Loose sections of fence propped up against a wall or fence at a 45-degree angle are also extremely easy to climb. If you can't find any handy props in the vicinity of tall fences or walls around a site, you might consider using your car, your bike or even your tripod to give yourself a boost.

Another important part of climbing tall fences and walls is knowing how to fall, since urban exploration is one of those hobbies where you occasionally find yourself hanging in mid-air wondering why you aren't at home playing a good videogame. When you have to fall from a height, do your best to land on the front of your feet and then try to relax your body and let it fold up smoothly, distributing the energy of

Some abandoned buildings are more hole than wall.

the impact rather than resisting it.

Barbed Wire and Razor Wire

In most situations involving barbed wire or razor wire (or razor wire's even nastier cousin, concertina wire), your best bet is probably to find a way under, through or around the fence. Take a good, thorough look around the perimeter before you give up on this idea, since you'll probably kick yourself if you cut up your ankle and then later realize that the lock on the main gate wasn't actually closed.

If you decide you really do need to go over the top, there are a few possible strategies you can use. All of them require you to have thick gloves and sturdy, snug clothing. The one technique you've probably seen in the movies involves throwing a thick blanket over the top of the wires as a bit of shielding. Razors will probably cut through most blankets if enough pressure is applied, but this method at least provides a little peace of mind. If, on the other hand, you're travelling light, you can try holding the wire still by grasping it between the barbs or razors with your gloved hand. As you move over the wire, be careful to get not only your body but also your clothes over the wires without snagging. Razor wire cuts through most work gloves and other clothing quite easily, but some protection is better than no protection as long as you're well aware of its limitations. Don't forget to wash your cuts out with soap, antibacterial solution or at least moist towellettes once you reach the other side of the fence. Those barbs and razors get dirty and rusty. And try to leave an easier way. Fortunately, it's often easier to get out of fenced-in compounds than it is to get in, unless you're visiting a prison or something of that sort.

Getting In

All right, you're at the site, through the perimeter barriers and now you just need to find your way inside. Sometimes this is the easy part; sometimes it's the hardest part of all. Unless you see or already know about an easy entrance, start by scouting the perimeter and evaluating your potential entrances in terms of concealment and ease of accessibility. At many abandoned sites, particularly those that attract a lot of visitors, getting inside is a simple matter of walking in through a missing door or wriggling in through a hole in the wall — in some places, there is more hole than wall. Other times you'll find unlocked doors; sometimes these are jammed shut and require some persuasion by your group's expert strong guy. If doors don't work out, you may be required to hoist yourself up and in through a broken window, ideally while wearing work gloves and being careful to avoid any remaining shards of broken glass around the edges. Other times you'll have to haul out the rope and lower yourself into an unlit and partially flooded basement and work your way up from there. If your entrance requires some planning, plan it in advance rather than working it out as you go, since from a getting caught perspective you're at your most vulnerable while you're in the midst of entering the premises, and these things often go faster with a little advance planning.

If a thorough check of the perimeter doesn't yield any possible entrances at ground level or in the basement, it's time to set your sights a little higher. The second storey is often much less secure than the first, and climbing up one storey of a building is rarely much more difficult than climbing over a wall. For starters, look around for easy routes up. Low-hanging fire escapes are the most obvious routes; in their absence, gates, drainpipes and trellises should all be viewed as substitute ladders. If you're making a difficult climb using rope — for example, if your group's best climber is trying to help the rest of your group climb up to join him or her — try tying knots in the rope every two feet or so to give yourself handholds and footholds on your way up; this makes a huge difference. If possible, loop the rope around the railings on a staircase or a fire escape and try climbing up while bracing yourself on the wall with your feet. (Incidentally, be very careful about using ropes left behind by previous visitors, as they may have deteriorated a fair bit since they last supported a lot of weight.)

Another possible route into some buildings — or a fun activity in and of itself — is buildering, or scaling buildings from the outside without the assistance of ladders. Buildering can be a very dangerous activity, so I recommend you get a great deal of practice in safe places before you try it anywhere dangerous or in less than ideal conditions. Finding a spot where you're unlikely to hurt yourself if you fall off, try gradually hauling yourself up to a

Always make sure doors won't lock behind you before you let them shut, or you could get trapped, as I was at this under-demolition wing at Toronto General Hospital.

ledge, window or low rooftop, using the building's indentations and decorative flourishes as hand- and footholds. Running jumps can provide a lot of help or a lot of pain, depending on your technique. As you're climbing, it's helpful to visualize your next several steps, see exactly how you're going to climb and know precisely where your hands and feet are going to be at each stage; some people do this instinctively, while others need to think it through. In some situations you may be able to make progress by chimneying, pressing your back against one wall and your feet against the other and slowly pushing yourself up the wall behind you with your legs. Again, get good at doing this somewhere safe before you do it somewhere dangerous.

If you can't get at the main building you had your heart set on, consider turning your attention to nearby buildings. Neighbouring buildings may provide a good indirect route into your dream building, either

While explorers don't leave graffiti, but we do often get a kick out of samples like this one at Detroit's Michigan Central Station.

through underground tunnels, or, if they're directly adjacent to the building you're interested in, by hopping from one building to another. You shouldn't attempt any miraculous 10-foot leaps, obviously, but sometimes it's a simple matter of stepping from one roof to the other, or gently lowering yourself down from one building's fifth-storey window onto the other building's directly adjacent four-and-a-half-storey roof.

Navigation

Getting around abandoned buildings is generally fairly straightforward, since under normal circumstances you should have all the time you need and no particular worries about locks, alarms or cameras. In theory, at least, you should eventually be able to make your way to every area you're interested in. There are, however, further safety issues to consider, on top of the aforementioned problems with collapsible floors and ceilings.

Sometimes it's hard to make sure you see everything, especially since older buildings tend to have more character and thus more chaotic layouts than modern buildings. It's probably not necessary to resort to mapping but, if you have the time and patience and desire to see as much as possible, it's a good idea to tour in a methodical fashion rather than simply racing to the good parts and then trying to fill in the gaps later. Generally it makes sense to tour a building from the bottom to the top, since exploring each floor provides a nice break from climbing the stairs or ladders, so I recommend starting in the deepest subbasement and working your way up from there.

Sometimes underground utility tunnels connect various buildings in abandoned complexes — like asylums, hospitals, schools and factories — and these tunnels are the easiest way or the only way to move from

Basement flooding can pose an obstacle during the warmed months.
During the coldest days of winter, it may be possible to trust your weight to
the ice, but never trust the ice too much.

building to building. While such tunnels are very interesting, they can also be quite dangerous, since they're generally totally unlit, and since you'd be much less likely to be found in an abandoned tunnel system than in an abandoned building. Such places are often flooded, and in winter you should be very wary about trusting your weight to the ice. If you do, you're better off spreading out your weight by crawling rather than walking. At all times, you should watch out for cracked asbestos insulation, mould, sharp metal, badly rusting ladders, hostile wildlife and other nastiness occasionally found in abandoned utility tunnels.

If you feel the need to climb up stairs or ladder rungs that are rotting or have faced fire or water damage, (a) don't, (b) if you do anyhow, at least stay close to the more supported sides of the staircase or ladder. The middle of a staircase is usually the most dangerous part. If applicable, hold on tight to the metal railing along the side of the stairs. These railings aren't designed to be load-bearing, but they might help you out in a pinch. In some circumstances where the railing is built out of sturdy metal while the stairs are merely built out of wood, you might want to place more faith in the railing than in the stairs themselves — indeed, if a few a steps are missing, you can climb the railing instead of the stairs. But please don't do any of this if you're the kind of person who might be inclined to fall and die. Wooden stairs in abandoned buildings are dangerous things.

If, during your ascent, you find certain staircases are broken or bricked off and don't take you everywhere you want to go, you might try turning your attention to the elevator shaft, on the off chance that it's climbable. If that doesn't work out, you may need to consider coming back with thick climbing rope, a collapsible ladder or an elevator at another date.

It's likely that at some point in your tour of an abandoned building you'll make your way out to the roof. Obviously this is a good place to be careful, in terms of not falling through the roof, not falling off the roof and not being seen from outside. When you're done with the roof, make sure you take the trouble to properly reseal the roof hatch, as rain damage can destroy a building faster than almost anything else except fire. (In fact, if you find roof entrances open, you might consider closing them. It's an exception to the rule "take nothing but pictures, leave nothing but footprints", but a noble one.)

Dealing with the Supernatural

While I esteem ghost hunters and paranormal enthusiasts as fellow intrepid adventurers in off-limits locations, bluntly, I recommend not concerning yourself with ghosts or hauntings until such time as a poltergeist actually walks up to you and says hi. I'm not suggesting that you actively refuse to believe in anything supernatural, merely that you take an agnostic approach and don't believe it until you see it. There's no real down side to doing this, since ghosts, unlike gods, aren't known for punishing people for their lack of faith. If they're real and they want you to know they're real, they'll let you know.

In the meantime, don't worry about it. Urban exploration is cool enough and tense enough as it is without forcing in fantasy elements or other imaginary sources of extra tension. Staying grounded in reality not only gives you one less thing to worry about while you're exploring, it will also remove that tiny nagging voice in the back of your head that says maybe your excitement is rooted in self-delusion. Not actively believing in or seeking out the supernatural doesn't need to diminish your exploratory experiences, as you can still be fully tuned into the powerful vibes and spirits of the places you visit and still savour their very real creepiness. There's just no need to attribute those feelings to

KING EDWARD HOTEL

It was the 100th birthday of Toronto's King Edward Hotel, and Harpocrates and I decided to stop in to wish it our best. The palatial hotel opened to the public on 11 May 1903 as part of George Gooderham's evil scheme to keep the centre of Toronto from drifting west, away from his considerable holdings in the east. While this plan failed, at least it produced one hell of a sexy hotel.

The part of the hotel we were most interested in was actually the slightly younger 1921 addition to the hotel, the portion featuring the abandoned Crystal Ballroom. Once the social centre of Toronto's elite, the ballroom has stood abandoned since the late 1950s. Today, the elegant room once restricted to the rich and famous stands empty except when it is used for indoor fly-fishing lessons.

The plan was to blend in as businessmen as we effortlessly navigated our way to the top of the hotel, but this plan encountered its first hitch before we even started. Exhibiting his usual knack for dressing for the occasion, Harpocrates showed up unshaven, dressed in a sweatshirt and carrying a large tripod. I sighed and tried to feel grateful that he was at least wearing shoes. As we strolled from the subway to the hotel, we dismantled his tripod and stashed it in our bags, covered up his sweatshirt with a jacket and pulled his employee ID badge out from under his shirt and over his jacket to more fully convey his drone status. This quick makeover would have to do.

We arrived at the hotel's front doors too deep in conversation to acknowledge the doorman as we strolled into the busy lobby. Neither of us was familiar with the layout of the hotel, but we attempted to move through it and find the elevators with the deliberateness of people who considered the building a second home. Turning a corner and finding ourselves confronted with washrooms rather than elevators, Harpocrates went in to use the washrooms while I picked up a nearby payphone and had a brief conversation with a friendly dial tone.

When Harpocrates returned, we got down to business and purposefully strode across the lobby to an elevator. Stepping inside, we saw that the elevator only went down. We had no interest in going down, but we didn't want to be seen backtracking. We decided to go down and try to find another route back up.

As we emerged into a basement conference room, an employee greeted us almost immediately with the dreaded words "Can I... help you?"

I lamely explained that we'd actually been trying to go up, but had accidentally taken the wrong elevator. Harpocrates asked if there was another bank of elevators down here that would take us up. The employee, who must have thought we were awfully stupid to have pressed the "B" button in the hopes of going up, told us we'd have to take the same elevator back up to the lobby and then transfer to the main elevators from there. We thanked him and left. As we rode back up, we chastised ourselves for our sloppiness. Being CIHY'd within our first five minutes was pretty embarrassing.

Finally stumbling upon the correct elevators and getting in with a few other hotel guests, Harpocrates pressed the button for a floor near (but not suspiciously near) the top of the hotel. "That presentation today went better than I thought it would," he led.

"I was worried about that one too," I mumbled.

"It turned out not to be that big a deal. Steve actually did a pretty good job. It basically covered the same material as that project I e-mailed you already — did you get that?"

"I'm not sure... which one was that?"

"Oh it was a Visio file about the Equinox Project."

Astoundingly, we managed to keep straight faces as we bantered for the rest of the ride. Getting off the elevator, we switched to the service staircase and climbed up a few flights of stairs. Pulling back a door, we found ourselves in an all-but-empty room, and the photo harvest began in earnest.

There were few spaces at the top of the King Eddy that were less than spectacular. The vast, empty Crystal Ballroom, with its multitude of gigantic picture windows peering out on the city and

Active buildings, like Toronto's King Edward Hotel, often contain magnificent abandoned areas, such as this former 1920s ballroom.

the lake, is but the most breathtaking of many dozens of gorgeous rooms, attics, ramps, hallways and stairwells. The balcony overlooking onto the Crystal Ballroom, where a luxuriously carpeted staircase juts up into the middle of a rocky, rubble-strewn floor, throws the contrast between opulence and decay into high relief. Nearby storage rooms are filled with a wide assortment of craziness, including tires, old Christmas decorations and bathtubs standing on end.

There's much more to the top of the hotel than just the Crystal Ballroom and environs; there are actually four and a half storeys of fun up there, though both the roof and the uppermost mechanical room are kept locked behind doors labelled "grandmaster only". Sadly, neither Harpocrates nor I have yet attained this rank. But many doors that seem like they should have been locked were not. By passing through a half-height red door, it's possible to enter and climb around in the very large attic over the Crystal Ballroom, though you might choke to death on the dust. The unlocked, still-functional elevator and mechanical rooms are filled with monstrous, primitive equipment that has somehow been coaxed into continuing to function smoothly for more than 80 years.

After about an hour of climbing around the upper storeys of the hotel, we decided to head back to civilization. After taking the stairs back down to the inhabited part of the hotel, Harpocrates and I paused in the stairwell to pack up and make ourselves look a little less suspicious, making a fair bit of noise in the process. When I opened the stairwell door, I was very surprised to see a middle-aged woman standing on the other side of the door, also with her hand on the doorknob. She stared at us with surprise as we greeted her and walked past her, and rather than going through the door she began to follow us down the hallway. The three of us then filed into the elevator together, joining a girl who was already in the elevator and heading to the lobby.

"So, did Steve manage to make it to the meeting?" I asked Harpocrates.

"He did, but he hasn't made a decision yet. He said you should call him when you get there."

"That's great. You know, I feel really good about what we've accomplished here today."

As the elevator doors slid open, we made our way through the lobby and out the front door of the hotel, where we stood beside the doorman surveying the rain outside. "Do you want to take a cab there?" Harpocrates asked.

"No, after being cramped up inside all afternoon I think I could use a walk," I replied.

As we did up our jackets, we heard the girl who'd ridden down with us speaking into her cell phone behind us. "That's good... It sounds like it... Do you think we should go to the gallery now or later?... Well, I'm going to get a cab..."

Gesturing back at her as we walked away, I admitted, "She's good."

ACTIVE SITES

Many explorers I've spoken with complain about the lack of "UE sites" in their area, and generally seem to agonize over the difficulty of finding targets. I can only conclude that these people either (1) live in the wrong parts of the world, such as the Congo or Nunavut, (2) aren't paying enough attention to their surroundings or (3) need to expand their definitions of suitable targets. In Toronto, where I've been living and actively exploring for the past decade, I have the sense that I've seen maybe *(maybe)* five percent of what the city has to offer, and I *always* have more potential targets to explore than I have time. I don't think this is just because Toronto is great city to explore, either: when in other big cities, I see a constant, seemingly inexhaustible stream of opportunities for exploration. And they keep building and digging more!

So, if you live in or near an actual city and bemoan the lack of places to explore — by which you almost certainly mean abandoned buildings and storm drains — you're defining the hobby too narrowly, limiting your horizons and missing out as a result. Open your eyes! See beyond the abandoned buildings! For most of us, I think, what draws us to abandoned buildings (aside from the reduced risk of being caught) isn't the abandonment itself so much as the beauty, the neglect, the charm and the authenticity of the place, which strikes us simply because we're so used to cities and suburbs that are full of the disposable, generic architectural junk that's been the norm in North America since WWII. While the qualities we seek out in abandoned buildings are indeed special and rare, they can certainly be found in many places that aren't yet abandoned.

When we visit abandoned buildings, our senses are so heightened by the idea of having earned a glimpse of something unique and forbidden that we intensely savour the splendour and wonder of the place. But cities are full of beautiful, neglected, charming and authentic places and these aren't all inside abandoned buildings — not by a long shot. Some of the city's most surprising and impressive places are hidden inside old schools, hotels, churches, factories, power plants, courthouses, theatres, libraries, museums, stadia, office buildings, hospitals, transit stations and similar buildings that are still more or less open for business. Just about any interesting old building is worth a look and so are a lot of newer ones. Go in and find their secrets. Climb every ladder. Open every door. Summit every rooftop. Etc.

Safety Issues

For the most part live buildings are safer than other potential exploration sites, since at least their main areas have been built (and are
maintained) with public access in mind. Behind the scenes, or above or
below the scenes, there may be fewer handrails and warning signs. On
rooftops, in basements, in mechanical rooms and so on, you may
encounter a few live wires, uninsulated pipes and threats of that nature,
and elsewhere you might have to worry about falling hazards and
things like that. But at least in live buildings you rarely have to worry
about being flooded out, having the roof collapse or being hit in the
head by a stray girder.

Some particular sorts of live buildings pose a few special risks,
most of which you can deal with using common sense. Avoid engine
rooms that are so loud they're likely to damage your hearing, or electrical rooms that are filled with sparks. Stay away from scientific experiments in universities and laboratories. In hospitals you'll want to be
careful around garbage, fluids and anything marked with the radioactive or biohazard symbols. I encounter radiation warnings pretty frequently in universities and hospitals and my usual practice is to try to
take the same precautions the employees or students seem to be taking.
If I see them walking in and out of an area marked "radioactive" without a care in the world, then I will do likewise. I leave rooms that I've
never seen in use alone. I would probably also leave a room alone if it
were populated only by skeletons.

Security Issues

There's a greater chance of run-ins with security in live buildings than in
any other sort of location. If you explore live buildings often, you will
almost certainly get caught once in a while, whether by guards, employees or janitors, but this is usually a very small deal if you're exploring
somewhere vaguely welcoming of the public, such as a mall, a train station, a hotel, a school or even a hospital during operating hours. Even in
most government buildings, employees can be expected to have the apathetic "not-my-department" attitude you might expect of civil servants.
There is a fair risk of being questioned ("can I help you?"), but unless
you're doing something exceptionally suspicious or naughty, there is very
little chance of having any sort of confrontation worth writing home
about. If someone questions you and doesn't like your answers, you'll
probably just be asked to leave. The odds of actually facing any negative

Not to alarm you, but someone may have let the dogs out.

consequences are slim unless you do something stupid or exude an attitude that makes people want to punish you. (Of course, airports and railway stations can be a significant exception.)

If you *are* caught while doing something suspicious, such as exploring after hours, or if you are caught somewhere suspicious, such as out on the roof, in the steam tunnels or near high-tech equipment, you might face slightly more serious punishments, ranging from having your ID collected and your personal information recorded to being banned from the premises for a period of time (usually three months to a year, but occasionally for life). It's highly unlikely that someone will go to the trouble of calling the police and having you charged with trespassing unless you're really suspicious, or you've made the mistake of compounding your trespassing with some other crime, or they really don't like your attitude.

Security at active buildings is likely to be higher in areas where crime is higher because the income gap between the people inside the buildings and the people outside the buildings is outrageous (whether because the people inside are ultrarich and the people outside are middle-class, or whether the people inside are middle-class and the people outside are poor). Security is also likely to be higher in areas that can easily be reached by people who don't own cars, such as buildings within easy walking distance of the subway, since poor people can take the subway.

Finding Active Sites
Unless you happen to live in a ghost town (which I think is technically impossible), you'll probably find tracking down interesting active sites much easier than locating interesting abandoned sites. While a "live site" is technically anything that's not abandoned — including places such as active storm drains, utility tunnels, transit tunnels and construction sites — for the sake of convenience the term is usually reserved for occupied buildings. Many active sites worth a second glance are tricky to infiltrate, since they're strictly reserved for certain types of people: bank towers are strictly for bank employees, factories are strictly for factory workers and so on. This makes it much easier to stand out and get caught. This isn't to say you should never try to explore such places, but you should probably get good at what you're doing first. Better places to start out are malls, stadia, large churches, schools, hotels and hospitals, as these places are populated by ever-changing groups of people who won't think anything of seeing an unfamiliar face. The older the institution, the better the chance that it has accessible rooftops, tunnels, basements and other vast neglected realms waiting to be explored. Older institutions also tend to have less intimidating surveillance and access-prevention systems.

Many people who explore live buildings are focussed on reaching the summit, and thus head straight for the upper mechanical rooms, elevator rooms, attics and rooftops. Rooftops especially are favourites of those who came to the hobby by route of photography, since the views are often extraordinary, but rooftops don't have to be just about the view. Many rooftops have lots of different levels and interesting stuff to poke into and climb around on, and some can be used as effective routes to different buildings or sections of buildings.

When to Go
Most explorers tend to go out a lot more often during warmer weather rather than cold, but active sites provide an excellent way to keep busy while you're waiting for the abandoned buildings to warm up or the drains to thaw out. Live buildings are generally kept toasty warm, except perhaps for their parking garages, shipping and receiving areas and rooftops. They're also often air conditioned in the summer. And some of them have pools. So, really, they're right for any time of year.

If you don't mind being around all the people, weekdays are usually easier than weekends. In most buildings, visiting on the weekend will

Wait — if the area is alarmed, then why would one stop there? It seems like the sign should say, "Get the hell out of here. Area is alarmed!"

force you to overcome special sign-in procedures, elevators on restricted access and other needless hassles. While exploring live buildings at night can be extremely fun — as well as being your only option in some cases — under normal circumstances it's easier to get around a live site during the day on weekdays, either during or just outside of its regular operating hours. In my experience, the absolute optimal time for infiltrating an office tower or similar place of business is between 4pm and 6pm on a Friday night. Between 4pm and 6pm, all the employees are taking off, but the cleaning crews and evening security patrol haven't yet been around. And Friday afternoon is by far the most laid back time at virtually any business — it's the day when people wear their regular clothes instead of suits, order pizza for lunch and spend most of the afternoon focussing on their plans for the weekend and playing Minesweeper.

Another good idea from a timing perspective is to consult relevant newsletters and websites to find out about special events, scheduled construction, fire drills and so on that might present interesting opportunities and then jot them into your date book. It might be significantly easier to sneak into Sinistercorp's world headquarters if you show up during their annual Bake Sale and Fun Fair.

Tailgating

While most active buildings keep at least the doors to their front lobby open during business hours, some places — mostly office buildings and the like — that feel vulnerable but lack security guards will simply lock themselves up entirely, requiring employees to let themselves in with keys or cards. Other buildings, such as schools, leave their front doors open during the week but go into lockdown mode on the weekend.

Unless you can find some more creative method of entry, as described further on, the most common way of dealing with this situation is tailgating, or slipping through a door that someone else has opened for you. While most people think of tailgating in terms of a stowaway following a group or an individual into a building, it's often easier and less suspicious to arrive at a locked door at the same time someone else is leaving since, if they're leaving, then you are clearly not their problem. Finding an open door usually isn't too tricky if you make your attempt on a weekday around 9am, noon or 5pm, since these are the times when entrances and exits see the most use, but coming at a high-traffic time isn't always possible.

To effectively stalk a door that isn't getting a lot of use, summon up tremendous reserves of patience and alertness and take up residence somewhere within a few metres of one of the building's main entrances, preferably one that isn't under camera surveillance. Disguise your alertness as aloofness by using a payphone or your cell phone and calling a friend or by reading something. Try to wait somewhere out of sight of people inside the building, and aim to watch the door only out of the corner of your eye. Have your key ring or wallet handy for fumbling when you get near the door.

When someone finally exits the building, wait until the door is open and they're already on their way out before you try to make your way in, since if they see you waiting for the door, they may decide to challenge you. If, on the other hand, you notice someone getting ready to head into the building, continue reading or talking on your cell phone and pace yourself so you'll arrive at the door just after they do. You can then react to the person's body language and either play it distracted, only half noticing that someone else let you in, or play it friendly, smiling warmly and thanking the person (keeping in mind that you're thanking them not for providing your only possible route into the building, merely for saving you a moment's trouble). Once you're on your way in, if they seem to have noticed you, you might try heading off their queries about your presence by asking, for example, where the building directory is, or if they happen to know where the superintendent's office is. In any case, once you're inside, move quickly and confidently in one direction or another. Looking lost, confused or in any way hesitant is quite likely to inspire the person you came in with to ask you some question or other. Questions are bad, unless you're the one doing the asking.

Tailgating a group of employees entering a building at the same time is usually much easier than trying to squeeze through the door at the same time an individual is entering or exiting, since the people in a group are likely to be paying attention to each other rather than to you. Try to be not just near the group but part of the group; listen attentively, smile or laugh at their jokes, assume their pace and mannerisms. Think of yourself as one of the gang. If they happen to notice your sudden appearance at their periphery, each person in the group is likely to assume that you know someone else in the group and to simply smile and nod at you, if they acknowledge you at all. And even if they do sense that you're an overly familiar weirdo, the odds of them having the nerve to confront you about it are slim to none.

Passing Security

Sneaking past security into off-limits buildings is incredibly easy, once you learn a few tricks of the trade, like avoiding security cameras and motion detectors, using shipping and receiving docks, taking the stairs instead of the elevators and using the employee walkways. This is amazingly simple in places like malls and hotels, but sometimes buildings such as condos, apartments, government institutions and office towers require one to pass by a security desk on one's way in. While in most cases the people manning these security desks are simply ready to help and perhaps keeping an eye out for undesirable types, in other cases they take a more active stance and try to pay attention to every person entering the building. They may ask for ID from anyone who looks out of place, or from anyone they don't recognize, or even, if there is some special perceived threat, from absolutely everyone entering the building.

People often ask me what the best tactic is for getting past a security desk. The answer is to just walk past the security desk. There, now you know my secret. Obviously smiling, looking confident and knowing exactly where you're going — or frowning and looking flustered, perhaps while speaking on a cell phone — can be a big help. Wearing

suitable attire that doesn't attract attention is a plus. It's also quite helpful if you can manage to come in at the same time as someone else, or
perhaps a small group of someone elses, and look like you're with
them. You don't even need to actually speak to the strangers for this to
work — staying near them and using friendly body language should do
the trick. If you're in a situation where you're theoretically supposed to
be showing an ID badge as you walk in, try to stay on the far side of
your group with full hands — a cell phone and a coffee will fill your
hands nicely — and make a show of making the appropriate fumbles
even as the motion of the group carries you helplessly past the desk and
on to the elevators.

Entering a building without a coat or jacket on a cold, rainy or even
snowy day, perhaps with a hot cup of coffee in hand, is a good trick.
You're obviously not just walking in off the street, because it's too cold
for that sort of madness, and, even if your ID badge isn't on display,
your businessy attire (and tie, if you're a fella) is right out there where
people can't help but see and that's *basically* the same to most security guards. Roughly two-thirds of the time, the guard will assume you
just stepped out to have a smoke, grab a coffee or see a client out to her
cab and that you accidentally left your badge or your swipe card with
your coat. It's your choice whether you want to actually smile and nod
at the guard or simply look cheerfully and confidently oblivious as you
stroll past the security desk to the elevator bank. If the guard does happen to call your bluff, no big deal. You've never misrepresented yourself. Apologize and make up an appropriate excuse, or, if you can't
think of anything better, say you just wanted to see the view from the
top floor.

Operable Opening Entry
Operable openings — that great family of entrances including doors,
windows and transoms — provide the most straightforward routes into
most buildings.

External doors are probably the most common method of ingress
into active buildings, being the preferred entrance of 99.999 percent of
the population. During operating hours, it's hard to beat them in terms
of convenience. After hours, doors can still be your friends. Buildings
with many doors, such as stadia or malls, sometimes accidentally leave
a door or two unlocked. Some doors are designed so that they are
locked from the outside, but a motion detector just inside the building

Ventilation shafts really can be used to move from room to room, and in large ones crawling on your knees and elbows is not normally a necessity.

automatically unlocks the door so those who are still inside can leave. In these cases, slipping a piece of paper through the crack in the door, near the top, will allow you to trigger the motion detector and unlock the door from the outside.

Windows and transoms (hinged windows atop doors or other windows) can also provide easy routes into buildings; the only real disadvantage to coming in through the window or over the transom rather than through a door is that, if you're caught, it's significantly harder to claim you didn't realize you were trespassing. But otherwise windows are almost as easily accessible as doors. Sometimes outside windows are left completely ajar after hours, but more commonly you'll find a window that's been left open just a crack, and be able to open it up to person size yourself. Always take a good look at what's on the other side of the window before you lower yourself in or hoist yourself through: it's possible the room on the other side might be occupied, alarmed or under surveillance. If you're travelling with a group, it normally makes sense for only one person to go in through the window and to then open a door for the rest of the group, as this is considerably less suspicious.

Creative Entry

Sometimes, particularly after hours at higher-security sites, the front door isn't the best way into the building or area you're interested in exploring. Often, if you can gain access to any other part of the complex, you can get from there to where you really want to be. This can be as simple as walking down the parking ramp, into the parking garage and taking the elevator up from there, or as complex as climbing the building from the outside and entering via a roof hatch. Virtually every building has at least a few chinks in its armour, and it's often an infiltrator's greatest thrill to identify and exploit these weaknesses.

Parking garages and shipping and receiving areas should be among the most secure areas at any given site, but in reality they're often extremely vulnerable to explorers who are willing to confidently stroll past the attendants, convex mirrors and surveillance cameras and head straight to the stairs or the elevator. You're probably on camera in these locations, so behave accordingly. In some cases, the doors to the stairs may be locked and the elevators may be on limited service, in which case you can try some of the elevator tricks described below. If neither stairs nor elevators work, you might consider ascending through the ventilation shafts. Concrete ventilation shafts in parking garages are often large, comfortable and easy to climb, and they're rarely locked up well.

If the parking garage yields no points of entry, turn your attention to the shipping and receiving area, which is normally open to the world except perhaps late at night. Shipping and receiving areas are normally under a great deal of surveillance, but in many cases this is really all they have in the way of security. It's easy to find some stairs or hop onto the freight elevator and get somewhere interesting. I've often found buildings that are otherwise in total lockdown mode can be easily penetrated through the soft underbelly of their shipping and receiving area.

On some occasions, determined explorers will employ awkward and narrow entry and exit points to get where they want to be. Through the creative use of narrow passages such as crawlspaces, elevator shafts, dumbwaiters and dumbwaiter shafts, large chimney flues, air conditioning ducts, heating ducts or the empty spaces above drop ceilings, agile explorers can often squeeze their way from the less secure parts of a complex to the more interesting areas. (Don't worry, travelling through air ducts isn't always as claustrophobic as they

make it look in the movies —
in some large buildings, the air
ducts are big enough that you
can easily stand up in them.)
Such little-considered routes
are very rarely locked,
alarmed or secured in any way
— the explorer's bulk is normally the only limit to his or
her progress.

Another creative entry
technique is what security
forces refer to as hiding in,
which involves entering a
building during operating
hours, finding a comfortable
out-of-the-way spot and camp-
ing out there until after the
building is closed, when you
can have free run of the place
(provided after-hours security
is minimal, of course). While

Dumbwaiters can be a creative means of travelling from floor to floor — and they aren't really all that dangerous.

this requires you to have enough patience to sit around for at least half
an hour while waiting for the building to empty out, it isn't very difficult. Explorers are generally much better at finding concealed nooks
and crannies than security forces are at patrolling them. (A tip: don't
hide in the janitor's closet. The janitor is the one person who's likely to
still be around after closing.) And if you're caught inside shortly after
closing you can normally just say you didn't hear the announcement
that they were closing, or that you fell asleep on a bench somewhere.

Provided you can find a way to the top of the building, the roof can
often provide a good, stealthy route inside. Rooftop alarms are relatively rare, and getting onto the roof need not necessarily involve scaling the building from the outside: when new buildings are built, the
older buildings don't always react to their newly adjacent neighbours,
and it often isn't difficult to get from one roof to a neighbouring roof,
or to climb out one building's window and onto the roof next door.
Once on a roof, seek out the square roof hatches that will most likely
provide your way inside. In some cases, roof hatches are locked from

the inside, but more commonly they feature a lever that can be pushed to the side to pop the hatch. After doing this, it's a simple matter of climbing down the ladder and shutting the hatch behind you as you make your way in, generally to the top of a staircase.

Know Your Codes

As you study buildings, you will gradually get a sense of how different edifices from different eras tend to be put together, getting a sense of roughly how many entrances and exits you can expect and where they'll be, how access to the building will be controlled, where the mechanical rooms will be, how the stairwells will function, where the security cameras and alarms will be and so on. You can hone this sensibility to the point where you almost intuitively know the best methods to approach a building the first time you go inside, and thus look like you know what you're doing even on your first visit.

Being familiar with building and fire codes can give you some valuable clues about how particular sorts of buildings will work, outlining basic policies about entrances, exits, electromagnetic locks, stairwells, roof access and information of that sort. While very few buildings comply with codes in their entirety, safety codes give you useful rough outlines, such as that floors with 100–500 occupants require a minimum of three exits, or specific details on how certain access features must work, such as that manual door releases must unlock a door for a minimum of 30 seconds.

Canadian explorers should pay a visit to the website of the Canadian Commission on Building and Fire Codes (*http://www.nationalcodes.ca*), which features brief summaries of both the National Fire Code of Canada and the National Building Code of Canada. The fire code covers policies related to hallways, stairs, doors, fire exits, signs and so on. The building code covers policies on construction, renovation and demolition, providing outlines about safety, health, accessibility, acceptable and unacceptable hazards and so on. It looks like the full codes may go online shortly; if not, you'll have to read them at the library. Reading the full codes will give you an idea of the government's specific — usually *painfully* specific — policies on things like fire escapes, noise protection, the containment of hazardous substances, minimum numbers of urinals per floor and so forth, though unfortunately you'll have to wade through language like "a dwelling unit containing more than one storey shall have an exit door or an egress door opening directly into a public access to exit from the uppermost storey and from the lowest storey of the dwelling unit so that each storey is served by an exit or egress door...." Okay, okay, I'll stop. Sorry about that. While the codes in Alberta and Quebec deviate slightly from these national codes, none of the variances are significant and reading these documents will give you a good idea of what to expect nationwide.

American explorers should head over to the online headquarters of the National Fire Protection Association (*http://www.nfpa.org*), which contains hundreds and hundreds of documents related to

Crossover floors, whatever their signs may warn, should be unlocked in compliance with fire codes. They're good routes out of stairwells.

fire protection and building policies in the United States, from NFPA 1 (the Uniform Fire Code) to NFPA 101B (the Code for Means of Egress for Buildings and Structures) to NFPA 520 (the Standard on Subterranean Spaces) to NFPA 5000 (the Building Construction and Safety Code). Some can be read online for free, while others require a viewing fee. There's a lot of good stuff in the huge, unsorted pile, including detailed information about elevator rooms, mechanical rooms, stairways, ventilation shafts, underground structures, fire exits, vacant buildings and more. These codes (and their various drafts, amendments, errata and so forth) are most definitely not light reading, but some sections provide some interesting insights, such as Section 4.4.3.2.2 of the Uniform Fire Code, which states "No lock or fastening shall be permitted that prevents free escape from the inside of any building other than in health care occupancies and detention and correctional occupancies." Section 10–14.3.6 decrees that in any given stairway, "Roof access or no roof access shall be designated by the

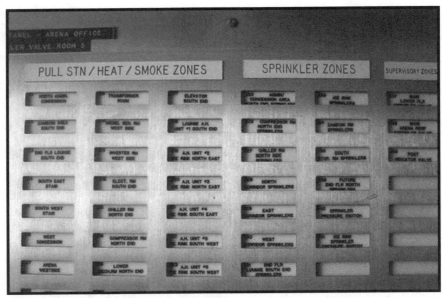

Usually located near the front entrance, fire annunciator panels provide useful checklists of all the interesting areas to examine within a given building.

words 'Roof Access' or 'No Roof Access' and placed under the stairway identification letter. Lettering shall be a minimum of 1 in. (2.5 cm) high bold block lettering."

Speaking of constant, flagrant violations of the law that are so constant and flagrant as to render the law meaningless, reading both the Canadian and American codes makes it quite clear to anyone who has done some exploring of such sites that no construction, renovation or demolition enterprise has ever or will ever take place on this continent without being in violation of at least a dozen sections of the building and fire codes. I mean, there's just no possible way the workers on a site are following every policy or have every permit they require. So if there's a project you strongly oppose, you might consider familiarizing yourself with the code and then sneaking into the site with a camera, a pen and a notebook. Bring a thick notebook.

Warning Signs
You know the videogame Pole Position? Most people just drive along the track, taking the curves, staying on course until they finally reach the finish line and die (the videogame doesn't actually show the driv-

ers dying, but we can assume). If you deviate from the set course at all, you quickly crash into roadside signs that bar your escape from the track and prevent you from ever visiting those beautiful scenic mountains in the distance and the wide world beyond.

Real life is a lot like that, except in real life when you encounter the signs at the side of the designated course you don't explode. In real life, the signs just warn or threaten you, and then, if you'd like, you're free to go past them anyhow and see all the wonderful sights that lie beyond the beaten track.

In the wise words of *Infiltration 2:* "Many of the most fascinating and fun exploration sites on earth are not guarded by locks, cameras or security guards. Often all that lies between a merry band of infiltrators and exploration paradise is a simple, two-dimensional warning sign. A warning sign that cruelly informs all who gaze upon it that it holds no love for them; they are unwelcome; whatever lies behind the sign is too good for them. Though our eager explorers would think nothing of parking beside a 'no parking' or 'employee parking only' sign and later claiming that they didn't see the sign, or didn't think the sign applied to them, they would never think of taking such a chance here. And so, though our explorers have never signed any document agreeing to obey all signs they may encounter, they brush off a tear and turn away. Well, no more! We have allowed these signs to repress us for too long! It's time to do some serious disregarding!"

The word "disregarding" might have been a bit strong, and I apologize to anyone who is now in prison and/or dead as a result of that advice. (No hard feelings?) Warning signs should certainly be regarded, closely and carefully, though of course it's also a good idea to take them with a grain of salt. Signs lie — a lot — and create false impressions even more often.

The very lousy policy of security through dishonesty often begins at the front entrance to a building or site, with the notice that the premises are protected by ABC or XYZ Security or whomever. Hiring a security company to monitor your premises costs anywhere from $30 to hundreds of dollars a month, whereas a packet of stickers *saying* that some phoney security company monitors your premises costs maybe $5. Establishments that put up a security company's "premises protected by" stickers in honest circumstances are very unlikely to make the removal of those stickers a priority when they later decide to terminate their contracts — as demonstrated abundantly by the high number of businesses that, if you took them at their word, would seem to have simultaneous contracts with three or four competing security companies, two of which went out of business in the 80s. Similarly, when new owners move into new premises, they rarely bother to tear down the stickers advertising the last tenant's security company of choice.

Just as the bullies who spend the most time talking about how tough they are are the most likely to be cowards at heart, the establishments that brag most loudly about their use of alarms, dogs, cameras or alarmed dog cameras are the least likely to effectively employ these measures. When someone installs a real security camera system, they might put up one or two small signs subtly mentioning the presence of those cameras to the public; on the other hand, when someone spends $30 on a dummy camera from Radio Shack, they're probably going to put up a dozen large signs boasting about how effectively they've removed their customers' privacy. Similarly, a site that posts a dozen signs about its free-roaming packs of ravenous, ferocious guard dogs is clearly overcompensating for something. A site that's *actually* guarded by guard dogs doesn't need a lot of signs — the dogs bark, run at the fence and attempt to eat passersby, and that's really all the sign the place needs.

In many buildings, the most blatantly inaccurate and most easily disprovable signs are those that state "Emergency Exit Only: Alarm Will Sound" or make some similar claim about an alarm sounding if a door is opened or a particular point in a stairwell is passed. Unfortunately, I can't say that such signs are always false — I wish I could, really — but they often are. I can think of at least 100 doors in downtown Toronto that claim they'll scream like a banshee if anyone touches them but are attached to no alarm. If doors such as these are not connected to the door frame via wires (usually at the top of the door; these are sometimes concealed on the inside of the door frame), or do not have an obvious speaker attached to the door handle, the sign is probably bluffing. It's kind of a giveaway when you watch the employees walk through the supposedly alarmed doors without a care in the world. It's not clear whether such signs were always bluffing, or if they were once true, until the building security companies or until the alarm started going off so often that they decided to disable it. Usually, the trend is consistent throughout a building, so if you find one lying door they're probably all lying doors. I hope this doesn't sound prejudiced.

It frequently breaks my heart to see people (even, on occasion, fellow explorers) turn away from doors labelled "Emergency Exit Activated By Fire Alarm" or similar phrasings. People read those big red words "Emergency Exit" and "Fire Alarm" and just sort of jumble them together into a vague idea that an alarm will go off if they tangle with the door. But if you read the sign carefully that's not what it's saying at all — what it's getting at is that in the event that the door is locked, it can be opened with a fire alarm, so if you're fleeing a fire and find the door is locked, you should simply head back and hunt around for a fire alarm. During operating hours, and often after hours as well, such doors are often unlocked and should be used freely. Similarly, you shouldn't feel shy about using doors labelled "emergency exit" or "fire exit" or even "no exit", as long as no alarm is threatened. There probably isn't an alarm, or they'd brag about it. And if an alarm *does* go off and someone gets upset about it, well, they should've warned you. Besides, the sign didn't say "emergency exit *only*", did it? Well did it? I didn't think so.

Signs from the "Danger: Do Not Enter" genus often exaggerate the threat posed; usually, the only real danger is that the general public will enter an area the person who put up the sign doesn't want them to enter. As I've noted before, this sign is kind of like a sign saying "Tasty Food: Do Not Eat". It presents two very separate ideas, but then fails to draw any connection between the inviting statement and the prohibitive statement. If this sign were written in proper English, it would say "There is danger ahead, so do not enter unless of course you like that kind of thing and think you can take care of yourself." And you do. So go ahead.

Interior Doors

While the basics of using doors are understood by many, there are several advanced door manipulation techniques that will allow you to take your door-using game to a whole new level.

One skill you'll gradually develop is a sense of which doors are and which doors are not locked, which will allow you to save time and make yourself appear less suspicious by checking fewer doors in active buildings. Getting a sense of which doors are almost certain to be locked isn't just about spotting the deadbolt before you bother turning the knob; over time, you'll come to recognize the types of knobs and handles that are likely to be locked, as well as the tell-tale upside-down

Doors such as this allow explorers to turn the "autolock" feature on or off with the push of a button.

or sideways positioning of key-holes on locked doors. You'll come to recognize and give thanks for the sorts of knobs and handles that are almost always open. You'll also learn which colours of LED mean "locked" and which colours of LED mean "open" at a given site. (Don't assume the colour scheme is the same at every building. Some sites use green for "go" and red for "stop"; others use green for "secure" and red for "insecure".)

Experience — hopefully not of a horrific nature — will also teach you what sort of doors are likely to close and lock behind you, though it doesn't do much harm to take a moment to double-check this kind of thing on any given door. To determine if a door is set to lock automatically or not, hold it open and test the knob or handle from the far side, and make sure turning the knob or pressing the handle causes the bolt to retract. If it does-n't, first check the knob and the inside of the door frame to see if there is a mechanism (either a small switch or two buttons) that will allow you to toggle the door out of automatic locking mode. If not, you may want to consider improvising something to prop the door open. Ideally, the door should be propped open just enough so that it doesn't lock, but not so much that someone casually strolling by would notice the door was propped open. Small stones, pen lids and items of similar size and incon-spicuousness work well. These should be wedged into place at the base of the door, where they won't drop and make a noise if someone walks through the door without noticing that it's slightly ajar.

While I recommend explorers avoid carrying lock picks for practi-cal reasons, occasionally it's possible to persuade a door or two to become unlocked without the use of picks. Everyone's seen the ease with which TV cops and spies use credit cards to slide curved bolts back into the door frame — well, once in a while, on older door locks, that actually works. Sometimes, using either a credit card or a pocket knife, you can even persuade deadbolts to move out of your way. Doing this is a fairly risky business, from a legal point of view, so only attempt it when you're confident that you're alone and not on camera, and be careful not to damage the door, the lock or the frame in your attempt. If you're interested in more advanced sorts of lock picking, I recommend searching for the "MIT Guide to Lockpicking" online, or

Doors can often be propped open with just a pen or a pen lid.

picking up the latest edition of the informative, well illustrated and up-to-date *Visual Guide to Lockpicking* from Standard Publications (*http://www.standardpublications.com*). And then I recommend avoiding carrying or using lock picks in any situation where you might conceivably be caught, unless you're okay with the idea of going to prison.

In certain situations, such as when you encounter a locked door away from a populated area that looks like no one has used it for years, you may want to consider carefully and temporarily taking the door off its hinges. (Providing, of course, that the door opens towards you and its hinges are accessible.) You can do this by tapping the hinge pins loose using a hammer (or a rubber mallet if noise is a consideration) and a screwdriver. This is best accomplished by two people — the first person tackles the hinges while the second person keeps the heavy door from falling on the first person's head. If you're successful, open the door and then tap the hinge pins back in place — yes, *before* you go down the tunnel or make your way out to the roof. After all, there's no guarantee you'll wind up coming back the same way.

Finally, always bear in mind that an open door is a beautiful thing, particularly when the door *should* be closed and locked. Whenever you see a very slightly ajar door, that is a gift, and you should accept it. If your side of the door lacks a handle, grab it by the top edge and pull. You can grab it by the bottom edge if you're too short to reach the top, but be aware that crouching looks a little more suspicious than reaching up. If the door is missing a knob, fiddle with its locking mechanism and try to open it. If someone else has smashed a window either beside or set into the door, feel free to reach your hand or a coat hanger through the glass and try to open the door from the other side (while bearing in mind that if you're caught you may be blamed for smashing the glass). But don't pass up an opportunity to open an openable door. There are so many locked doors in this world that it would be a real shame to let an openable one go to waste.

Alarms

Some areas of some buildings will attempt to hinder your exploration through the use of alarms of some sort. Alarm systems employ a wide variety of inputs and outputs, but they all work by the same basic principles. All alarms consist of a sensor, a central circuit and an output device. The alarm sleeps peacefully while the sensor relays a steady on or off signal to the central circuit, but if the sensor should suddenly report a signal that differs from all the rest then the output device is activated and all hell breaks loose.

Alarms come in generalized and zone annunciator flavours. Whereas generalized alarms simply report that an alarm has been tripped within the building ("ALERT: BADNESS"), zone annunciator alarms use an alarm annunciator panel to pinpoint the zone (or even the exact door or hatch) that triggered the alarm ("ALERT: BADNESS AT GROUND FLOOR BACK DOOR"), permitting security to respond quickly and directly. Perhaps obviously, zone annunciator systems are only useful to on-site security, not to remote monitoring companies or the police, who won't have a full panel display at their disposal. On-site security can respond quickly, but off-site security generally knows little more than that there was a problem somewhere in the building or complex of buildings.

The most common sort of door alarm sensor you'll encounter will be the magnetic reed switch. This simple device features two bits, one of which is attached to the top of a door and the other of which is attached to an adjacent position on the door frame. The half on the door contains a magnet, while the half on the door frame contains an electrified circuit that's engineered to be affected by the magnet. While some older versions of the switch were designed so that the magnetic field kept the switch open (a faulty design that allowed burglars to bypass the alarm by simply cutting the wires), in most cases modern switches are designed so that the magnet holds the circuit closed, so that electricity can flow through the circuit freely. If you separate the switch from the magnet by opening the door, you break the circuit, halt the flow of electricity from one terminal to the other and trigger the alarm.

These supposedly alarmed doors are sitting slightly ajar, indicating that the alarm isn't doing much.

There are no perfect tricks for getting past a magnetic reed switch. It's theoretically possible to temporarily unscrew both the magnet and switch and bind them together with duct tape or electrician's tape to make sure that they stay in close contact with each other even after you go through the door, but this is an intricate and risky procedure that's likely to go wrong and get you in a lot of trouble. Ditto for bringing along your own magnets. But the nice thing about magnetic reed switch alarms is how often they're disabled. Employees, students and perhaps even irritable security guards tend to get annoyed by the frequency with which magnetic reed switch alarms interrupt something they'd rather be doing, so it's common to find smashed alarms and snipped wires in any installation that's more than five years old. In other cases, you may stumble upon a magnetic reed switch alarm where the door is already slightly ajar, but the alarm isn't ringing. That's a good sign that this building may have disabled its alarms and just kept

Notices such as this alert explorers to possible opportunities to try doors that might be alarmed.

the useless sensors around for looks. It's a surprisingly common practice.

Though it's something you'll develop an instinct for over time, when you're new to the hobby guessing whether or not a particular door will be alarmed with a magnetic reed switch can be a tricky business. Certainly, many doors that claim to be alarmed are not, but there are also a handful of doors out there that don't even bother to warn you that they're alarmed until it's too late. In many cases, the door's context within the building will give you a clue as to whether or not it's alarmed. If the door looks old and neglected, it's probably safe. If the door seems like it is near something sensitive or valuable, it may be alarmed. If the door is an exit to the street and it isn't on camera or supervised, well, there wouldn't really be any point in alarming a door like that, so it may be safe. And so on. Specific warning signs to look for are wires, or narrow metal conduit tubing of the sort that might house wires and make them slightly more difficult to cut, near the top of the door frame. In some cases, you'll be able to peer through the crack at the top of the door to check for signs of a magnetic reed switch on the other side, with the caveat that not seeing an alarm is not a guarantee that there isn't one in place.

Much more obvious door alarms are those from the Detex or Arrow families, often used to keep people inside a building from accessing the roof except in emergencies. These alarms typically feature a lever/door handle, sometimes painted bright orange so you don't miss it, labelled "Emergency Exit Only: Alarm Will Sound", with a speaker actually mounted on the door handle itself. These alarms aren't kidding, and they are very loud. The one nice thing about them is that they are not typically connected to any sort of security station, so security probably won't come running unless they happen to hear the alarm. Still, these alarms should be avoided except in the most drastic circumstances.

Motion Detectors

The second most common variety of alarm you'll face is the motion detector. While there are some freakish motion detectors out there that employ thermosensors, photosensors or ultrasonic sensors to detect movement, nine times out of 10 the devices you'll encounter are passive infrared (PIR) motion detectors, which are by far the cheapest and most common variety of motion detector. Unlike various active motion detectors, which fire waves all around a room and then monitor to make sure the waves are reflected back in the proper pattern, passive infrared detectors just relax, sit back and take snapshots of the infrared pattern in a given room. This casual approach makes them smaller and much more energy efficient than any of their competitors, and also makes it easy for an establishment to guard a room with multiple motion detectors without worrying about how the fields of two or more overlapping detectors will interfere with one another.

Passive infrared detectors work very simply. Once each given time interval, say once every second, the sensor takes in an image of the pattern of infrared light, or heat, in its area. In theory, any motion within the room should cause a change in the pattern of infrared light. If two consecutive infrared snapshots vary by an amount greater than the detector is set to allow (that is, the moving object is determined to be bigger and more mobile than a breadbox), the central circuit triggers the output device.

When the alarm is in its calmer, more peaceful mode, normally during the day or during business hours, the output device will usually just be a little green or red LED that lights up for a second or two each time motion is detected. Sometimes overhead lights or spotlights are also connected to motion detectors, either for security reasons or simply for convenience. Playing with detectors when they're in light-up-but-stay-quiet mode will give you a good idea of how sensitive a motion detector you're up against; motion detector sensitivity is adjustable, since some security guards get fed up with chasing mice and blowing leaves after a while. Unfortunately, even on the least sensitive setting, you'd have to be incredibly skilful and extremely patient to ever slide past an infrared motion detector without triggering it.

This is especially important to remember after hours, when the lights are off and when the alarm is in its much more stern mode. Unlike during operating hours, triggering the alarm after hours will not only light up the LED — an alarm countdown will also begin. This countdown can be anything from two minutes to two seconds, depending on how much hustle the people who set the alarm expect you to use in disarming the alarm or leaving the area. Some alarms will emit tiny warning beeps in advance of the major squeal, while others will immediately flip from total silence to total noise. The most insidious alarms won't make any local noise at all — they'll just notify the police or the on-site or remote security company that some unsuspecting victim is waiting for them. Unless you happen to notice the LED flashing — which you may not, if you're not in complete darkness and the motion detector is overhead — you'll probably have no idea you tripped the alarm until it's too late.

You might think that wearing a cold wetsuit or wrapping yourself in aluminum foil would let you stroll past a heat-detecting alarm with impunity, but you'd be both wrong and silly-looking. Your body temperature would still differ from the surrounding air. And although it's true that passive infrared detectors function better at regular-to-low temperatures, they can still get the job done even in uncomfortably hot areas, so heating the whole room above body temperature won't do the trick either. The only known reliable method for disabling a passive infrared detector is to block the sensor with something thick and opaque, such as a piece of wood or cardboard, while it is in mellow mode. When you return later when it is in armed mode, it will be so busy monitoring the constant temperature of the wood or cardboard that it won't even notice you're there. You hope.

Of course, situations in which such a trick would work are rare. In most cases, your focus shouldn't be on defeating motion detectors, but on spotting them and avoiding them. If you constantly keep an eye out for motion detectors at all times and in all locations, you'll gradually get a sense of where they're installed, and learn that you have to be especially careful near important doorways, roof hatches, outside exits, the tops and bottoms of stairwells and similar locations. And you'll get familiar with the slightly more out-of-the-way routes that can be used to avoid them.

The second-most common type of motion detector you'll encounter is a microwave/infrared detector, which can usually be identified as such by its use of three differently coloured LEDs instead of just one. In addition to doing everything a PIR detector does, these devices issue and map microwave signals to compensate for the few potential shortcomings of infrared detection. As you'll find if you play around with these, they're even more sensitive and trickier to defeat than regular PIR detectors. They're also significantly more expensive, so an institution that uses these detectors is probably fairly serious about access prevention. Try to avoid these.

If your urban exploration career involves a lot of visits to active sites, you'll probably accidentally set off a few alarms. When you do hear that unbelievably loud and nasty squeal, it's important not to panic and run. Think about what someone who worked for the organization would likely do if he or she accidentally set off an alarm door — maybe sigh, maybe apologize to the air, maybe feel a little embarrassed, but certainly not sprint away like a foiled burglar. It'll be very hard to stay calm the first couple of times you set off an alarm, but it does get easier and easier with practice. (Note: don't get too much practice.)

When you're exploring live buildings, you may wish to take note of any signs you see announcing days and specific times when they're going to be testing the fire alarms. Those may be good times to come back and try your luck with some of the "alarm will sound" doors, as employees will be accustomed to ignoring alarms on those days. Keep in mind, though, that any on-site security guards will probably notice the difference between a fire alarm and a security alarm.

Surveillance
Explorers of active buildings must know how to handle security cameras. Offices, hotels and commercial enterprises often use cameras to defend their valuables, and hospitals often have them for safety reasons, since they deal with a lot of drugs and desperate people.

There are three basic breeds of cameras: covert, overt and dummy. Covert cameras, as you might guess from the name, are "spy" cameras designed to secretly catch people doing naughty things. These often pinhole-sized cameras can be hidden easily, and are designed to either stay hidden or at least not to be noticed until it's too late. Fortunately for explorers, covert cameras are normally used to spy on employees or otherwise violate the privacy of known individuals, rather than strangers, and are less popular for security purposes.

Overt cameras, on the other hand, are often large beasts designed to be obvious and create an exaggerated sense of the security force's

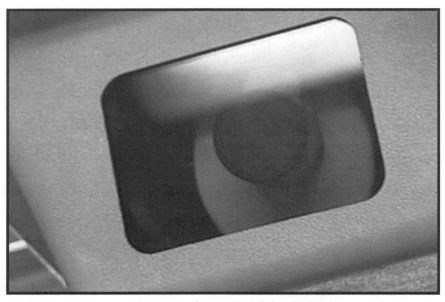

Security cameras aren't necessarily monitored, hooked up or even uncapped.

omniscience. The most common sort are tinted dome cameras, which come in a wide variety of shapes and sizes for mounting on walls or ceilings. Tinted dome cameras give the impression of constant 360-degree surveillance, but usually just contain a normal camera looking in one direction and struggling to peer through the tinted glass. In unusual lighting conditions, one can see where the camera inside a dome is pointing and sometimes the camera is aimed at a blank wall or staring off into space. Almost as bad are big bulky hanging cameras. In this age of cheap miniaturized electronics, these ludicrous relics serve no purpose other than to exclaim their presence in the most obvious way possible. Sometimes these will also feature blinking lights or even an accompanying monitor or sign to further demonstrate that all who pass are being watched. Only slightly less blatant than the dome camera and the bulky hanging camera is the very common ceiling-mounted camera. These cameras hang from ceilings inside triangular casings, and often feature a red power light just to make sure they aren't too subtle. Generally, these cameras exist not to monitor, but to create an impression of monitoring.

While overt cameras are primarily designed to be deterrents rather than useful tools, they do at least function. Dummy cameras don't even

Unmanned banks of monitors are a very common sight in most buildings.

go that far. Although real security systems have fallen drastically in price in recent years, some prefer to stick with the even cheaper dummy cameras, which retail for under $30 at Radio Shack. These dummy camera systems generally include a supply of signs stating that the premises are being monitored by closed-circuit television. Whereas the cameras themselves are merely deceptive, the accompanying signs are flat-out lies. In a bizarre twist on dystopian science fiction, the powers that be are ridiculously eager to convince us that they are violating our privacy, even though they aren't willing to shell out the cash to do it properly.

While truly dumb dummy cameras are nowhere near as popular as they used to be, many fully functional overt cameras are nothing more than dummy cameras in reality. Businesses and organizations have installed many thousands of cheap overt cameras over the past decade or two, but few establishments have actually hired additional staff to repair the cameras when they break, or indeed even to monitor their output when they're working. It's quite rare for an institution to have more than one person watching its closed-circuit monitors at any given time. In many situations, no one is assigned to watch the monitors, as employers may view it as a waste of manpower and employees view it as a tremendously mind-numbing chore. Think of all the unmonitored camera banks you've seen yourself. It's incredibly rare for someone to actually sit and do nothing else but watch the monitors. Further, often one monitor flips between the input of a dozen or more cameras. This means one has a one-in-12 chance of being seen or less, if anyone's even watching.

While you shouldn't abandon all hope of successfully exploring buildings with cameras, it makes sense to take simple precautions. In any building known to have cameras, assume you're being watched at all times unless you know for a fact that you are not. As soon as you stroll in through the front doors, you should be on performance at all times. If you stay in character during your entire exploration, even to the point of engaging in mock conversations with your partners, you'll gradually develop mannerisms and minor details that will not only look good on camera but make your story much more believable should you ever need to tell it to someone in person. Acting is a more important skill than lying; if you can act out the little things correctly you won't be placed in a situation where you need to lie. If you're ever in a camera building and you do wind up in a situation where you need to lie, remember to only lie about why you did something, not about what you did, since chances are security has all your naughty deeds on film.

Camera awareness is a valuable skill every explorer should cultivate. You and whomever you're exploring with should actively scan corners and ceilings for cameras every time you enter a new room or hallway, and mumble "camera" or "we're on TV" to each other as a warning. It's better if you and your group don't pay attention to or look at the cameras directly, since security will be more inclined to trust you if they think you're behaving yourself not because you know you're on camera but just because that's the kind of people you are.

Sometimes you'll want to head through a room, hallway or stairwell that's off-limits and monitored by a camera. In many cases the best way past such a camera is to calmly walk past the camera. Certainly, this will work more often than snipping the wires, cycling the video feed or any other elaborate spy stunts.

Access Controls

While it's difficult to say whether or not modern automatic access controls have made entering buildings more difficult for explorers, they've certainly made life more interesting, adding a whole new set of puzzles and challenges to what was already a fairly puzzling and challenging business. While both access control systems and intrusion detection systems use clever mechanical and electronic gadgets to thwart intruders, the two should be considered separately, since they serve different functions. While intrusion detection systems are designed to detect unauthorized entry, access control systems are designed to prevent it altogether.

Older buildings are more likely to lack effective automated access control, since access control systems can be more easily incorporated into new buildings than retrofitted into older ones. It's common to see the main entrances of older buildings manned by a single security guard, who often winds up functioning as a concierge/receptionist/information desk more than as a guard.

The use of automatic access control systems is more common in newer buildings, especially outside of normal operating hours. Except in high-traffic buildings and buildings where a human presence is seen as a desirable amenity (apartment buildings and condominiums, for example), decisions about who gets in and who stays out are normally made by circuitry rather than people. Maintaining a door that only opens with a correctly entered code or the swipe of a smart card costs a lot less than a security guard's salary, and the presence of a closed-circuit camera that records to tape is often thought to be a cost-effective substitute for a human presence. Many large buildings that employ a human guard at their main entrance will use some form of automated access control combined with closed-circuit cameras at their secondary entrances.

Unfortunately, in my experience, it's often tougher to get past these automatic barriers than to get past human barriers. Duplicating the magnetic stripes in smart cards is an advanced business far beyond what most casual interior tourists would be interested in pursuing. While there are many people who have many suggestions on how to beat punch code locks (often involving powder, fingerprinting, surveillance and such super spy stuff), the truth is that your odds of opening such a lock stealthily are slim to none, unless someone's been tremendously careless. Normally, the only way through such barriers is to somehow find a human element in the system and make it work for you, either by sneaking in when someone else is careless or asking someone for a favour.

Of course, there is the hope that they've left the punch lock set to open with the default access code; in fact, this happens surprisingly often. On 5-button Simplex locks, the default code is indeed simple: hold down the 2 and 4 buttons at the same time, and then follow it with 3. (Note that if you *really* have your heart set on getting through a particular door secured by a Simplex lock and have a hell of a lot of time and patience, a list of all possible combinations to Simplex locks from *2600* magazine can be found online at *http://www.totse.com/en/bad_ideas/locks_and_security/simplex.html*). On electronic keypad locks, the default codes vary from manufacturer to manufacturer, but they're never very sophisticated. Codes like 0000 (or 0000#, or 0000*) or 1234 (1234#, 1234*) are good places to start. If these codes have been changed from the default, they may be quite tough to crack.

Navigation

While it's generally harder to get lost or stuck or trapped in an active building than in some other urban exploration sites, navigating active buildings effectively does take some degree of skill, particularly since one's mistakes are much more likely to be noticed in an active location. It's not only embarrassing but suspicious to confidently stroll up to a door to the stairs only to find out it's locked, or to hop into a crowded elevator and push the button for the penthouse, only to find that that floor requires a swipe card you don't have. If you are seen repeatedly hitting dead ends, looking confused or walking past the same area too many times, it could lead to questioning by an employee or even security. Being noticed trying doors, climbing ladders or entering or exiting sensitive areas can lead to calls to the security department. All of this is especially true if there are three or more people in your group, if you're inappropriately dressed or if you're carrying large bags or backpacks.

That said, it doesn't take that long to figure out how to blend in at active sites — a little experience combined with the judicious application of the advice in this book should quickly get you to the point where it is very rare for you to be questioned or even given a second glance. Your main challenge then will become locating and getting into the tasty bits of the building, and there are a few good tricks for this.

Many active buildings that are open to the public, especially landmark buildings, offer hand-out maps to visitors, either in a free-for-the-taking pile or by request, and buildings of sufficient complexity will often feature maps of their public areas on a panel somewhere in their lobby. In some cases, basic maps may also be available online.

Scanning, photographing or downloading such public maps can provide you with a head start on making a full and proper explorer's map of the site. Additionally, fire evacuation maps are normally located on each floor of the building, and these often provide more honest, useful information about stairs and service areas than the normal public maps, which generally prefer to pretend that such areas don't exist. Often, these evacuation maps can be studied inconspicuously while you wait for an elevator.

Fire alarm annunciator panels often provide very tempting menus of venues located within particular buildings. Normally located either just inside a main entrance, by a security desk in the lobby or in an engineering area, these light-up panels labelled with the names of various areas within the building are commonly used to help firefighters find the exact location of a problem. They can also be used as "to-discover" lists by explorers, since secret places that don't make it into the official maps and tour guides, like "west steam tunnels", "second level subbasement" or "north tower attic", often have lights and labels all to themselves.

If you're after basements and tunnels, the first routes to try are the public stairs and elevators. If those won't take you as low as you want to go, go up a few floors and then try to find your way into the service stairwell or the service elevator, since these are likely to be easier to find and access once you're off the ground level. As a bonus, there's also likely to be less supervision.

If you're after mechanical rooms, look at the building from the outside and count how many levels up to the floors with no windows. It's surprising how often the public stairs and elevators will take you right to these levels, but if they won't, there's a good chance that the service stairs or elevators will. Often the easiest way to find the mechanical levels is to look for the levels that are skipped on the public elevator: if the floors one can select from the public elevators are 1, 2, 3, 4, 5, 6, 7, 8, 11 and 12, then by all means it's time to track down floors 9 and 10. (Note that a missing floor 13 is nothing to get excited about, as that's likely just superstition at work; in buildings with high Asian populations, floors 4, 14, 24, etc. may also be missing as some eastern cultures associate the numeral 4 with death.) In some buildings, you may encounter many sorts of individual mechanical rooms, including air conditioning rooms, heating rooms, boiler rooms, chiller rooms, telephone rooms, meter rooms, fan rooms, electrical rooms, elevator

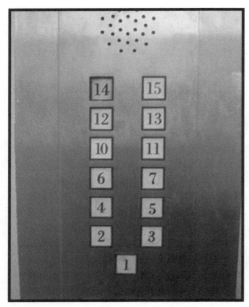

Obviously the challenge here is to visit floors 8 and 9 — probably mechanical floors.

rooms, generator rooms and more, but in most buildings with sufficient space these different functions are all fulfilled in one or two large, generic mechanical rooms, usually found in basements or attics. Some skyscrapers will also locate mechanical rooms halfway up the building, or every 10 floors or so.

If you want to find disused or under-construction areas, look at the building at night and count how many levels up to the floors with solid lighting patterns. If you more or less have the place to yourself, you might also just try opening the elevator doors on every floor, or taking the stairs to every floor.

If you're after the roof, start at the floors a few levels down from the roof and find the staircase that goes all the way up by the process of elimination. Every building has at least one stairwell that goes to the roof (or to a ladder that goes to the roof), though unfortunately it's fairly common for this roof exit to be electromagnetically locked. You may need to climb around some cages or climb up a ladder or two to actually get to the panel leading out to the roof.

Stairs

Although they have proudly served humankind since prehistoric times, in the last century or so stairs have become the poor step-siblings to escalators and elevators. While many two-, three- and four-storey buildings still partially employ stairs for everyday use, most taller buildings regard stairs as an embarrassing holdover from an earlier, more primitive age, and keep this secret shame hidden away only in case a fire or power outage forces them to overcome their prejudice.

In spite of this attitude, pretty much any building worth getting to know will have at least two staircases in order to accommodate fire codes. In some cases, some stairs will be designated public staircases and others will be designated service staircases, but in buildings with both passenger and freight elevators it's more common that all staircases will be regarded, either officially or unofficially, as "fire stairs", not to be utilized by anyone except in an emergency. In most establishments, even if the building doesn't actually mark the staircase as off-limits, people using the stairs will be considered vaguely suspicious — after all, why

Any infiltrator who can't get past this locked stairwell door has not yet mastered the art of creative problem solving.

would anyone want to get a bit of exercise on real stairs when they could just as easily use a Stairmaster at their gym? Regardless of the common biases against stairs, explorers should take to the stairwells often, if only because they are the road less travelled, and are likely to go to some places the elevators don't.

Where fire codes allow, it's becoming increasingly common for buildings to lock the entrances from stairwells to all floors but the ground level, or perhaps the ground level and a few evenly distributed crossover floors (that is, floors where the doors from the stairwell to the building *aren't* locked — in an 18-storey building, levels 5, 9 and 14 might be crossover floors). Fire stairwells often only exit through a single ground level exit that is supervised by a guard or at least by closed-circuit cameras. While this limitation on free movement is an obvious potential fire hazard, it's considered a shrewd move from an asset protection standpoint, and asset protection is the main concern of most businesses and security forces. The idea is to force potential thieves to leave the building through supervised entrances, so they can't steal anything big.

Fortunately for explorers, rooftop exits aren't often considered risky from an asset protection point of view, since few thieves have the budget for a rooftop helicopter. In most regions, fire codes require that buildings have at least one stairwell that leads to an unlocked, or unlockable, roof exit. More secure buildings will generally pursue the "unlockable" option by installing an electromagnetically locked door that unlocks by alarm only.

Elevator Action

While the stairs are more likely to take you to the most interesting places than public elevators, occasionally elevators are your friends, especially if you know their tricks.

Looking unsuspicious is a big part of using elevators for exploration. If you're on the ground floor and you want to go down, or if you're near the top of the building and you want to go up, it may be in your best interest to push the wrong button, just in case a guard or employee joins you. You can change your mind and your direction once the elevator arrives, providing it's empty. If you're sharing an elevator with others, if you worry that others might get on part way through your ride or if you simply worry that you're looking suspicious, you may want to send out similar miscues about what floor you're visiting when you hop onto the elevator. If you seek the roof of a 50-storey building, hit 36. If you have the elevator to yourself when you arrive at 36, hit 47, and walk up from there. (If you look and feel confident, you needn't take these sort of precautions — these tips apply only when you feel out of place or out of your league.)

If you're going somewhere with high security, or if you elect to visit a moderately secure building in the evening, you may have to deal with elevators on restricted access — for example, you may encounter an elevator set to only travel to the first three floors of a 50-storey building unless one employs a pass card. One way to get around this problem is to simply hop in an unsupervised elevator that goes to the levels you're interested in, push and hold "door close" and wait for someone on one of the higher floors to summon your elevator up. Stand right at the doors and pretend to be surprised when the doors open and someone else makes to get on as you are getting off. Yes, you lose the ability to plan your route, but dealing with the surprises can be fun.

Additionally, in most buildings more than a few storeys tall, elevators have "home floors", usually somewhere around halfway between

Freight elevators, while they can be intimidating, are just as effective a means of travelling from floor to floor as regular elevators. Just don't get caught.

the top and bottom of their route. For example, an elevator that serves a ten-storey building will often return to and hang around at the fifth floor when not in use; an elevator that serves the bottom half of a 60-storey building will loiter at the fifteenth floor. What this means to you, the elevation enthusiast, is that if you get on at the first floor, step inside, push "door close" and wait, the elevator may automatically take you halfway up its route — possibly deep inside restricted-access territory. You need only push the "door open" button once you get there. Often, just getting above the first few floors — outside the "public zone" — will give you access to the service stairs or a freight elevator, thus giving you everything you need to get wherever you want to go in the building.

There are several tricks for taking greater control of elevators. Whereas newer elevators require a key for every special function, older elevators often just hide their magic buttons behind a metal panel that's left unlocked. You can switch the lights and fan on and off and, more importantly, take the elevator in and out of service mode. Putting the elevator into service mode is like hiring a taxi for the night — if you push the right buttons and flip the right switches, it will take you wher-

Some elevator shafts, such as this one under construction, provide ladders for easy climbing.

ever you want to go and then patiently wait there for you. Another nice trick most older and some newer elevators will let you get away with is going into express operation. To do this, simply hold down the number of the floor you wish to go to at the same time as you hold down the "door close" button. If it works, the elevator will take you there expressly, not stopping to let anyone else — such as a nosy employee — join you. Often, an elevator set to express operation will also take you directly to floors that normally require a key or pass card, such as the penthouse, mechanical levels or subbasement.

When not in service mode, elevators are often configured to sound an alarm buzzer or bell if their doors are propped open for longer than a minute. To prevent this unwanted noise while holding an elevator, either find a way to put it in service mode or allow the doors to shut for one second and then immediately reopen them every 50 seconds or so.

Just as service stairwells are superior to regular stairwells, service or freight elevators are generally superior to regular passenger elevators, as they're more likely to go to staff-only areas. The touchy part about using service or freight elevators is that if an employee happens to get on while you're riding one, you may have some explaining to do, since it's usually quite clear that such elevators aren't intended for public use. Indeed, freight elevators often have very prominent signs proclaiming that they should be used by licensed operators only, although they really aren't that tricky — you just have to make sure you haul the appropriate doors and gates shut before you go, and remember to close them behind you after you get out, if you want other people to be able to summon the elevator. Often, loud buzzers or bells will sound if you forget a step, making it that much easier to remember. In very old freight elevators that predate the "push button" days you may also have control of the

Older, cooler elevators may lack up and down buttons and instead have one lever that controls speed and direction.

speed and direction of travel, and have to do your best to line the elevator up with the floor outside. This is very, very fun, providing you don't get caught.

Sometimes elevators will refuse to open their doors at a particular floor; for example, in a hotel with an abandoned third floor, the elevator button for "3" might be out of service, or even blocked with a metal plate, and the car might try to go straight from two to four. Sometimes, if you have the right sort of elevator, getting onto floors like this just takes a little timing, a little strength and a little luck: you need only haul open the elevator doors at the right moment — possibly using the "open doors" button to help you with the outer doors — and then, provided you're somewhere near the floor, hop out. When you're done, you should probably try to exit via the stairs.

Occasionally an elevator shaft might be the only possible route to a particular area of a building. Such shafts can sometimes be accessed through an escape hatch in the top of the elevator; other times, you'll need to find a way to open the elevator doors while the car isn't present. A small hole, about the size of a peephole, is often found on the outside of elevator doors. If you're able to fashion an appropriate key out of a coat hanger (or purchase one on Ebay), you can open the doors to the elevator shaft when there is no car present. Opening the outer door will stop the elevator in the shaft wherever it is, temporarily stranding any passengers in the elevator at the time. Don't do it unless you know the elevator is empty. This is usually done for the purpose of getting on top of the elevator car for the purpose of elevator surfing — something I've never tried myself and thus can't recommend or condemn. But they say it's pretty dangerous. On elevators with front and back doors, being on top makes it possible to open the unopened door on floors where one half is ostensibly secure.

Party Crashing
Ah, fancy people parties. Whether it's an opening party for a new gallery or club or business, a wedding reception or just some people getting together to celebrate the fact that they can afford a lot of cheese, high-society shindigs are always fun to pop in on. At most soirees, the only barriers to intruders are social barriers easily scaled with the ladder of audacity.

Dress sharply, not neglecting to shine your shoes. If someone appears to be collecting invitations or checking a list of names at the entrance to the party, there are several routes you can take depending on your assessment of the situation. First of all, if you have a coat or a jacket other than a suit jacket, go find a good place to stash it. Fire hose closets, pianos, drop ceilings and a thousand other places make great improvised lockers.

Now you can decide if you'd like to wear your explorer's hat or your social engineer's hat in order to make your entrance. If the former, now's the time to find the back door. There's bound to be at least one emergency exit from the party, probably accessible via a stairwell somewhere above or below the party. It's likely that there's an open door to the outside to accommodate smokers. It's almost a sure thing that there's an entrance to the party from a kitchen, and if you can find an entrance to the kitchen you're pretty much in, since it's unlikely that a confident-looking person in a suit or a dress would have any trouble strolling through a kitchen. The people who work there will either assume you're capable of getting them in trouble or just dismiss you as not being their problem.

If you prefer to go the social engineering route, find an inconspicuous spot from which you can study the entrance without being obvious to the people guarding the door. Pretending to talk on a payphone or a cell phone is a good way to stall while you suss out the situation. If things are busy enough that you think you'll have no trouble slipping into the party unnoticed, watch the entrance and time your arrival so you show up at the same time as another group of guests. If you're infiltrating the party as a male-female couple (which is ideal), arrive at the same time as other couples; if you're flying solo, try to arrive at the same time as a more motley assortment of attendees.

If things aren't busy enough and you think your bluff is likely to be called, check your coat as described above and then keep a steady pace as you approach the entrance, making it clear that you don't intend to stop and check in, and as you pass by smile warmly at the person and say "hello again".

Once you're in — and you really should be able to get in, unless you're trying to sneak into the Academy Awards or something — stay alert while looking cheerful and calm. If you came as a couple, talk to your partner to ward off unwanted inquiries. If you're flying solo, you're probably better off presenting yourself as a shy date left alone rather than one of the people who actually belongs at the party. As always, don't make up a more elaborate story than is necessary. Enjoy the entertainment, eat the food and drink the drink — but don't get tipsy. Unless you really savour the challenge, avoid the dinner portion of a party with assigned seating, as this is when you're most likely to be caught.

If you are caught, stay calm, as you're unlikely to get in serious trouble. Apologize and say that the gentleman at the door didn't mention that the event was invitation-only, or, if you're at a venue with multiple shindigs (such as a hotel or a wedding factory), apologize and say you accidentally came to the wrong party. Whether they actually believe you or not, they can't really prove you wrong.

Running for It
If you spend any time exploring live locations, you're going to occasionally run into employees and guards, or have them run into you. While in most cases humbly pleading confusion or curiosity is your best bet, occasionally you'll find yourself confronted in a spot where it's clear that you were quite deliberately poking about somewhere off-lim-

its. In such a case, running for it *may* be an option, providing that you're certain it's necessary and you're confident that you can outrun your pursuer.

Don't run unless you're sure it's your best way out of a situation. Running is not just an admission of guilt, but of serious guilt that can't be explained away. If you run, your pursuers are likely to assume you were up to something much more serious than just harmlessly looking around, and this will increase their determination to catch you. Furthermore, if you make someone go to all the trouble of chasing you, this will almost certainly increase their determination to punish you if they do catch you, since no one wants to do all that work for nothin'. People get cranky when they're hot and sweaty.

When you run into employees or guards in off-limits areas, try to quickly gauge your opponents' expressions and body language to determine if they're the kind of people who will actually be upset that you're deep inside the steam tunnels or if they're the sort who are happy to look the other way or just testily chide you to leave the area before someone who cares comes along and gets you in trouble. (In my experience, a single person is much more likely to be easy-going in these circumstances — when you encounter two or more people, it becomes more important to them to do things by the book.) If they say something to you, that can be a great indicator of how they're likely to play the encounter. If they lead with "Are you lost?"; "Are you looking for the elevator?"; "Looking for the parking garage?"; or something of that nature, then clearly that's what they'd like to believe, and you shouldn't shatter their illusion by running away. If they ask what you're doing or what you're looking for, they're slightly more suspicious but still not convinced you're up to no good — if you have any talent for fast-talking you should be able to get out of there without having to run for it, though you may have to endure a tongue clicking or two.

Things are probably more serious if they lead off by issuing a command, such as "stop", or if they demand ID. Cold, professional responses like these may indicate that the people you're dealing with are proud graduates of an "access control practices" seminar, avid readers of security memos or perhaps just big fans of the TV show *Cops*. If they do issue a challenge like this, it's good to note whether they say "stop!" or "stop...?" since the former communicates certainty and determination while the latter displays reluctance and hesitance. This provides a handy bit of insight, since these are probably the exact same traits they'll display while they're chasing you, which, indeed, they're probably doing right now. I'm just assuming you started running as soon as they said "stop". If you didn't, what are you waiting for? By ordering you to stop, they've pretty much shown their hand. If all social interaction can, indeed, be boiled down to an elaborate game of rock-paper-scissors, this is the equivalent of yelling "rock" in advance of boldly presenting one's balled-up fist, so it's pretty obvious you'd better turn around and paper the hell out of there. I mean, they've obviously already decided you're guilty, because who goes around yelling "stop" at potentially innocent people? That's just obnoxious.

Perhaps you haven't started running yet because you'd like me to elaborate on those other things I said you should consider before running away. Fair enough. Even in a situation where the person has yelled "stop", thereby indicating that they're pretty darn sure you're a bad kid and they are eager to bring you to justice, it may not be in your best interests to run if you do not feel confident that you can outrun your opponents.

Fortunately, there's actually a fairly basic mathematical formula for determining this. First, take your estimated familiarity with the terrain on a scale of 1 to 10 and subtract it from your potential pursuer(s)'s familiarity with the terrain on the same scale. Next, take your estimated running speed in kilometres per hour and subtract your potential pursuer(s)'s estimated running speed in kilometres per hour, basing these figures on your swift analysis of your comparative weights, encumbrances and levels of fitness and coordination. Award a bonus if either of you has special shoes with a pump or gel or air in them.

If your calculation yields a positive number, that's good and you should go for it. If it yields a negative number, that's bad and you should try to talk your way out of it instead. If it yields a 0, well, maybe ask the guy if he'll give you a minute so you can re-do your calculations and — Okay, okay. There's no actual formula. It's a gut instinct thing. If you're out of shape or likely to wind up at a dead end, don't run for it. If you're a pretty good runner and you know the place like the back of your hand, by all means, get goin'. If you know the place well, you're better off running through a lot of twists and turns while aiming for a more obscure exit rather than heading straight for the main doors. And if you *really* know the place, you need not necessarily head straight for the exit — a reliable hiding place is just as good, or perhaps even better, if your pursuers have radios and may be in communication with guards near potential exits.

When you do leave the premises, you can relax a fair bit, knowing that it's rare for anyone to pursue a simple trespassing case where the person hasn't been caught red-handed, but do keep in mind that you were seen and possibly videotaped (and, indeed, that you may still be on camera even outside the building). Get out of the area, and don't head straight for your car, if you brought one — take a nice, long indirect route.

Patience

Yoda once famously said, "There is no try, only do." As much respect as I have for the Jedi master, I wouldn't want to go exploring with him because, in my humble opinion, that jockish sort of "failure is not an option" nonsense has no place in urban exploration. Determination and continued striving for success are noble and good, but forcing success is a mistake. It's sometimes necessary to just admit that you're out of luck for the day, and you may have to come back half a dozen times or more before you see everything you were hoping to see. Sometimes you might drive three hours to see a building only to find out there's really no non-destructive way in, and you just have to deal with that. If you're the kind of person who thinks, "I didn't drive three hours for nothing, I'm getting in no matter what", then I would humbly suggest you stop driving three hours to get to places and stick to exploring local sites where you'll find it harder to justify smashing your way in. If you don't have the necessary patience and feel determined to get in "by any means necessary", please consider taking up another hobby, because the people who force things to work are the people who smash windows, get caught and ruin things for everyone, possibly hurting themselves or winding up in jail in the process.

If you don't have the patience for other types of exploring, you definitely won't have the patience for active sites, since infiltrating active sites generally takes considerably more patience and a greater willingness to fail than visiting less secure unpopulated areas. You must often wait five minutes for someone to get out of the service stairwell, or wait half an hour for a janitor to finish in a particular hallway, or wait through a week or two of frequent repeat visits for someone to finally forget to lock the door you're interested in. You need a willingness to endure the "error" part of "trial and error".

Additionally, progress through an active building can be much slower than progress through an abandoned building, tunnel or drain.

While certainly not all areas of all active buildings require you to walk on eggshells, infiltrating the non-public areas of active buildings generally requires more care and patience than other sites. There are many areas where it is necessary to move about quietly, slowly and deliberately, especially in the most off-limits areas, or when you're visiting outside operating hours. Before advancing into unknown, risky territory, you need to carefully listen at doors and peek through their cracks for signs of people, alarms or cameras. It's often necessary to stop and listen for footsteps, or to wait a while near a particular door or stairwell to get a sense of how often it's used. And of course you have to know when to strategically retreat and live to explore another day. For all these reasons, it often takes a lot longer to really get to know an active building than it would take to get to know an abandoned building of equal size, so if you don't have the patience, please don't do it.

UP, UP INTO THE OCAD BUILDING

Whether you prefer to think of it as the ugliest building in the world or merely the weirdest building in the world, Will Alsop's expansion to the Ontario College of Art and Design makes a strong impression. The dramatic part of the project, officially called the Sharp Centre for Design but more commonly called the tabletop, is a nine-storey structure that has forsaken storeys one through seven in favour of large, colourful crayons and empty space. Personally, I find it creative and playful and like it a lot, but I think the architect and I are about the only two people in the world who feel that way.

After doing some initial scouting trips of the bizarre project during its construction, Avatar and I were determined to find a way up for a sneak preview — Av doing so in spite of his immense distaste for the building. Usually exploring a construction site is a simple matter of hopping the fence and finding a way in, but since this project began seven storeys in the air it required a less direct approach, through the old building and up into the new. Sneaking past an inattentive guard into the older part of OCAD one night, we began to scour the building for possible routes into the under-construction part of the building, but at first encountered nothing but an endless series of locks and chains. The old building was empty aside from security guards, but we encountered three of these in our first 10 minutes, so we didn't feel too lonely.

After trying many doors on many levels, we eventually found a complex route into the big, white, empty hall in the middle. Knowing that two of the guards we'd stumbled upon earlier were watching the hall from above, Av and I moved about very slowly, quietly and carefully in search of a route up. After failing to get past a locked door in the stairwell, we decided to take a risk and see if by any chance the elevator was in working order. We hit the button for the elevator and hid — a moment later, an empty construction elevator appeared with a mercifully quiet "ding". We quietly hopped in and pressed the button for the top floor (nine storeys up, but labelled level six because of the missing levels).

The OCAD extension begins seven storeys up.

We were inside the half-built tabletop now, but we didn't have it to ourselves. Some voices down the corridor sounded like they were coming towards us, so Av and I scurried off into a small, dark room to wait for them to leave.

Instead, the voices grew louder and louder until I realized with dread that they were actually coming into the same tiny room that we were in. There was nothing to hide behind, so Avatar and I turned away and pressed ourselves into a dark corner, where we watched the workers fumbling with some supplies through a reflection in the glass. They were only about five feet away from us but, amazingly, they didn't see us. Afterwards one fellow went to work in the hallway immediately outside the room we were in, so Av and I ran out past him when his back was turned and took the elevator from the sixth floor down to the fifth.

We had the fifth floor to ourselves, and took the time to explore and photograph it thoroughly, paying special attention to the incomplete outside walls and the half-finished metal staircase. When we were done, we found another staircase and took it up and out to the roof, where we left a huge mess of footprints in the thick snow while we circled the roof and took pictures of the gorgeous view. Afterwards, we headed down the stairs and played around in the scaffolding jungle on the fourth floor for a bit before heading out. We were surprised to find the door we'd come through to get into the construction area had locked behind us, but fortunately it wasn't too difficult to navigate our way out by a different route. The guard at the front door scarcely glanced at us on our way out.

CONSTRUCTION SITES

Construction sites can be boring or fantastic. Buildings-in-progress that are identical on every level above the third floor, like built-from-scratch condos or office towers, tend to be dull except for the view from the roof (and perhaps from the nearby crane, if you're in a climby mood). More complex buildings, like schools or hospitals or movie theatres, are more fun to poke around in, especially when you're dealing with additions or renovations to existing buildings rather than construction from scratch. Under-construction subway tunnels, utility tunnels and major parking garages are a lot of fun. I like that construction sites change pretty drastically every few weeks, so each time you revisit them you have to do all your problem solving in a different way, and you see different things as a reward. Once the place is complete, you also feel a certain special pride at having beta-tested it, as well as feeling a certain special connection with it from having watched it grow up.

Safety Issues
People often tell me that construction sites are dangerous, but they're actually the only exploration site where I haven't injured myself, in spite of having actively and regularly explored them for more than two decades. But I admit there are certain opportunities to hurt yourself if you're so inclined.

Construction sites are full of holes and hazards, and generally lack the guardrails and warning signs members of the general public have come to expect to warn them about any potential hazard. You really have to keep your eyes open at a construction site — if you're going down a staircase, for example, you can't just assume that it continues around the corner, because maybe they're not building that section of the staircase until tomorrow. Construction crews are often composed of fairly laid back people who conform to codes and follow proper procedures when an inspector's around but otherwise prefer to do things the way that seems easiest, which often isn't the way that's safest.

Because of low overhangs and falling objects, hard hats aren't just good credibility props, they're also useful from a safety point of view. The only drawback to bringing your own hard hat to a site is that it may be difficult to explain if you are caught; unless you have some sort of proof, the worker or guard may not take your word for it that it's your own hard hat, and may wish to confiscate it or (even worse) have you

There are no guardrails at most construction sites, so watch out for deep pits.

charged with theft. And if they do believe you that it's your own hard hat, that kind of ruins your whole just-wandered-in-to-see-what-was-going-on routine.

Security Issues

Security precautions at construction sites vary according to their type, location and degree of completion, but generally they're not among the most secure locations you will find. In the evenings and at night, construction projects outside of well populated areas will often be left totally unguarded; sites in the city may be fenced up and occasionally patrolled by one or two guards. Measures beyond this are unusual.

Fences around construction sites tend to be psychological barriers at best; they're normally temporary, flimsy and simple to scale or wriggle beneath. Sometimes you can just temporarily undo the little clasps holding the sections of temporary fence together while you slip through the temporary opening between two sections. Usually construction fences don't serve much point beyond keeping out cars and giving the construction company a place to hang its no trespassing signs.

The security agencies and guards assigned to construction sites tend to be those that aren't well trained in the art of dealing with the

public. In most cases, their primary concern isn't so much risk prevention as warding off potential thieves and vandals. Perhaps for these reasons, in my experience, guards on construction sites are much more
likely to just yell "get out of here" than try to question you or nab you.
They'd prefer to avoid an actual confrontation. Of course, this is only
a general observation, and sufficient boredom could probably inspire
just about any guard to become a pain in the neck.

Finding Construction Sites
Construction sites generally aren't too hard to find, though sometimes it's tricky to find one worth exploring. Most under-construction
houses are quite dull, unless there's something special about them,
though it can be fun to explore the drains and sewers of a new community before they're first put into use. While I grew up thinking
under-construction houses were among the most exciting places in
the world, that was only because everything else was so incredibly
boring that they were exciting in comparison. Usually generic condos,
under-construction plazas, restaurants and stores don't really have
much personality.

The sorts of construction projects that are more worthy of your
attention are those for distinctive buildings, like movie theatres, opera
houses, churches, libraries, hospitals and schools, and anything subterranean, like new storm drains, water tunnels, utility tunnels, subway
tunnels and so on. Additionally, anything really big is worth exploring,
because really big stuff is cool. Older buildings undergoing major renovations can also be extremely interesting, even if they're just being
turned into condos, both because they have more history and character and because renovations generally require more elaborate and creative solutions than building something new from scratch.

Unlike some exploration sites, construction sites are not normally
concealed from the public eye. Not only are the people building the
projects usually pretty excited about what they're up to and eager to
brag about it, but generally the projects involve a lot of noise and mess.
If you live in a decently bustling town, just wandering around and
keeping up with local news will probably leave you well supplied with
potential sites to check out. Keeping up with minutes of city council
meetings will let you hear more about some of the less-publicized projects, such as new sewers and the like. If you can't be bothered to do
any of that, a web search for your town name and "construction" will

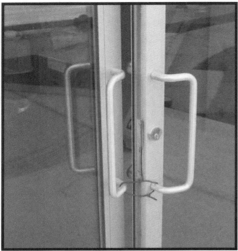

*Construction sites don't always bother
wih top-of-the-line security measures.*

*Some construction sites only worry about
keeping cars out, not people.*

probably yield a fair number of hits. Ideally not all of them will be half-completed websites from the early 90s featuring that animated icon of the little construction worker. If you live in a constructopolis like Toronto or Chicago, you can be pickier and search for "major construction project". The Emporis Building Database (*http://www.emporis.com/en/bu/*) is also a good place to look.

Changeportunity

You may have heard before that the Chinese word for "change" is the same as the Chinese word for "opportunity". Personally I think the Chinese have the right idea and that we should replace the English words "change" and "opportunity" with the much catchier word "changeportunity", but I haven't been able to get the people at the *Oxford English Dictionary* to write me back.

Regardless of their stubbornness, change *is* opportunity to an explorer. Any time something slightly unusual is going on, it's going to create some slightly unusual new possible methods of ingress. Buildings undergoing remodelling or renovation are extremely easy targets, since they tend to be populated by a wide variety of workers and contractors from different companies, none of whom really feel a sense of responsibility towards anything but their own small segment of the project and who can't possibly all know each other. An entirely different set of security procedures is normally put in place during special events, presenting new opportunities to retry all possible entrances as well as new chances to social engineer your way in. Newer security procedures are more vulnerable than practices that have been in place for some time, since they're generally conceived in an office and have not yet had a chance to

Scaffolding can provide a handy route up or down at renovation sites.

evolve in accordance with real-world experience. Even in those rare situations where the guards actually care, it takes a while for security forces to notice and recognize their blind spots. Explorers can usually do so much more quickly.

It's important to bear in mind that changeportunity is not limited to situations where access restrictions are relaxed. Often situations where security is theoretically beefed up actually present additional opportunities, and if you're creative enough in your thinking you can probably find the silver lining. If public access to a building is sealed off during a special event, for example, that just means that once you get inside you won't have to worry about being seen by other members of the public. If more security guards are brought in to a location, that just further dilutes the responsibility of each individual guard, since each guard can blame the two guys beside him. If security cameras or other electronic devices are installed, they're likely to make the guards cockier and more complacent. Every change offers new possible ways to solve the puzzle.

An important lesson that most explorers learn early is to take opportunities while they're there. This rule is especially true of construction and renovation sites, since they change so much so quickly, but it applies to pretty much every sort of infiltration. If the door is ajar, the gate unlocked or the guard post unmanned, that's the site's way of telling you that it is welcoming visitors *now*, so, if you have a friend with you, get the hell in there. Do not leave and make plans to come back with a camera the next day. Personally, I'm a little superstitious about this, and I think one of the reasons I've been given so many lucky chances is that I almost always take them when they arise. Opportunity is fickle, jealous and immature; if you hurt its feelings by not paying it enough attention it will soon stop speaking to you altogether. In spite of its personality problems, opportunity is a very good friend to have, so remember to demonstrate how happy you are to see it whenever it shows up, even if you're dressed all wrong and the timing is terrible.

If you're walking down the street and some guy wearing a hard helmet comes out of an unmarked door on the side of an unmarked building, smile at him, grab the door and walk through. Sure, there's a good chance a bunch of maintenance or construction workers will shoot you confused looks on the other side, but a few confused looks never hurt anyone, and you're not going to be charged with anything for just walking through an open door from the street. If you encounter people, you can just apologize and leave. And what if instead you find a long metal ladder leading up the inside of a tower, or a damp cement staircase leading down into the darkness? It happens — mostly to people who seize the door.

Navigation

The techniques for navigating construction sites vary drastically according to the type of site being explored; exploring an under-construction skyscraper obviously requires different procedures than exploring an under-construction utility tunnel system. There are, however, some common elements between the various sorts of large construction projects, including weak barricades, concrete, heavy equipment, scaffold staircases, ladders and cranes.

In most cases, entering a construction site is not a great challenge. The wooden hoarding and the metal, wooden or plastic fencing surrounding the site is temporary and generally looks that way — it's usually more intended to delineate a boundary than to actually prevent

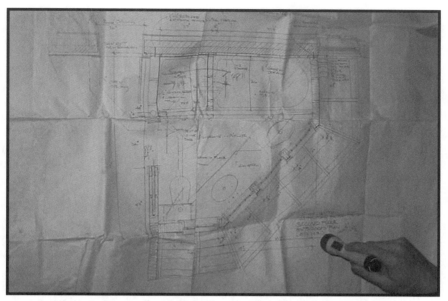

Construction sites are often well stocked with detailed blueprints of what's underway and what's planned for the future.

access. Normally, it's easy to slip through two poorly connected sections of fence, roll underneath a gate, scale a short fence or hop through an oversized viewing hole and get to the good stuff. It's rare that a thorough perimeter check won't reveal some major weakness in the barricades.

Once inside, the dominant features of most major construction projects are steel and bare concrete. (Note that many people use the terms concrete and cement interchangeably, but cement is merely the binder in concrete, the other ingredients being sand, gravel and water.) Most structures these days have at least their skeleton built out of steel, while their floors, walls and elevator shafts are all most commonly fashioned by pouring wet concrete into pre-made molds. Both steel and concrete are good, sturdy materials to walk on and climb around on, providing the concrete is dry, of course. Avoid stepping in wet concrete, as it will harden around your footwear and slow you down. Concrete slabs are commonly strengthened through the addition of a grid of long, skinny steel reinforcing bars (rebar) — sometimes you'll encounter rebar grids that haven't yet had concrete poured around them, and these can probably hold your weight if you have decent balance.

You'll likely find lots of heavy machinery on the site of most major construction projects, often with the keys still in the ignition. As tempting as it may be to take a little ride, you're much better off doing nothing more than posing with such toys for a photograph. Starting an engine not only makes a fair bit of noise, but could perhaps lead to charges of criminal mischief or even attempted grand theft.

Before proper staircases are brought in, construction workers normally move from level to level through temporary freight elevators, metal scaffold staircases and wooden or metal ladders. The freight elevators are not normally accessible to explorers outside of working hours, so we normally get around with the temporary stairs and ladders. The rickety scaffold staircases are wobbly but generally safe, as long as you don't place too much trust in the guardrails, while the ladders are straightforward. In cases where neither staircases nor ladders are present, it may still be possible to ascend or descend by hoisting oneself up on large equipment, scaling scaffolding or climbing cranes.

While personally I'm more of a solid roof man, some people who are fans of heights view construction cranes as the cherry on top of the entire site. In those cases where the cranes are not spectacularly spotlit at night, it may indeed be possible to climb up to the cab at the top of the crane via metal ladders set into the crane's main pillar. From the cab, the main and back booms of the crane are technically accessible, but it would be pretty foolish to attempt to walk around on these precarious booms without a proper safety harness and training.

Since most major construction projects do have at least some on-site security, after possibly drawing attention to your presence by doing something like summitting the building, climbing a crane or accidentally using light or a camera flash at night, it's a good idea to leave the site quickly, preferably through one of the less obvious exits.

THE CORPSE SLIME DRAIN

A fellow named Mike got in touch with me and invited me to come check out a drain in uptown he'd visited. (Mike referred to the drain as the St. Clair drain, but it's subsequently been renamed for one of its unusual features.) Mike was a very interesting fellow; he was part of some sort of special operations unit in the Canadian army, and he had done a lot of amazing things and been in a lot of amazing places. He struck me as pretty much ready for anything, so I tried to follow his lead.

On the night of the exploration, we pried open the two-metre-wide grate to the drain without much difficulty and proceeded up the pipe. Before long, we passed through a very old-looking (1918) section of drain made of huge stone slabs. Some portions of the roof and walls had fallen onto the ground. We then came to a stretch where some very unpleasant yellowish brown slime was dripping down the walls and forming stalactites on the roof. Some of the slime had completely enveloped the rungs of a nearby ladder. Mike informed me that at this point we were under the cemetery, leading to speculation that this slime had something to do with decomposing human bodies.

The drain had a lot going for it besides its age and its corpsy goodness. It was far more interesting to navigate than an average suburban drain, being very curvy and having a good number of shape changes. The water was cold but clean and well below boot level, and the drain didn't have any unpleasant odour. There were many potential turn-offs away from the main tunnel, but we stuck with the main route. After an hour or so of twists, turns and tunnels not taken, we wound up in a horseshoe- or mummy-shaped tunnel, something I'd previously only read about in *Il Draino*.

Moving right along, we soon came to a section of the drain that was quite flooded with deep, cold, rapidly flowing water. Mike told me that this section wasn't usually so flooded, and that he wanted to press on and see if the water level went down enough that we could continue to an interesting exit he knew about. I was feeling pretty sick for some reason. I didn't want to get soaked, but I also really didn't want to go back the (long) way we'd come in, so I

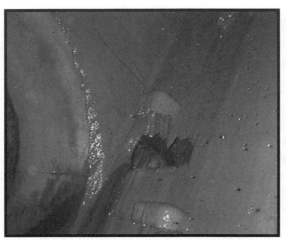

Yellowish brown slime coated all surfaces in the area beneath the cemetery.

accepted Mike's offer to scout ahead and see if we could continue. We agreed that he'd take a glowstick, and that he'd either come back if the route was impassable or give me a signal if I should follow him up the flooded drain.

So Mike set off while I leaned against the side of the drain and watched the beam of his flashlight slowly move further and further away until I couldn't see it anymore. I stood there feeling cold, wet and sick, and, as time passed, more and more concerned about the fact that I was alone in the drain with no idea how to get out. After around 20 to 30 minutes of this, I noticed a green glow coming down the pipe towards me, fast. Soon enough, my glowstick had floated all the way back to me. I eagerly snatched it up and slightly less eagerly plunged ahead into the deep, rushing water. After about 15 minutes, I saw a flashlight beam up ahead, and soon I had joined Mike before the entrance to a very, very small side tunnel.

I say "side tunnel" but I'm being generous; in actuality, this thing was just a thin pipe, not more than two feet in diameter. A raccoon could walk through it easily enough, but it was clearly not meant to accommodate humans. In fact, if Mike hadn't tossed his backpack ahead of him and begun to wriggle up the pipe, I might have assumed it wasn't humanly possible. I thanked god I hadn't had a lot to eat that day and began to slither up afterwards, thoroughly battering my knees and elbows in the process.

About 10 minutes later we popped out of a manhole in the middle of a parking lot — cold, exhausted, soaked, scraped, bruised and triumphant.

DRAINS

Metres below the busy streets above, a hidden concrete utopia snakes its way from the downtown core out beyond the suburbs, creating what is probably the second most popular realm for most urban explorers after abandoned buildings. Drains — sometimes called stormwater drains or storm sewers — are underground tunnels, usually made of brick, stone or concrete, that are used to transport stormwater, rather than household water or human waste. For many people, they're an accessible substitute for natural caves. They can stretch on through the subterranean darkness for miles and miles, and can be filled with all sorts of interesting sights to see and twists and turns to investigate. They stay cool in summer and warmish in winter, and inside the air is thick with the sweet aroma of wet concrete and the relaxing sound of running water.

While not exactly drinkable, having run through puddles of pesticides and gasoline exhaust on its way into the gutter, drain water is often clean enough to support fish and other wildlife, including insects, spiders, crayfish, crabs, turtles, eels, snakes, raccoons, rats, bats, skunks and more. The water is not normally very toxic or germ-filled unless people have illegally hooked their sanitary waste up to dump into the drain, or there has been overflow from an attached sewer system.

Sadly for drainers, in many municipalities, particularly older ones, the drainage system and the sewerage systems are not completely separate. Some older cities are drained by combined sewers, wherein stormwater and sewer water travel through identical pipes either at all times or just in cases where the water level passes a certain point. Combined sewers either fully combine the city's sewage and drainage systems or simply allow the contents of sewers to spill over into the stormwater drains when there's a heavy rainfall through a process called Combined Sewer Overflow (CSO). CSO drains are terrible for cities, since they allow untreated, bacteria-rich excrement water and industrial wastewater to gush out into the rivers and lakes, and they're terrible for explorers as well, since they add sewagey nastiness to what otherwise could have been perfectly nice drains. That said, they're still not as bad as full-on sewers.

Sewer systems — or sanitary sewer systems, as they're sometimes called, in what is undoubtedly the greatest euphemism in the history of euphemisms — are just as extensive and as easily accessible as drains, though they're usually smaller than drains in the same area and are nowhere near as popular with explorers. While most explorers just avoid any manhole cover labelled "sewer" or "sanitary", a few hardy souls do go in for that kind of thing and have some pretty amazing adventures down there. According to their accounts, sewers tend to be slimy and filled with murky grey water with many small bits of toilet paper floating about. The ground is slippery, and in some places the water levels are high and the currents strong. Frequently, long, glutinous stalagmites explorers have dubbed "snotsicles" hang from the ceiling, eager to escape to freedom by riding out in the hair of an unsuspecting victim. The air is filled with noxious fumes and droplets of sewage likely to infect those who breathe enough of them with any number of nasty diseases, including campylobacter, typhoid fever, hepatitis, E. coli, encephalitis, gastroenteritis, giardiasis, leptospirosis, methaemoglobinaemia and possibly some others that are even harder to pronounce. So, generally, you should avoid going into a sewer unless you have a damn good reason for going in there, like if you lost your dog.

It should be stressed that neither drains nor sewers have any connection to the water supply system — both are strictly used for getting rid of wastewater. This may make the authorities less jumpy about finding people in them. Other water tunnels, including buried rivers, aqueducts and other water transport tunnels, also tempt explorers, though the ones that relate directly to the water supply tend to be a little better guarded, less accessible and more likely to get you in real trouble should you be caught there. Generally I recommend sticking to drains, though much of the advice below applies to any sort of water tunnel.

Safety Issues
First things first. Follow the traditional slogan of the Cave Clan: when it rains, no drains. Check weather forecasts before you head out. If there's a chance of rain (or a sudden snow melt), put the expedition off, or you risk being flooded out. Water levels in drains can rise very, very quickly, and a fast-flowing drain can whip large rocks, pieces of metal and mangled explorer corpses down the pipe like it ain't no thang. So, don't risk it. Always check the forecast and then look for warning signs once you're draining. Inside a drain, look at the walls for signs like discolouration and bits of debris that give you an idea of the normal highwater mark within the drain. That's the point you have to be able to get above quickly if the drain floods.

There are several other safety concerns to be aware of while draining. Some of these are fairly straightforward. Watch out for slippery surfaces and low overhangs. Leave the potentially rabid wildlife alone. Try not to step on broken glass or hypodermic needles, and watch out for deep-water pools. It's not at all uncommon to fall over in a drain, but when you do, try not to scrape or cut yourself or accidentally swallow any water, since even non-CSO drains can be home to some fairly nasty bacteria and diseases. Even after exploring clean drains, you should still treat yourself to a nice, hot, soapy shower when you get

Stepirons set into the concrete at the side of the drain are often used in place of ladders.

home. Your dirty shower water will then drain out into the sewers, where it will be properly treated before it is sent back out to sea so the whole beautiful nature-driveway-nature cycle can begin again.

Unfortunately, many people don't understand the difference between sewers and drains, and ignorantly pour nasty things into their gutters, not understanding that drain water, unlike sewer water, flows directly back to nature. Many people wash their cars in their driveways or drain their pools into the gutter, and all their chemical nastiness combines under the streets. Some careless people go so far as to add paint, turpentine, ammonia and other nasty solvents into the mix, and occasionally some people who really just don't give a damn about the rest of the world will illegally hook up their plumbing so their home's sanitary waste spills out into the drains instead of the sewers. Industries can also be rather contemptuous of the world in terms of dumping foulness in drains. Obviously odd-smelling air or odd-smelling or -looking water should be avoided, and if you see anything really nasty you should probably anonymously report it to your local water board.

As well as bad water, it's also important to be aware of bad air. The term "bad air" actually encompasses several distinct hazards, including the threats of insufficient oxygen, combustible gases like methane and even poisonous vapours like hydrogen sulphide. The simplest way to avoid these problems is to stick to drains that are obviously well ventilated and filled with clean, running water and perhaps some evidence of animal life, and avoid fully enclosed pipes with foul odours and stagnant air and water. These threats won't always be obvious, of course. Naturally, bad air tends to be invisible and not all noxious air has an odour. True natural gas has no odour; the "rotten eggs" smell you're accustomed to is artificially added to the gas by the gas company to make it easier to detect. Unfortunately, municipalities can't do this with naturally accumulating explosive and suffocating gases like methane, which can collect wherever natural materials decompose in an enclosed space. Sometimes a drain's air quality will deteriorate as you wade through it and kick up nasty substances in the mud. If you're ever draining and start feeling out-of-breath, dizzy, confused, nauseous, headachy or faint, exit or get back to good air immediately. Any symptoms such as these should be taken extremely seriously when exploring any confined space.

As with many other potentially dangerous types of exploring, when you go draining it's a good idea to tell someone who isn't coming along where you're going and when you expect to be back. You can't count on a cell phone working deep inside a drain, but you may want to bring one along in case you happen to wind up locked on the wrong side of a grate or manhole cover where you're able to get some reception. A lot of people go draining by themselves, but for the sake of safety it really does make sense to recruit at least one other person to come along for the trip, especially since drains are one of the few urban exploration locations where the chance of getting caught by security doesn't increase exponentially the more people you bring along.

Security Issues
Only a very small percentage of those who venture into drains and sewers ever have any dealings with the authorities, but it does happen, particularly to people who insist on being noisy and like to pop out of manholes near busy intersections (including me, in my younger and more foolish days). In some cases you'll be able to talk your way

In some cases, grates to drain outfalls have been completely removed.

out of it, if you can convince your opponents — police, municipal workers or whomever — that you didn't damage or deface anything and that you thought drains were public property (which, indeed, they are, although your region or municipality may have laws against entering this particular sort of public property). In other cases, this won't work, and you'll be given a ticket for trespassing. You'll probably face more serious penalties if breaking and entering, vandalism or some sort of perceived threat to the water supply is involved.

Finding Drains
Drains are pretty much everywhere, so unless you live somewhere weird, you should be able to find a few. One basic technique for finding explorable, human-height drains is to look for outfall grates in areas where storm water could potentially run free and escape the city in favour of strange fringe areas known as meadows, marshes, creeks, rivers, ravines, marshes, ponds, lakes — a gallery of horrors collectively known as nature. These unholy concrete-free zones are normally completely dull and repulsive to urban explorers, but tragically these primitive wildernesses are often exactly the sort of places one must visit to find the grated entrances leading to storm drains. You

know you're on the right track when you find a small or narrow stretch of green more or less totally surrounded with asphalt, cement and other impermeable land. When you're lucky, this can be ridiculously easy — sometimes you just spot suspicious-looking slabs of concrete adjacent to a river or pond while you're out and about. Other times it can take horrific amounts of traipsing through plant-filled suburban forests of poison ivy or wandering up and down insect-filled riverbanks searching desperately only to come up dry.

The best way to avoid wasting so much time and energy is to do a little advance research. While you might try phoning your city engineer's office, it's unlikely that they'll be too eager to turn over the information unless you have, or can effectively bluff, some credentials. An easier method is to go to a reference library or city archives and look at topographical city maps — particularly hydrological survey maps, if you can find 'em — and look for long, narrow stretches of green or undeveloped land, paying special attention to areas where greenways give way to rivers, or where rivers suddenly stop dead as they come up against roadways or built-up areas. These places are very likely to have some good drains, so slap on some bug spray and head over on a quest for grates and manholes. If you can find older topographical maps and compare them to the newer ones, you may also be able to discover spots where creeks or rivers have been buried in tunnels and converted into drains.

Unfortunately, not all drains are explorer friendly. The size of a drain is typically measured in millimetres, with sizes from 1600mm and up accommodating most explorers without too much discomfort. Sizes from 1800mm and up are better, and in some cities, if you're lucky, you will occasionally encounter 3500–5000mm monster drains. Sometimes, a drain's size and effectiveness is measured in terms of how often it will fail — for example, the size of a 50-year-flood drain will probably prove insufficient and cause flooding twice per century, whereas a larger 100-year-flood drain will fail half as often. Some municipalities are dry and cruel and rely almost entirely on tiny little drains. Some explorers are willing to crouch a fair bit in order to explore a drain, but no one wants to spend a whole evening crawling around on wet cement. So, sadly, finding a drain isn't really much of an accomplishment unless that drain is large enough to accommodate people.

When to Go

Although drains are dark enough that they require a flashlight during either day or night, they're typically much brighter during the day. A few beams of sunlight poking in through tiny holes in grates and manhole covers can make a big dent on total darkness. While painting with light can be artform in itself, for the most part, those interested in snapping long-exposure pictures of drains should favour daytime draining.

Draining can be enjoyable during either the warm months or the coldest months; in the summer, drains are pleasantly wet, shady and cool, and in the winter they're

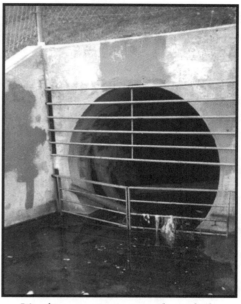

It's often easy to squeeze through the grates at a drain's outfall.

protected enough from the elements that they're generally warmer than the outside. As long as one takes extra care around stairs and ladders, draining in winter is fairly safe, and frozen drains can be incredibly beautiful sights. Other than avoiding rainy days, the one time of year that is dangerous for draining is during the spring thaw. Exploring in slush and water that's just above freezing temperature is asking for hypothermia, exhaustion and other sorts of trouble. Stay clear of drains until the weather warms up, and keeping your clothes dry isn't a matter of life and death.

Entering

With drains and sewers, most of the work lies in the finding rather than the entering. Once you've found a human-sized drain and located the point where it ends (the outfall, or catch basin, where the drain water dumps back out to nature), chances are good that you'll be able to get inside.

If the drain entrance is grated, as they normally are, and there's no

*Some drain entrances, such as this entrance to the drain named Limbo,
require some creative squeezing.*

unlocked doorway in the middle of the grate, try to figure out a way to
bypass the grate without damaging it. They don't build these things as
carefully as jail cells, so if you're skinny you'll often be able to squeeze
through the bars. Sometimes the grate will be bolted to the concrete
tunnel, and it'll be possible to temporarily unscrew half the bolts (either
the bolts at the bottom or the bolts on one of the sides) in order to pry
the grate back far enough that you can squeeze inside. If you're dealing
with a heavy grate, you may want to use some sort of strong metal rod
to hold the grate open while everyone slips through the entrance. If
you're dealing with a very heavy grate, you may need some sort of tool
just to help you pry it open (noting, of course, that forced entry may
lead to more serious charges if you're caught). A car jack works. If you
have no luck with the grate, follow the drain backward at street level
until you come to a manhole cover, possibly labelled "storm" or something along those lines. If water is pouring out of the outfall, you
should hear rushing water below; if the drain is dry, you'll have to do
without this aural cue.

    If you feel confident that you can take the lid off without being seen,
you can very carefully give it a whirl — keeping in mind that manhole

covers can be very heavy and can quite possibly mangle your fingers if you accidentally let them slam shut at the wrong time.

If the lid is light and full of holes, you may be able to grab it and pull it up with your bare hands. If the lid is heavy and only has two small, square lift holes (as many manhole covers do), you'll probably need what drainers call a popper, a tool for opening manhole covers. You can purchase an excellent and thoroughly portable one of these called the Lift-o-Matic from the Melbourne Cave Clan, but most people just make do with homemade solutions. Crowbars are popular, though

Some drain outfall grates look solid but can actually just be swivelled or pushed aside.

obviously very suspicious if you happen to be caught (something that is not at all unlikely if you spend significant amounts of time prying open manhole covers). Bent metal bars work decently. An Ontario-based explorer named Quick has come up with a great little trick for opening manhole covers using nothing but a sturdy pair of pliers. One handle of the pliers is inserted into the hole in the lid, while the other handle is used to pull the lid back and off. This is an especially nice trick since pliers are both lighter and considerably less suspicious than a crowbar or similar length of metal. After you've got the popper in place, remember to lift with your legs rather than your back.

Once you have the manhole cover off, smell what lies below. If you smell sewage — a fairly distinct aroma — you are looking at either a sewer or a contaminated drain. If that's more than you bargained for — and it probably is — lower the lid securely back into place slowly and carefully, watching your fingers and making as little noise as possible.

If, on the other hand, you don't smell anything you can't deal with, take a look down at the ladder or step irons, metal rungs jutting direct-

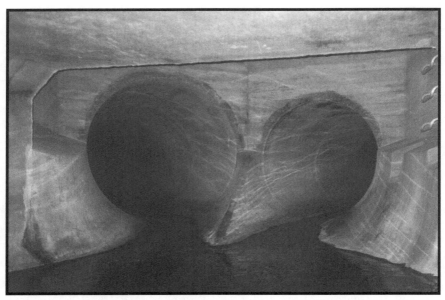

Junction rooms are the areas in drains where various branches of a drain converge.

ly into the side of the drain. Are the rungs all there? Are they rusty? Are they firmly attached to the wall? Try your weight on them before you trust your weight to them. If they snap or dissolve, you should probably pass, unless this is some dream pipe, in which case — if you know what you're doing — your friends can help you secure yourself with ropes and ease your way down. Remember that — in theory — it takes at least four people to haul someone up by a rope. When climbing down, expect that the ladder rungs may be slippery, and grow more slippery towards the bottom.

Ideally, if you're new to this, a friend should be holding open the manhole cover for you while you ease yourself down. Unfortunately, someone always has to handle the slightly awkward task of closing the lid behind the group. Be extra careful when you're doing this with a square lid because, unlike the safer circular lids, square lids can potentially be dropped down the shaft. After holding the lid open while you ease yourself down into the manhole chimney, angle and slide the lid a little ways to the side of the hole, so you won't have to worry about the lid suddenly falling into place before you're ready. Then, once you've steadied yourself inside the shaft, reach your arms up, keeping your hands away from the sides of the lid, and gently lift or push it back into place, making as little noise as possible. While you're doing this, both you and any people standing below you should avert your eyes to avoid getting them filled with rust and dirt. Now you can climb down and turn on your flashlight or headlamp and find out if this drain is human height or not.

Navigation

There are those who think drain exploration is unbelievably dull, and in some cases it can be. In the least interesting scenario, you'll find yourself in a round concrete pipe (RCP)

Many drains contain interesting changes in shape and construction material.

that goes straight for miles and miles, and never changes in size, shape or building materials, while never encountering a single noteworthy feature or even any graffiti to break up the monotony (yes, I maintain that tagging is dumb, but I'm less opposed to artwork and commemorative pieces deep inside a plain concrete drain, where they're unlikely to spoil anything for anyone).

That said, at their best, drains can be beautiful and fascinating places to explore. While most drains these days are made of concrete, some older drains are fashioned out of bricks or even carved blocks of stone formed into arches. Occasionally you may encounter pipes built with more exotic materials, such as plastic or corrugated metal. As you move up the pipe, water levels will rise and fall — ideally, they shouldn't rise beyond the tops of your boots. Some drains are filled with pits of deeper water designed to collect trash or other large debris that accidentally washes into the drain, and that might otherwise clog it up. You can usually get past these pits without swimming.

Other changes in elevation can also result in interesting features. When one segment of a drain is higher than another, the two can be

connected via a slope (commonly called a slide, and quite often a popular place to slip and fall); steps (designed to break the water's speed,
not to make life easier for explorers); or, if the first drain simply spills
down into the second, a waterfall. Sometimes several times as tall as a
person, drain waterfalls can look quite spectacular, even more so when
they're frozen. Provided the water isn't too polluted, they can also be
fun to play in and climb through. Sometimes drains change elevation
drastically, and tall metal ladders — sometimes several storeys high —
are in place to assist you in climbing from one level to another.

Very occasionally, you'll find homemade wooden ladders or ropes
left behind by previous visitors. While these people were almost certainly trying to do future explorers a favour, it's a good idea to give these
gift horses a thorough dental examination before trusting your weight
to them, since the drain environment can be fairly corrosive over time,
what with the humidity and people occasionally dumping nasty chemicals into the gutter. Sometimes you'll have to get a boost or climb up
a wall to get to a slightly higher section of drain (when you do this, be
careful not to gash yourself, as the drain water probably contains some
upwardly mobile parasites that would love to make a beautiful new
home in your intestines).

Drains are often filled with natural formations such as stalactites,
stalagmites and flowstone, all of which should be left alone and appre-
ciated from a distance, as they're part of the happy process by which
the drain will eventually come to look more and more like a natural
cave. Many drains will change shape, from round to square to rectangular to ovoid to horseshoe and so on, or change size, generally shrink-
ing as one moves further up the pipe and the pipe has to accommodate
less water. The sad fact is that drains often don't end well. They go on
forever, or they just get really small. Very rarely is there a big chequered
flag or a trophy waiting for you at the end. The reward really has to be
in the doing, rather than in the completion.

In almost all drains, the main pipe is fed with water from a variety
of smaller side pipes. These side pipes are often explorable themselves,
though getting through them may involve some pretty rough-on-the-
knees crawling, and large people probably won't be able to pull it off.
Claustrophobic people almost certainly won't be able to pull it off.
Side pipes are usually too small to let a person turn around, so if you
come to a dead end or have a surprise encounter with a rabid raccoon
you'll just have to crawl back to the main pipe backwards. Most side

Small sidepipes in drains are often humanly accessible but not comfortable.

pipes eventually lead to the shafts beneath gutters, which are rarely bolted shut and can be used as emergency exits from a drain — though of course one should keep in mind that they may be at the side of a busy street.

While most drains are relatively straight, or only slightly curved, some are more pleasantly labyrinthine, splitting apart or coming together at junctions and sometimes spanning several levels. Bringing along a rough map and a compass can be fun and useful for mapping purposes, but even in the more complex drain systems it's difficult to get truly lost. In most cases you can just follow the water flow upstream or downstream, as appropriate. Even when this isn't possible, as in a patch of drain that's dry or filled with stagnant water, it's not usually difficult to find the main pipe and determine which way is which. If you do find yourself in a real maze, scribbling a few chalk markings on the walls will probably enable you to sort it out by dinnertime.

Most drains are filled with vaults (for manholes, usually), junction rooms (where multiple pipes come together), grill rooms (where the ceiling itself is a grill which admits water, light and fresh air) and other sorts of rooms, all of which can provide a welcome break from drain-walking. Manhole chambers provide nice places to stretch out and get some slightly fresher air, as well as an opportunity to exit the drain, if you know for a fact that the manhole doesn't lead out to the middle of a road. If you hear an evil-sounding metallic thwump-thwump echoing down from above every so often, that's the sound of cars going over the manhole cover, and you should definitely steer clear. Conversely, if you don't hear any cars going over the cover, that doesn't necessarily mean you've found a safe exit — you might just be underneath a road that isn't used very much. But, as the old saying goes, one semi truck in the face can ruin your whole day. Except in unusual circumstances, drains should be exited either by manholes you know to be safe, such as the one you came in through, or through the infall or outfall.

Exiting through a manhole is not considerably more difficult than entering through a manhole. Again, it's important for you to be well braced inside the manhole chimney, to keep your hands away from the edge and to avert your eyes from the falling rust and dirt. If you find you don't have the strength to lift the lid with your arms above your head (nothing to be ashamed of — some of those lids are insanely heavy), try recruiting a friend or two to join you at the top of the ladder to give you a hand. If that doesn't work, try contorting yourself into such a position that you're able to brace your back against the lid and use the muscles of your legs pressing down on the ladder rungs to open the lid. If none of that works, it may be time to try a different exit — but again, don't exit through mystery manholes.

The only times you should consider exiting at a point other than the outfall or a known, safe manhole or gutter box are when you see, hear or feel signs that — contrary to the weather forecast you undoubtedly remembered to check before you decided to go draining — it has started to rain. As mentioned, a flash flood is the worst thing that can happen while you're in a drain. If you hear rain outside the drain, see a sudden increase in the water pouring in through the side pipes, notice the main pipe's water level rising steadily, hear a loud and increasing noise coming from further up the pipe (while you stay still) or feel a sudden, intense change in the air pressure inside the drain, it's time to leave — head for the nearest known safe exit or head up a ladder towards a potential exit. Get above the flood line left behind the last time the drain flooded. It's not likely that the water level will suddenly shoot up all the way to street level, so you need not actually pop the manhole until you're fairly certain that the water is indeed rising to a dangerous level, but you do need to be ready to get out of there if necessary. Unfortunately, it is not only possible but likely that any randomly chosen manhole cover you head towards will be bolted or rusted shut, or have a car parked on top of it, in which case you and your group will just have to stand on the ladder rungs at the top of the manhole chimney and hope the storm doesn't last more than a few days.

CLOSE CALL AT LOWER BAY

The CBC TV show *Big Life* wanted to film a segment on *Infiltration*, and I let them talk me into it, part of the temptation for me being that I would get a high-quality video copy of our journeys to places like the tunnels leading to the abandoned Lower Bay subway station. On the night of the scheduled expedition to Lower Bay, I met up with the interviewer and her cameraman in advance and briefed them on the sorts of hazards I figured we'd be likely to face, including all the usual safety warnings as well as a few extra cautions because the TV camera would make us extra conspicuous as we headed into the tunnels.

But entry into the tunnels from Museum station proved no problem at all, and even the fairly long and nerve-wracking journey down the unlit tracks to Lower Bay station went without a hitch. We paused to film in nooks and crannies along the way where we wouldn't be crushed by any passing trains and everything was going smoothly when we finally saw the fluorescent lights of Lower Bay before us.

We climbed up the maintenance stairs and emerged onto the dingy platform of the abandoned station and had just started to take in our surroundings when suddenly we heard a very unexpected noise: a train racing into the station at high speed through the opposite tunnel from the one we'd just exited. I yelled "Hide!" and did my best to conceal myself behind a pillar, but I watched the cameraman scramble around for a while before he finally found anywhere to take cover.

The train was empty except for the driver, who was presumably just using Lower Bay as a switching point so he could move his train from one line to the other. This driver clearly saw us as he pulled into the station, and he sprang from the train and began very angrily yelling for us to come out. I caught the eyes of the interviewer and the cameraman and pointed towards the exit, and we began sprinting up the stairs that go from Lower Bay back to Bay proper, the in-use part of the station. We could hear the driver yelling behind us as he gave chase, so we continued up from the station and out onto the street via one of the unattended exits.

Shortly after being spotted and yelled at, my companions and I headed up the stairs leading from Lower Bay to the regular level of Bay station.

Once out on the street, the interviewer and I realized we'd somehow become separated from the cameraman, and looked about for him frantically as we tried to hail a cab. Already we could see transit supervisor vehicles cruising around the station, and within minutes they were joined by police cars. Finally spotting the cameraman, we joined him and the three of us hopped into the first cab that stopped and slunk down low in the back seat. The cab driver may or may not have known we were hiding, but he willingly drove us past the many security vehicles in the area and off to freedom.

Not surprisingly, the CBC never used the incriminating footage, nor were they ever willing to give me a copy of the tape.

When I later reflected on how narrowly I'd avoided being killed by a high-speed train that evening, I resolved to stop visiting Lower Bay via the subway tunnels. I imagine the CBC folks did too.

TRANSIT TUNNELS

While most people probably think of subway tunnels when they think of transit tunnels, the broader definition of transit tunnels includes any sort of tunnel that was originally built for, or later adapted to, the purpose of facilitating traffic. As well as subway tunnels, this includes covered light rail tunnels, automobile tunnels, freight train tunnels and even covered waterways.

People who like exploring transit tunnels also usually like exploring the various service and mechanical areas adjacent to the tunnels and the stations between the tunnels, particularly in cases where those stations are not in public use. Finding a not-in-use line or station feels like stumbling upon your own private transit museum, and gives you a wonderful feeling of being in on the secret workings of the city.

Safety Issues
It must be stressed that transit tunnels, at least ones that are still in use, are among the most dangerous locations you can possibly choose to explore, from a living-and-dying perspective. If you want to do a lot of things with your life, do the other things first. I'm serious — *you can go into a subway tunnel alive and come out dead*. The trains themselves are probably the greatest threat, as they travel at unpredictable intervals and at very high speeds, and will not be able to stop for you if you get in their way. If you see a train coming towards you, there is a good chance that you will be unable to get out of the way before it hits you, or at least slices off your leg. Many people imagine that they can count the minutes between trains and thereby determine a safe window for tunnel running, but trains don't always stick to a schedule or routine — an empty train will often be sent express between two regular trains, for example. Nor is there any guarantee that a station that's not normally in use won't be visited by a train making a special detour, or being used for training a new driver, or even for filming a movie or commercial. It's important to bear in mind that unexpected trains can suddenly appear on any electrified (or live) line — and you should always assume that a line is live unless you have a good reason not to.

Although many people do survive accidental contact with electrified rails (the voltage of which varies dramatically from city to city), it's better if you avoid them altogether. Certainly don't imagine that rubber soles will protect you. Electrified rails are sometimes referred to as "the

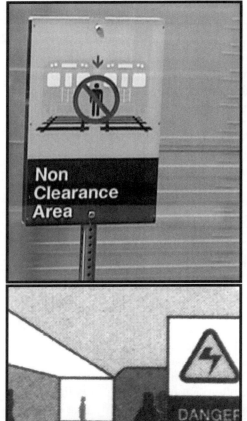

The narrow gaps between two trains and the electrified third rail are two good places to avoid.

third rail", but this nickname is less appropriate in systems like Montreal's Metro or London's Underground, where there are multiple electrified rails. In most cases, the electrified rails will be somewhat shielded, perhaps with wooden boards, providing a little bit of protection for workers who stumble while working on the tracks. Be grateful for these boards, but don't assume that they'll keep you safe from electrocution. It's still quite easy to make contact with live rails. Certainly, it would be a mistake to trust your weight to these potentially damp-and-decades-old boards — they're an emergency backup and nothing more.

Other hazards to watch out for include uninsulated wires and, in some cities, rats. Don't pet either. In a longer-term way, you may want to worry about the effects of breathing underventilated tunnel air for hours at a time. You'll notice that subway tunnels and everything in them tends to be black. This isn't black paint; it's a thick coating of steel dust particles that have been ground off the train brake linings over the years. While you probably don't need to go so far as to wear a face mask (most tunnel workers don't), it's a good idea to breathe through your nose rather than your mouth. Your nose — specifically, your nose hair — acts as a natural filter against at least some small amount of the particulate nastiness in the air around you. If you doubt me, blow your nose at the end of a trip

Some good advice.

and look at the blackened tissue. Yes, I forgive you for doubting me.

The phenomenon of people living in transit tunnels only exists in New York City (and possibly Moscow), and the numbers of people living in tunnels under New York have been steadily declining since the problem first attracted media attention in the mid-to-late 1980s (much to the frustration of local pseudo-journalists). This exciting lifestyle trend hasn't caught on elsewhere, though it's a popular subject of urban legends.

Security Issues

The punishments for entering transit tunnels are very severe, especially since 11 September 2001, and often go far beyond $500 fines and all the way to jail time or worse. In New York City, there was an orange-alerted period where many subway stations were guarded by men armed with submachine guns, indicating that the city was almost certainly not going to adopt a "boys will be boys" attitude towards curious tunnel runners. Use your common sense and don't explore in locations where tensions are high. (Unfortunately, at the time of this writing, this warning encompasses the entire US, but perhaps this will change in the future.)

Exercise extreme caution while entering and exiting transit tunnels, paying attention not only to the eyes of other passengers but also to surveillance cameras. Keep in mind that even lines and stations not currently in use may be under surveillance. Sometimes under-construction subway lines connect their security systems before they power up the electrified rails, and it's certainly not unheard of for an out-of-use station to have a camera or two still keeping an eye on things. Generally these surveillance systems are installed more to monitor for violence and vandalism than to watch for tunnel runners (as is clear if you pay attention to their usual lines of sight), but it's still wise to keep their presence in mind when you're making your move.

While in the tunnels, you need to stay out of sight of passengers, drivers and any maintenance workers that may happen to be in the tunnels at the same time as you. Meeting workers in the tunnels at random is very rare, but dodging workers could be an important concern if you're taking advantage of a service outage, a track renovation or some similar special opportunity (ahem — *changeportunity*) for exploration.

Finding Transit Tunnels
While active transit tunnels are obvious and easy to find, if you don't mind the whole huge-risk-of-dying-or-going-to-jail business, finding the more interesting and out-of-use parts of your local mass transit system (or former mass transit system) may require a bit more researching and searching. Subway tunnels that are under construction are amazing exploration sites, and transit systems often do explorers the courtesy of printing maps showing "planned stations" a year or two in advance. Transit systems are also pretty good about informing customers in advance when particular stations, segments or lines will be closed for track maintenance and similar work. Pay attention to special opportunities like these: the best time to explore transit tunnels is when they are neither in use nor electrified — though not-in-use but still electrified tunnels do present a pretty juicy opportunity.

Finding out about older, half-built or abandoned stations and lines may require some online and library research, and will probably result in a few wild goose chases before you begin to hone in on the real thing. Personally, I followed many false leads before getting the real story on, and finding out how to access, Toronto's abandoned subway stations. (The transit-geek-filled newsgroup *misc.transport.urban-transit* turned out to be the most reliable resource at the time, and is still a good source of information today.)

Navigation
There are two main varieties of tunnel you'll encounter: cut-and-cover tunnels and machine-bored tunnels. Cut-and-cover tunnels, which are generally rectangular, are created by digging down from the surface,

hollowing out a space, wrapping the space in concrete and then putting the earth back in place atop it. Machine-bored tunnels, which are generally tubular, are created by driving a large tunnel-boring machine (TBM) through the earth, drilling a tunnel-sized hole and snapping metal or concrete fortifications in place as it travels. Cut-and-cover tunnels are generally more explorer-friendly than machine-bored tunnels, as their design often makes it possible to cross back and forth between two parallel tunnels if you hear an oncoming train, and presents more opportunities for hiding as well. Machine-bored tunnels tend to keep the two parallel tunnels completely separated, reducing your options for hiding and evasion.

Provided you remember your flashlight (and your backup flashlight), the odds of becoming hopelessly lost in transit tunnels are relatively slim, since the distance between two stations is rarely more than a kilometre or so. Personally, I've never had any trouble navigating my way through transit tunnels, but then Toronto's subway system is extremely straightforward. In some of the slightly more complex systems involving multiple levels, wall signage indicating which station is in which direction may help reorient you should you somehow lose your bearings. Graffiti may also provide helpful clues. In more complex systems, bringing along (or creating) a track map — containing some of the information that a standard route map omits for the sake of clarity — may prove useful. Transit geek websites are good places to hunt for existing track maps, which you can then embellish with details of interest to explorers.

UNDER THE YORK POOL

Back in the days when my exploring partner Pablo and I were first charting the hazards of the northern and southern tunnels under Toronto's York University, we learned to take the stories about the school's utility tunnels with a grain of salt. No, students didn't live down there. No, a guy named Burd hadn't died down there. No, the Sasquatch Tunnels were not actually inhabited by hairy hominids. It seemed reasonable to conclude that the legends about a set of tunnels leading to a viewing gallery under the school pool were equally ludicrous.

Or were they? When my friend Kowalski rejoiced that he and his exploring friend had recently spent most of an entire night touring the tunnels under York and searching for a variety of the school's famous sights, I had only one question for him: did they find the pool?

Kowalski offered to *show* me his answer, so a day later I took the bus up to York to meet him. The entrance he and his friend had used had been sealed off, but they'd had the foresight to prop another entrance open while they were down there. We headed to this backup entrance, and were soon deep inside the familiar maze of tunnels.

The tunnels had acquired a little new graffiti, and were a little brighter than I remembered them, but otherwise they seemed to be doing fine. We made our way south and west, towards a rhythmic thrumming noise that Kowalski billed as "the throbbing heart of the university". As we got closer, the noise throbbed more and more intensely, until we finally came upon the heart itself: a damaged ventilation fan. Obviously, Kowalski was quickly picking up the York tradition of giving grandiose names to minor landmarks.

Soon after this, we arrived at a door to a mechanical room and headed into the darkness beyond, closing the door behind us.

The room was filled with the sound of sloshing water and completely unlit except for a pale blue glow coming in through some windows. And those windows had people on the other side of them. And those people were deep underwater. The main part of the room was several feet deeper than the deepest part of the

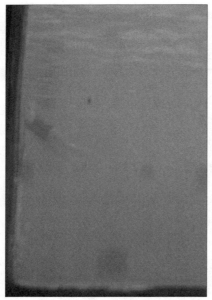

From the pool maintenance room inside the utility tunnels, we were able to peer up at the in-use pool.

pool's deep end; we had to climb up some stairs to peek through the windows and get a good view, and we did this very timidly. Although I'd been swimming in the Tait pool several times before, I'd never noticed the portholes before, so I had no idea if they were one-way or two-way glass.

Letting the poor swimmers have their privacy, we examined the odd machines under the pool for a bit. We then decided to return to the safety of the tunnels, but I heard Kowalski mutter the dreaded word "oops" as he tried the door handle. Locked.

Would we now have to bang on the glass and plead with the swimmers to let us out? I hoped not. That would be awkward for everyone.

Fortunately, it didn't come to this. We exited by another door, emerging in a public basement of the gym. After trying a few other possible entrances to the tunnels and finding them all to be dead ends, we recrossed the campus to return to our first entry point. As we headed back, Kowalski ran into a female friend of his. "Heading back to work?" she asked. "No, we just got locked out of the tunnels, so we're heading back to start again," he replied. I laughed. "She's been down there already," he explained.

The next site we saw didn't actually have a name yet, so I'll dub it, oh I don't know, the Fantastic Psychedelic Realm of Artistic Wonder. This was an old mechanical room that had somehow come into the possession of some art department; the room was filled with paintings, props and costumes. Old clothes, police uniforms and ballerina costumes hung from clothing racks. I suggested to Kowalski that if we heard someone coming we could quickly disguise ourselves as a policeman and a ballerina and then get away, but it didn't come to that.

We headed south to explore some areas neither of us had visited before, pausing to scour and photograph every mechanical room we passed along the way. In unlit tunnels, we waded through disorganized piles of cable weaving across the floor. Kowalski remarked that someone must have added an extra 0 to the cable order.

Some of the mechanical rooms were small and uninteresting, but others were enormous, multi-storey beasts filled with metre-diameter pipes and gigantic machinery, and oddities like an old Good Humor ice cream cart. Some mechanical rooms went several storeys up from the steam tunnels, while others went several storeys below the tunnels. One whole level of mechanical rooms seemed to be filled entirely with broken machinery that had never been replaced. And of course all the rooms were filled with the sort of bizarre signage we've come to expect — nay, demand — from the underbellies of large institutions.

After heading as far south as the tunnels would go and poking about in the dull basements of the graduate student residences (where I was very insistent on propping the door open behind us, even though Kowalski assured me none of the doors would lock), we turned back to take the other branch and poke about in the very hot area under Atkinson College, which one must pass through in order to access another short branch of tunnels leading south. We took this as far south as we could go and then headed back out to the main steam tunnels, sighing with relief as we shut the door behind us. "You know a place is hot when it's a relief to come back to the steam tunnels," Kowalski said.

After navigating tunnels, mechanical rooms and even some ongoing tunnel construction for several hours, we finally decided to call it a night, and headed out through the basement of the fine arts building, feeling that we'd come very close to seeing the whole system. Of course, there was that one ledge we couldn't quite get to....

UTILITY TUNNELS

The most popular tunnels for explorers are what are known as steam tunnels, college tunnels or utility tunnels. Traditionally, the idea behind steam tunnels was to generate heat for an entire institution in a central plant — often called the central utilities building or CUB — and then pump it out to all the outlying buildings in the form of steam carried in pipes, so as to avoid the expense involved in building and maintaining separate boiler rooms in each building within the institution. Water — both fresh and used — could also be transported through pipes in the steam tunnels, if a separate system wasn't in place. Typically, person-sized tunnels were built alongside the entire length of the pipes in order to allow engineers to service the system and make occasional repairs. Since the utility tunnels were already handily in place, it was natural for the engineers to simply reuse them for later developments such as electrical wiring, TV cable and network cables.

Safety Issues
Utility tunnels are most definitely not designed for public use, so minor injuries are a possibility, especially since the lack of keys sometimes requires explorers to climb and crawl through more dangerous areas never intended for human access.

Burns are the problem you're most likely to face in utility tunnels. Superheated steam is very hot. There's no need to test how hot it is by placing your bare hand in front of it when you come to a leak: it is very hot, I promise. It is so hot that you should avoid not only placing your bare skin anywhere near it, but even touching any pipes that might contain it. Pipes containing superheated steam need to be extremely well insulated; if the insulation is too thin or too worn, you can burn your hands right through the insulation. It should go without saying that touching an uninsulated pipe that might contain superheated steam is a very stupid thing to do. And yet, it is occasionally necessary to climb over some pipes in order to proceed down a given tunnel. In such situations the easiest way you can protect yourself from burns is to wear sturdy work gloves, but even when you're wearing gloves, it makes sense to avoid touching bare metal pipes, and to stay well clear of steam leaks.

Other safety hazards you're likely to face in steam tunnels include slippery surfaces, low overhangs and sharp surfaces. Because steam tunnels can be corrosive environments, you may also occasionally

Some utility tunnels are so clogged with pipes that explorers must climb over or under pipes in order to continue.

encounter badly rusted metal fixtures and crumbling ladders that you shouldn't trust your weight to. Expect to find very dusty areas and very poorly ventilated areas, and of course be well prepared for problems related to overheating and dehydration. Bring a lot of water — you won't regret it.

Asbestos
In some tunnel systems and mechanical areas, especially those that are abandoned or poorly maintained, there may be a risk of exposure to airborne asbestos fibres. Asbestos is a naturally occurring, fire-resistant family of minerals that, from the early 1900s until the last few decades, was a popular insulating material for pipes, floor tiles and ceiling tiles. Construction and manufacture using asbestos was largely banned in the early 1980s, when the mineral was conclusively linked to serious health hazards. Asbestos exposure has been linked to cancers of the chest and lungs, mesothelioma, gastric tumours and a fatal lung disorder called asbestosis.

It is uncertain how much asbestos people need to inhale before they'll become sick, particularly since the effects of exposure often don't

Avoid any areas labelled as having dangerous levels of asbestos. But don't assume the absence of such a sign means you are safe.

become apparent for several decades. It's tough to get practical answers about how much exposure is realistically safe. Many people are so paranoid about asbestos that they'll caution you against even thinking about it too hard. Governments typically warn people to avoid exposure entirely, unless they're trying to convince people to continue to work around asbestos, in which case they'll say the hazards for people who don't work with it daily are negligible. Though in theory a single asbestos fibre could prove deadly, some people who have worked with asbestos daily for many years have never had any problems. Luck seems to be a big factor, though people who don't smoke tend to have much better luck than those who do.

While it may be unlikely that occasional exposure to very small levels of asbestos will ever lead to problems, considering the potential suffering involved if you *do* get sick and considering the relative ease of protecting yourself against asbestos, you may as well take the appropriate precautions. As mentioned, dust masks and painter's masks won't do the job. Asbestos fibres are measured in microns, and are easily small enough to go through cheap masks like these. For real protection, you need a half-face respirator equipped with 100-rated filters of the type described in the chapter on equipment. The mask needs to form an airtight seal against your skin, so I hope you got rid of that moustache and beard like we talked about.

Even with the mask, however, it makes sense to try to avoid higher concentrations of airborne asbestos. Stay away from white dust or white insulation fibres in the vicinity of pipes. Don't climb on pipes with improperly sealed insulation. Avoid fallen ceiling tiles. Stay away from areas where asbestos abatement work is being done, as the air there is likely to be full of the stuff. When you're done exploring the area with asbestos, wash your hair and skin, rinse off the bottom of your shoes or boots thoroughly and either throw out your clothes or wrap them tightly in plastic bags for separate washing later. Take a bath at your next opportunity. Don't forget to wipe off your respirator before your next trip.

Security Issues
While tunnels are virtually never patrolled by security guards, some systems can be risky places to explore. Though relatively few institutions are overly paranoid about the idea of students getting too close a look at their steam pipes, unfortunately, utility tunnels can have slightly more nefarious uses as well. Because they connect most of the buildings on a campus or within a given institution, utility tunnels can be useful to people like thieves or animal-rights activists looking for easy entrances to and exits from secure buildings containing expensive equipment or animals for experiments.

Because of this potential threat to their property, in the last decade or two the administrators of some tunnel systems have installed door alarms, motion detectors and closed-circuit cameras aimed at either deterring or catching people who enter the tunnels without permission. Some systems are actually designed to trap students inside the tunnels until security has a chance to arrive. These systems are not foolproof, naturally, and some explorers delight in finding clever routes over or around the alarmed door or under the motion detector or camera. On those occasions when things go wrong and an alarm is somehow triggered, or you notice a flashing red light that you don't like the looks of, it is often possible to escape from the system before security has a chance to respond, since most tunnel systems are full of exit hatches and doors out to mechanical rooms.

Occasionally, however, tunnellers get caught. The administration policy is normally that students caught in the tunnels will be suspended or expelled while non-students are threatened with steep fines, but instances of tunnellers being seriously punished are few and far between. When people are seriously punished, it's normally because they pried something open and caused some permanent damage or grabbed something as a souvenir. If you are caught, you may be able to get off with a warning, provided you took nothing and did no damage. Some institu-

Sometimes the entrance to the utility tunnel system is obvious.

tions give everyone they catch a ticket for criminal trespass, regardless of their student status or their actions inside the tunnel system.

Finding Utility Tunnels

While many people assume that the best and most likely places to find such tunnels are beneath colleges and universities, these are really just the best-*known* places to find tunnel networks, since college and university students are curious, vaguely rebellious sorts who often have a lot of free time on their hands. In reality, utility tunnels — as such tunnels really should be called — can be found all over the place, in virtually any place where several buildings are owned by the same person or institution — and often in other places as well.

While colleges and universities that occupy multiple buildings almost always employ utility tunnels, so do many other sorts of complexes, including hospitals, asylums, government buildings, hotels and train stations. It's worth your time to investigate the basements of, and the manholes and grates surrounding, any large institution with multiple buildings. Sometimes this condition isn't even necessary, and you'll find a surprise utility tunnel between two or more buildings that don't even share a common owner but have come to an agreement to share a single heating plant and connect themselves by utility tunnels, as is the case here in Toronto with Union Station, Toronto General Hospital and the University of Toronto all generously donating heat to some of their smaller neighbours via steam tunnels. Other times a particular utility company — such as the gas, phone or cable company — will decide to build a unique tunnel system that will allow it to serve all its clients in a particular area. There are many clues that can alert you to systems like this. Some of the most obvious are spray painted markings on roads and sidewalks above tunnels, or manholes labelled "Utility", "Telephone", etc. Manhole covers that are elevated two or

Emergency exits within the tunnels offer a quick route to freedom, but are often alarmed and should generally be used as a last resort.

three inches above ground level are likely to be connected with the utility system in some way, as they obviously aren't intended to collect rainwater. In the winter, look for long patches of melted snow surrounded by snow that's still frozen, possibly indicating something hot not too far below the surface.

Finding Entrances

When checking basements in search of tunnels, head towards the heat and noise. If you see pipes running along the ceiling anywhere, follow them and hope they'll lead you back to their lair. Begin by checking any door that uses the words "utility" or "mechanical"; if those don't work out, or you can't find them, check every door. If they're all locked, come back on a different day, and at a different time of day, and try again. If there's any ongoing construction in the area, climb in and check out the basements. The new buildings will probably be hooked into the tunnel system and may not yet have security systems in place.

If you're checking a large complex, such as a university campus, bring along a map and use it as a checklist to make sure you don't leave a single basement unexamined. Mark any pipes and mechanical rooms you find on your map until you begin to get a pretty good idea of where the utility tunnels *must* be. Assuming all goes well, after many hours or days of searching you will eventually hear a choir of angels sing and a ray of sunlight from the heavens will shine down to illuminate a sign on a door reading "Tunnels". Unfortunately, this door will probably be locked. Keep looking.

If you feel sure you've tried and failed with every basement there is, you might try heading over to the central utilities building (CUB) itself, where all the steam is made and pumped throughout the system. You shouldn't have much trouble locating this building — it's likely to have a tall smokestack and will probably be louder than all its neighbours. It's almost a sure thing that the CUB will be populated, and while this means that you have a greater chance of getting caught, it also means you have a greater chance of finding some unlocked doors. You may even find doors propped wide open for ventilation, since the CUB tends to get a little warm on summer afternoons. If you're feeling up for some sneaking, this can be a nice direct route, provided you're lucky enough to find the right mix of unlocked doors and unpopulated areas.

If none of that works, or if you would rather avoid any potential human encounters, turn your attention to possible outside entrances. These entrances can be manholes, ventilation grates or emergency exit hatches. Take a second look at anything warm, any small circular or square patches of melted snow, anything billowing steam on cold nights and anything labelled "utilities" or "steam". Don't mess with any entrances that will require you to shatter a bolt or cut a lock, but look out for ones that appear to be openable. Consider inventorying and mapping these rather than simply taking the first viable entrance you find. Make notes about which entrances are secluded. You may have a decent start on a tunnel map before you ever enter the system.

If you're looking for tunnels under a school and can't find an entrance on your own, try visiting the construction updates or facilities management sections of the school's website — once in a while you'll get lucky and find useful maps or some nice tips. Try talking to students or staff members to see if they have any tips. This will be considerably easier if you attend the school, but if you're outgoing enough you may be able to pull it off even if you're an out-of-towner.

It's common to pass through puddles in the tunnels; when you do, be sure to dry your feet off throroughly before you continue.

It's an odd feature of most tunnel systems that, as impossible as it seems to find your first entrance, once you actually have your first great success and begin to explore the system, you'll probably find more and more possible entrances. The phenomenon is kind of similar to how it's usually much easier to complete a maze if you start at the end than if you start at the beginning. Once you have a clear knowledge and understanding of your goal, it becomes much easier to work backwards and find various ways to achieve it. So if the first entrance you find involves an unbelievably hot, long and hellish crawl, don't despair. There's a decent chance that you'll find a relatively cosy route in before too long.

When to Go
There's no magic time when utility tunnels are extremely easy to enter and safe to navigate, but there are a few factors that might influence your decision as to when to visit.

While utility tunnel systems are normally staffed 24 hours a day, you're much less likely to encounter people in the tunnels outside of regular working hours. If you're able to enter the tunnels at night without being unusually suspicious, this is probably the best time to do so.

As mentioned elsewhere, tunnels and especially tunnel entrances can be easier to find in the winter if you use patterns in the snow as clues. However, winter is also the time of year when the tunnels are hottest and probably their most dangerous, as this is when the steam output is at its

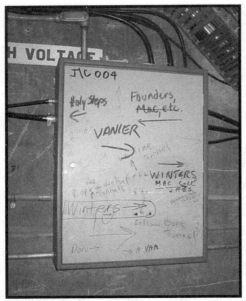

Directions left by past tunnelers can be quite useful, though they should be taken with a grain of salt. People make mistakes.

highest. During the summer, steam isn't needed for heating buildings so, while the idea of visiting steam tunnels on a hot summer day may sound rather unappealing, this is actually when the tunnels are at their most comfortable.

Navigation

It's definitely possible to lose your bearings after spending a few hours in a large steam tunnel system, particularly if it's very hot. While you may not be "lost" in the sense of being unable to find a way out, you may lose your place on your map or lose track of which sections of tunnel you have and have not visited before. The simplest antidote to this kind of confusion, first figured out by mariners and other explorers thousands of years ago (thanks, fellas!), is to keep track of which way is north. Unfortunately, being underground makes it tough for you to find the North Star, track the movement of the sun or get a proper reading from your astrolabe; GPS units won't work at all; and compasses will work less reliably when underground and surrounded with metal and electricity. What I'm suggesting is just keeping track in your head, or on paper. Chances are you'll know which way you're heading when you first enter the tunnel, and that you'll come to spots where you can refresh your bearings every now and then. When you make turns, or when the tunnel curves, don't think of the direction change as right or left — always think in terms of compass directions. Remembering that you get to the go carts by going forward, then left, then forward, then right, then right again is nowhere near as practical as remembering that from the starting point you go north, then west, then north, then east, then south. Right, left, forward and backward are useless if you're making a map, or if you approach the tunnel from another direction, or if you happen to come back to the exact same spot by lowering yourself down through a hole in the ceiling. Admittedly, a few non-90-degree turns can mess up your mental or physical map pretty quickly, but you're still more likely to be able to sort out the confusion if you're relating everything to fixed directions rather than the way you happened to be facing at the time.

Landmarks are another useful navigational aid. Although many sections of tunnel will appear very similar, there are always a few distinctive and memorable areas that can serve as signposts in your memory and on your maps. Anything distinctive can and

Sometimes utility tunnels change elevation drastically or even span over multiple levels.

should be noted: from unusual tunnel shapes to unusual noises, from staircases to large puddles, from the smell of chlorine to a patch of cold air. While you shouldn't leave any trace of your own presence, graffiti tags left by past tunnellers can be useful landmarks that help make all the twisty tunnels look less alike. Make notes about their form and content. Sometimes tunnels have street signs or signs indicating what building a tunnel leads to and these should certainly be noted.

Another important part of navigation is to constantly consider your escape route, in case you should suddenly set off an alarm, encounter someone or hear voices ahead. Pay close attention to all the doors leading out to mechanical rooms, and keep track of all the stairs and ladders leading out to public areas or the emergency hatches leading outside. Also pay close attention to possible hiding places. It's very difficult to talk your way out of an encounter deep inside a utility tunnel system, so running and hiding should be on your mind as you travel. As in abandoned buildings, make sure everyone in the group always knows the current escape plan and nearest safe exit.

LA GRANDE HERMINE

Just off the western shore of Lake Ontario, between the cities of Hamilton and St. Catharines, there rests a nautical enigma. The little-understood landmark is a large sailing ship, which lists strongly to one side as it half-rests, half-floats only a few metres off the shore in a small artificial cove. From up close, one can see that the vessel was once a floating restaurant called *La Grande Hermine* (The Big Weasel), after the ship Jacques Cartier used to sail up the St. Lawrence in 1535.

A few years before the lovely ship was mostly destroyed by arson, Scumbone, Liz and I wanted to know the boat's whole story, and, in the absence of a nearby tourist info booth, souvenir shop or explanatory plaque, we were left with no choice but to hop aboard and get to the bottom of things.

We headed to the *Hermine's* cove equipped with a pre-inflated *Explorer 100* raft with a carrying capacity of 120 pounds. None of us weighed a mere 120 pounds, of course, but the raft had only cost $18 and I figured it would stay more-or-less afloat long enough to get us aboard. My companions were less sure of this, so I was given the honour of making the first journey.

Armed with a flashlight, a camera, a rope and a couple of small boards to be used in place of oars, I lowered myself into the raft and headed out to sea. The raft clearly wasn't happy about supporting my weight, and it took in a little more frigid December water with each stroke I made, until my jeans and socks were so wet as to be worse than useless. Ten metres seemed like a surprisingly long journey while I was paddling against the wind with half-frozen hands, but eventually I docked, climbed aboard and tied the raft to the *Hermine*. Scumbone and Liz were clearly not going to trust their fates to the *Explorer 100,* so I made a quick scouting and photo-taking trip around the ship to make sure it was worth the money and effort to come back later in the day with a better raft. It was.

After I returned to the shore, the three of us headed off into town to warm up, eat and purchase the supplies we'd need for our

Reaching La Grande Hermine *required paddling out into Lake Ontario in mid-December in a rubber raft.*

second attempt. At Canadian Tire, we were assisted by a young fellow named Eric, who seemed intently curious about our mission once he ascertained that we intended to go out to sea in an inflatable raft. Thankfully, he put his concern for our safety aside long enough to hook us up with some more rope, a large $50 raft that went by the name *Windsurfer*, and a foot-operated air-pump. When he told us for the third time that it was really too cold to go rafting in the middle of December, I tried to put his mind at ease by purchasing some HotPads.

We headed back to the cove, where we took shifts pumping up the new raft as the sky grew dark.

By the time we were done, the sun had set and it was extremely cold. It was decided that I would use my greater boating experience to help my companions across, so I first ferried across Liz, then paddled back to pick up Scumbone. Liz then used the rope to tug the two of us back to the *Hermine*, where we docked the *Windsurfer* and turned on our flashlights to have a look around.

The experience of exploring an unlit, long-abandoned, strongly tilting, partially flooded, pirate-ship-turned-restaurant is eerie and wonderful. We started on the lower deck, where we headed to the stern and found a small metal cage that we decided was the brig. I had Scumbone and Liz climb inside for a picture (naturally I thought about locking them in and leaving them there to die as a joke, but I needed a ride home).

As mentioned, the ship listed very strongly to one side. At first this made walking, and particularly climbing stairs, quite difficult. After spending half an hour aboard the boat, though, we started naturally compensating for the angle until we pretty much forgot about it. Of course, this made for a very odd sensation when we peered out a window expecting to see the horizon and instead saw nothing but an expanse of dark water.

Virtually the entire ship was constructed of wood, so the indoor areas had a wonderful cottagey smell. It was also quite warm whenever we were inside. It would have been great to go back sometime with sleeping bags and have a sleepover party — there were even a couple of leftover mattresses lying around in the hallway, near two sets of washrooms that were helpfully designated as out of order.

Areas that were once living quarters were located near the stern on decks two and three; these were very small, but in a way that I'd describe as cozy rather than cramped. The quarters each had their own washrooms. The quarters on deck three also had their own little sundeck, where unfortunately the handrails had been mostly demolished, making for a creepy view.

After wandering to the top of the ship on the outside decks, we descended back to deck one and re-entered the indoor part of the ship through a shattered glass door. We found ourselves in the large main dining hall, which was actually quite easy on the eye. The walls were painted with tasteful murals of naked ladies touching each other's boobies, the wooden support pillars were nicely ornamentalized, and the shattered glass strewn across the floor caught the light in a pleasing way. Though beer bottles, melted candles and names and dates scrawled in the dust made it clear that the boat had been visited several times in the past, a few shattered mirrors and windows were about the worst vandalism we saw. No one had yet found it necessary to ruin the place with spray paint or light it on fire.

After a quick peek into some storage rooms behind the bar, we proceeded into the kitchen. Though the *Hermine* was once a restaurant, there was no longer any food aboard, which was probably a good thing. There were also no seafaring rodents, birds or even insects aboard, as far as I could see. The only real remnants of the restaurant were large appliances like ovens and freezers, and a rather large dumbwaiter that once shuttled food between the main kitchen on the lower deck and a smaller kitchen on the upper deck. We also noted an old metal mail drop here, marked *"lettres"* and *"enveloppes"*: only then did it occur to Liz that every sign aboard the ship was in French. Like good Canadians, we'd automatically translated *toilettes, hommes, dames, sortie* and the like into English without noticing.

The last area we investigated was the completely unlit lower deck. The starboard side of the ship was entirely flooded with deep pools of black water, which prevented us from walking down some hallways, as we didn't feel like sailing back to get another raft at this point. We did, however, get a good look at the furnace room, a mechanical/electrical room, four more *toilette* rooms and a special storage closet used exclusively for storing extra *toilette* bowls. (I think the former owner of the *Hermine* may have had a bit of a *toilette* fixation, to be honest.)

And so, after a very successful and satisfying expedition, we found the *sortie* and returned to civilization.

Wandering up the gangplank is the most straightforward way onto a freighter.

OTHER FUN STUFF

While this book has limited its focus to some of the most popular areas of urban exploration, opportunities to steal away and peek behind the scenes are all around you in the city and sometimes even beyond. These sites include, but are certainly not limited to, boats, bridge rooms, bridges, confined spaces, military leftovers, mines, smokestacks and towers, but really any seemingly out-of-bounds, neglected place that captures your eye is worth a closer look. Urban exploration is a very broad hobby.

Boats
Boarding a vessel at sea under the cover of darkness not only gives one the satisfaction of engaging in modern-day piracy, it also leads to whole worlds of exploratory delight. The ships you'll find tethered to the docks in a harbour range from modest tugboats and barges all the way up to gigantic floating industrial warehouses that could easily keep you occupied for hours. The simpler ships are easier to access, naturally, but even the real monsters have only token security, and (except for the international freighters) keep only skeleton crews while they're docked. Getting aboard is normally just a matter of avoiding drawing attention to yourself as you scale the unsecured gangway and emerge onto the main deck, where, if all goes well, you can quickly find a more suitable place to hide. The real action is in the deep darkness below decks, where you'll likely more or less have the run of the place — not that running is a good idea, because there are always lots of things to trip or bang your head on, and your light source won't normally do much beyond lighting up the few feet immediately in front of you. It's often tough to tell exactly how many football fields or 747s one could cram into a given space below decks, though you will get a general sense that you would be able to stash quite a few if push came to shove. (We can only hope this never happens.) Mammoth ships are great for making you feel totally small and insignificant, if you like that kind of thing. They're really lousy places to run out of batteries.

Dealing with people you'll encounter in shipyards requires a special finesse that you must try to refine while avoiding being suspected of terrorism. Crews of freighters are used to encountering boat geeks who photograph and chronicle the voyages of their vessels and generally tolerate this species, who, after all, treat them like rock stars. There's certainly a

When there is no gangplank available, boats can be scaled with rope ladders down their sides.

point up to which you can pretend to be a member of this known and harmless breed. Crews of international freighters, while they may yell rather excitably when they see strangers advancing up the gangplank, aren't familiar enough with or interested enough in the local language and customs to do much beyond raise a brief fuss. Often, even most English-speaking crew members are laid back and willing to let you off with a warning if you agree to leave the area, provided they don't find you anywhere too suspicious. Being spotted by the wrong sort of people — such as harbourmasters, ship captains, security guards and more paranoid crew members — may earn you the whole deal with the bright spotlights, the chasing and even the dogs. So don't be seen by those people.

Bridge Rooms

Bridge rooms recall those cheap chocolate bunnies your parents would get you at Easter. They're designed to look like a huge, promising mass of solid chocolate satisfaction, but upon oral inspection are revealed to be just a thin layer of waxy chocolate coating a hollow interior. Bridge rooms are the same, but with concrete instead of chocolate. And finding out that a bridge is hollow is more an occasion for joy than disappointment.

Because few construction companies want to spend any more on cement than they absolutely have to, hollow bridge rooms are almost as common as thick concrete bridges themselves. Bridge rooms aren't "built" so much as "left over"; they're just an unintentional by-product of the actual concrete-conserving construction. As such, bridge rooms aren't really designed to be accessed — but they often can be. Many bridge rooms feature doors or trapdoors to allow maintenance workers occasional access to utilities running through the bridge, or feature vents designed to allow wet concrete to dry properly. Doors to bridge rooms are normally supposed to be locked away from the public, but sometimes maintenance workers forget or don't bother, and other times more destructive visitors have simply snipped the bolts to allow themselves access.

Normally, the bridge room itself will be the extent of your discovery: while they're cosy secret places to hang out in, and some of them are surprisingly photogenic, bridge rooms aren't often connected to tunnels or other opportunities. Sometimes you can cross a river through a bridge room, but usually one is limited to hanging out and appreciating more anthropological finds such as the graffiti and litter of past visitors.

Bridges
Some explorers get a kick out of climbing bridges, for the challenge, the view at the top and the thrill of getting there. The techniques they employ range from free climbing and rope climbing — which are way beyond the scope of this book — to ascending the support cables and towers by a variety of means ranging from simple to near suicidal. Sometimes getting up a bridge can be as simple as walking up a lot of stairs and then climbing a ladder or two, as is the case with the Sydney Harbour Bridge, which actually offers (very expensive) tours to the public. More commonly, it involves climbing a lot of ladders, and climbing steel cables affixed to support bars or smaller, crisscrossed steel support bars in places where ladders are not available. Climbing anything but the easiest bridges requires a great deal of endurance and athleticism and is definitely not for amateurs; scaling the more challenging spans is best left to Alpine climbers or those who are comfortable with the idea of their own death.

Since 11 September 2001, Jinx and some other bridge climbers have officially ceased to climb bridges, for both their own sake and for the public good. While climbing bridges doesn't really endanger any-one so much as the climber, those who witness such a climb might overreact. Unfortunately, these days, the drive to get a nice view from the top could conceivably lead to charges of tampering with crucial public infrastructure.

Confined Spaces

Confined spaces can be roughly defined as cavities small and cramped enough to hinder free movement. Because such spaces are often asso-ciated with limited ventilation and other safety hazards, many juris-dictions require workers to have special confined-space training and acquire confined-space-entry permits before entering such areas. This training teaches workers how to eliminate or at least reduce threats associated with confined spaces, and how to rescue unconscious or injured colleagues if something goes wrong. For better or for worse, explorers who don't have this special training usually train themselves on the job, having a tough time staying away from holes of any sort.

While most explorers confine their attentions to the manhole cov-ers that are likely to lead to storm drains, occasionally everyone won-ders about the ones labelled "utility", "gas" or something similar. While these covers usually lead to nothing more than a small, fully enclosed cavern (a vault) containing a few connections of pipes and wires, just occasionally they'll lead to something more interesting, like a vast, interconnected maze under the city that would take weeks to explore fully. Other places confined spaces might be encountered are utility areas inside buildings or aboard ships.

Unfortunately, dealing with confined spaces can be a dangerous business. All the hazards of poisonous, combustible or suffocating air discussed in the draining section apply to an even greater degree in almost completely unventilated holes like these. When utility workers go into such manholes, they test them with explosimeters and then ventilate them with blowers both in advance and during their entire stay. They typically find that two percent of all manholes contain oth-erwise undetectable bad air of some variety — that's a one in fifty chance of death on every confined space manhole. Confined spaces may also have additional hazards of uninsulated wires, uninsulated steam lines, high temperatures, asbestos in the air and more.

So, if you decide to risk it and lower yourself down into a con-fined-space manhole, please take a few common sense precautions.

Never go in alone. Don't bring an open flame. Avoid sparking tools. Pay very close attention to your breathing, your heart rate and your brain, and if any of them seem out of whack, exit immediately.

Military Leftovers

Military leftovers — which run the gamut from abandoned bunkers to fallout shelters to military tunnels to observation towers to missile silos and more — are a huge sub-branch of urban exploration that really deserves more attention than I'm able to give it here. I plead Canadianity. Canada, being a peaceful nation situated far from the usual theatres of war, has a relative dearth of military leftovers. There are some abandoned bunkers in some of the coastal provinces, and one very famous/secret six-storey underground complex called the Diefenbunker in the town of Carp, Ontario, but usually we Canadians have to visit other parts of the world in order to see leftover war toys.

But the rest of the world has a real treasure trove of abandoned military sites, most of them underground, and many of them quite neglected by the governments that built them (or the governments that replaced the governments that built them). Bunkers are a favourite location for explorers across Japan, the UK and Australia, while Germany and France are more famous for the huge networks of tunnels that connect their bunkers and their above-ground forts and command posts. In the US, the primary objects of desire are the huge masses of abandoned missile silos scattered around the Midwest and Southwest, some of which are now on private land and a few of which are even available on the real estate market. Russia has a little of everything; well, a lot of everything, actually — Russia probably has more abandoned military properties than any other country. For details on where and how to explore such sites, however, I'm afraid you'll have to ask the locals.

Mines

While caves are, alas, too much a part of nature to be considered urban exploration targets, their man-made cousins, mines, fall within our realm of study. Mines are, however, among the more deadly sites an explorer could choose to visit, so you may want to place them on your to-do list only if you feel you have lived a full life. I've never explored a mine, and base the information here solely on what I've heard from others. Though I've certainly heard some stories and seen some pictures of mine exploration that have made me drool, I can't help but think about all the stories I'm *not* hearing from the casual mine explorers who were crushed in cave-ins, trapped after a fall or suffocated by bad air or near total lack of oxygen — more than 30 people annually, according to the US Mine Safety and Health Administration, and this figure excludes the dozens who were rescued after accidents that would have most likely been fatal. (Admittedly, 30 deaths a year is probably a small percentage when you consider how many thousands of people venture into mines each year, but 30 is still a lot of people, especially if they were all nice.)

If you choose to head into abandoned mine shafts, keep your wits about you at all times. Remember that mines are death traps. Worker safety was not a priority when most old mines were built in the first place, and decades of flooding and rotting haven't done anything to improve the situation. Bad air is the main hazard, and it's difficult for you to do anything about it other than pay very close attention to your breathing. Bad structural support is another main hazard — the vibrations of your walking may be enough to cause rotten wooden supports or flimsy stone pillars to collapse. If you see any evidence of past rockfalls, get out of the whole area. Don't trust your weight to wooden floorboards — they may be covering deep shafts. Similarly, don't trust your weight to old ladders and similar fixtures. Toxic chemicals are often left behind from the days when the mine was in use and should obviously be avoided. In some cases, dangerous animals such as bears and cougars may have taken up residence. Most mining areas feature steep shafts into which you could fall 100 feet or more to your death, and these are rarely fenced off or demarcated in any way.

Smokestacks

As the tallest part of many complexes, smokestacks, or chimneys, tend to get a little special attention from those explorers who have a thing for heights. Smokestacks often soar several hundred feet into the air — occasionally piercing the heavens at 700 feet or higher — providing incredible views and exhilarating experiences for those daring enough to scale them.

Normally, the safer method of climbing a smokestack found in an abandoned industrial location is to find the furnace room and scale the stack by means of the ladder going up the shaft from the inside. Being designed for occasional use by workers (workers in proper safety climbing harnesses, that is), this shaft will likely contain resting platforms every so often to allow you to catch your breath on the way up. Making a free-climbing ascent up the inside of a several-hundred-foot-high smokestack is less a thrilling expedition and more of a gruelling endurance test. Before you embark on such a monster climb, really consider the time and energy commitment you're making. Take food and drinks, and make sure you've relieved yourself before you start heading up. Take generous breaks when the opportunity presents itself and know when you should turn back.

Climbing a smokestack from the outside is a riskier proposition, and may bear a closer resemblance to scaling a mountain than simply climbing a really, really long ladder. But an outside ascent may be the only option if you're dealing with a smokestack that is still occasionally active. Climbing the outside smokestack with a (solid) ladder attached to the side, you face all the hazards of climbing up from the inside, and must additionally deal with exposure to the elements and the possibility of being spotted. Gusting wind becomes an increasingly challenging obstacle the higher one climbs — by the time you are 100 feet up, 20-mile-an-hour winds are not uncommon. Lightning and static electricity can be a real hazard. Jan van der Meulen heard clear static discharges while on top of an old power station chimney and descended immediately. The circular testing platforms on the outside are also likely to occur with less regularity than the resting platforms on the inside. In cases where a reliable ladder isn't present, only professional-level climbers should even attempt the ascent.

Towers
In their quest for the highest heights, some explorers are attracted by towers of various sorts, from water towers to electrical towers to radio towers. These days, any given tall, protruding thing is likely to be home to cell phone transmitters and the like, so even water towers and tall rooftops are often transmission towers of a sort. Sometimes towers can provide a nice view, but all too often they can instead provide unhealthy doses of radiation and similar unpleasantness, so they're best approached with extreme caution by those who know what they're doing and avoided altogether by those who don't.

Radiofrequency (RF) energy, in the form of radio waves and microwaves, is the main danger with most towers used for transmission. RF energy is very dangerous stuff, since it heats skin tissues quickly, beginning with the eyes and the testes, for those who have 'em. Radio and television broadcasting, cell phones, personal communications services (PCS), pagers, cordless telephones, commercial radio, police and fire department radio, amateur radio and microwave point-to-point links are all sources of RF energy. The most dangerous antennae are those that look like a large drum, which are often transmitting microwave radiation, but any sort of antenna should be avoided, since even the simple rectangular panels commonly mounted on rooftops can be dangerous if you stand near them for any length of time.

SHARING

Some magicians claim that good magicians never share their tricks. This is nonsense. Those who don't share can spend their lives feeling very proud of their five or six selfishly hoarded secrets, but those who do share will be shared with and will come out far ahead. All magicians worth seeing use the experience and advice of those who've come before them, and it's really the same way with explorers.

The motto of the Beavers, the junior branch of the Canadian Boy Scouts, is "Sharing, sharing, sharing," and it's a hard motto to argue with. Sharing knowledge of your finds, at least in a general sense, is a generous and noble thing to do, and produces lots of good karma. I know that there are many amazing places I would never have seen if I were not generous about sharing information about some of my favourite exploration sites.

What to Share
All of that said, it's important to share your information in the right way. While it's very kind to give your fellow explorers tips about particular spots they might want to examine, and perhaps even a hint or two about approaches they might try, it's easy to give away too much information and thereby diminish the other person's experience or cause other, larger problems.

Sharing a hint or two — or, even better, a warning or two — about a particular area or building with other explorers either online or in print is great, but please don't give away specific entrances or access points except perhaps to illustrate a general principle. Most explorers enjoy the challenge of finding a place and figuring out their own way in and don't like too much handholding. (Those who want step-by-step directions are the ones to watch out for.) It's a positive thing to encourage people to experience a wonderful building or tunnel system you've found, but it's needlessly prescriptive to suggest that they do so only by following precisely in your footsteps. This hobby is explicitly about choosing your own adventure, not about doing things step-by-step and colouring inside the lines, and overly detailed guides to specific sites spoil the fun.

Giving the general public too much of the wrong sort of information (say, on a public website or in a zine) can make a site more attractive and vulnerable to people who aren't primarily motivated by the urge to explore, such as vandals looking for tunnels to tag in, partiers looking for an abandoned building where they can hold a rave, thieves looking for a building to plunder, idiots looking for a place to burn down or other bad people of all stripes looking to make the world a worse place. If you perceive that a place is vulnerable to such threats, save your inside information about vulnerabilities for venues where you're fairly sure that your audience is on the same wavelength as you and will treat exploration sites with the reverence they deserve.

Finally, there are a few things that you really should just keep to yourself. As mentioned, you will occasionally come across houseless people squatting on sites. Not only should you not take pictures of their dwellings, you really shouldn't mention it to a wide audience, as it could easily lead to their eviction, and that's a devastating thing to happen to someone whether they legally own their dwelling or not. Squatters and explorers are generally on the same side, and it's in the best interests of explorers for things to stay that way, so go out of your way to make sure you don't do them any harm. Additionally, sharing information about certain sensitive government or military sites, or gang sites or drug labs for that matter, with the wrong people could get you in a lot of trouble. Don't put information like that up on the web, or brag about it to reporters: interesting as they are, those are the sorts of finds you should mention only to trusted friends, known fellow explorers and, perhaps, the police.

While it is unlikely that the powers that be will track you down based on your written recollections of a trip, it is not inconceivable. For this reason, you're generally better off being vague about dates as well as methods of entry, since the less specific information they have, the less likely they are to attempt to charge you with something. If you have reason to refer to the time of your exploration, say something like "one night this fall" rather than, say, "last Saturday". Combined with a date stamp on your post or text file, "last Saturday" could give the powers that be the information they need to check relevant videotapes and consult with potential witnesses.

What to Report

While some explorers are reluctant to involve the powers that be any more than necessary, sometimes it makes sense to put this principle aside for the sake of the common good. Since we tend to visit a lot of sites that other people haven't been to in years or even decades, explorers notice a lot of potential problems that might otherwise be overlooked. In some cases, it makes sense to mention these problems to people who can deal with them better than you. Australian Cave Clan members once found and reported evidence of a poorly designed drainage system that was needlessly torturing and killing waterfowl. Other explorers have found and reported — often anonymously — drug labs, major problems with drainage and sewerage systems, extreme fire hazards, toxic chemicals found in abandoned buildings and even the presence of human bones and other evidence of possible serious crimes. In these cases, even if the site has afterwards been secured, explorers have helped or at least potentially helped solve larger problems that would have otherwise gone neglected.

Some explorers have had to wrestle with more complex ethical issues, such as whether to report planned or ongoing acts of vandalism or theft (sometimes involving fellow explorers), what to do about a dangerous or vulnerable site that is too easily accessible or how to deal with squatters who persist in certain behaviours that are bad for a site, such as lighting indoor bonfires and the like. Unfortunately, there are no useful, infallible guidelines on how to handle difficult ethical dilemmas like these, except to suggest that you should be careful not to place what's best for you personally ahead of what's best for the site or what's best for the hobby as a whole, and that you should try not to involve force, including police force, as long as person-to-person discussion is still an option.

Using Aliases

A lot of explorers, myself included, prefer to write under aliases. But the use of aliases shouldn't be regarded as an integral component of the urban exploration tradition, especially since many of the world's most active and best-known explorers — including Vadim Mikhailov, Wes Modes, Petr Kazil, Julia Solis, L.B. Deyo, Steve Duncan and many others — use their real names exclusively. Nor is adopting an alias a necessary step in protecting yourself from trespassing charges. An alias won't help you if law enforcement decides to contact you about something: unless you actually go underground (in the metaphorical sense), the powers that be will probably be able to find out who you are without much trouble. Fortunately, the police don't normally invest significant resources in persecuting people for minor, victimless crimes, so as long as you confine yourself to harmless trespassing, it shouldn't be an issue. (Please note that I said *shouldn't*, not *won't*, and I confess that I am often baffled by the workings of the legal system.)

So, if you want to use your real name, go ahead. It probably isn't going to get you in any extra trouble; it makes you look less guilty; and it will spare you some of the unpleasant side effects of having multiple identities. You won't have to worry about accidentally signing an e-mail to your boss with your explorer name and such hassles, for one. As an added bonus, the hobby appears less shady when people don't seem to be embarrassed about practicing it.

Some people think using an alias is somehow an admission of naughtiness, but I think they'd have a hard time convincing pseudony-mous writers like George Eliot or Ellis Bronte of this. There can be many good reasons to adopt a pen name. Some explorers, like me, are just a little more private about what they do with their free time, espe-cially now that stalking people online is so popular and easy. Personally, I use an alias not out of some silly delusion that it will keep the police or any really determined person from tracking me down but in order to help me keep what I do with my free time to myself when I want to, and so that my co-workers won't be able to use Google to find out that the reason I'm exhausted on any given Monday morning is probably because I was out late exploring an abandoned brewery.

How to Share
There are many ways to share your findings with your fellow explorers or, if you feel you've found something of broader interest, the rest of the world. There are several existing database-driven websites that wel-come contributions of pictures and accounts of other people's adven-tures, including the Urban Exploration Resource (*http://www.uer.ca*) — the largest — and the Virtual Museum of Dead Places (*http://www.vimudeap.de*) — the oldest. These sites store both pic-tures and text, but are fairly heavily biased towards pictures. Other, non-database-driven websites devoted to the exploration of a particu-lar region may very well accept your contribution of stories related to their area of interest.

While it is both constructive and relatively easy to contribute your tale to an existing project, personally, I'm a big advocate of doing it yourself. I find people bring a personal flair to their own projects that just doesn't come across in a contribution to someone else's database. When you do it yourself, you provide the style as well as the raw pictures and words. You'll get a lot more positive feedback on your own site, zine or book than you'd ever get from a database entry. And it really isn't as hard or as expensive as you might think to make your own website, zine or even book. There are many helpful, free tutorials to each sort of publishing available online. (I look forward to the day when most bookstores have an "urban exploration" section, so I'd also be happy to help with any advice and information I can. Drop me a line at *ninj@infiltration.org*.)

I promote urban exploration enthusiastically because I can clearly remember the awe and wonder I felt when I first discovered it for myself. It's been inspiring to watch a community grow up around the hobby and see it shared with so many others. It's amazing to watch people get excited about the idea of really seeing the world around them, and my greatest ambition for this book is that it will have the same effect on some of those who read it.

ACKNOWLEDGEMENTS

I'm a very grateful person so this list could go on for half the book, but I'll try to keep it short. First I'd like to thank my (now extended) immediate family, who are all unbelievably supportive and amazing. I'd especially like to thank my parents for, probably inadvertently, teaching me that it's okay to ignore authority that is arbitrary or unworthy of respect. Sorry the cops had to come to our house that time.

My good friend Jim Munroe was an even bigger believer in *Infiltration* than I was in the early days; through his various self-publishing efforts he's inspired me more than he knows. Sorry about those alarmed doors, Jim. Thanks to my best friend Terri Ackerman, for her help in proofreading, providing rides and crawling up dark, wet side pipes that were too small for me. Sorry about the trespassing ticket, Terri. Thanks to those friends who were my most reliable exploration partners, who always kept coming back for more no matter how unpleasant the last trip was: Sean, Julie, Derek, Pete, Victor and Beth (some of whom you may know by their aliases if you read the zine). Sorry about all the various near-death experiences, guys. Thanks to my friends Bob, Marc, Jeremy and Oliver for generously donating time, tech help and server space for the *Infiltration* website. Sorry about the bandwidth, guys.

My greatest gratitude is reserved for my smart, funny, talented and beautiful wife Liz, who, besides being the most regular contributor and co-editor of the zine, has been endlessly encouraging and helpful with every aspect of this book. Liz, you are so awesome. Sorry about your leg.

Moving on to the people I know through exploring, my first thanks are to Dougo and Predator of the Cave Clan; Dougo, for treating *Infiltration* like a little brother to his much larger and more long-standing *Il Draino*, and Predator for his inspiring text files, most famously his "Approach to Draining". Sorry you had to go so early, Pred. Thanks to those trailblazing explorer-publishers who came before me, particularly L.B. Deyo, Lefty Leibowitz and Julia Solis, for sharing their enthusiasm and experience with me. Thanks to Avatar-X for creating and hosting a website that was of great help in constructing this book.

Extreme gratitude to Ben, Terri, Petr, Jim, L.B., Jessica, Derek, Emily and Liz for reading drafts of the whole book. Your corrections

GLOSSARY

This is a guide to some of the technical or obscure terms related to the hobby of urban exploration. We don't use code language or jargon to exclude anyone, but because it's a specialized hobby we've had to adopt or invent some specialized terms. Thanks to FiL for much of the draining vocabulary. If you think an oft-used term is missing, please let me know.

abseil <German> *v.* rappel; *see rappel*

back breaker *adj.* long, low tunnel in a drain

ball buster *adj.* round concrete pipe drain with wide section of water

BASE jump *v.* leap from *b*uildings, *a*ntennae, *s*pans (bridges and trams) or *e*arth (cliffs); not really exploring, but some explorers feel solidarity with base jumpers

buildering *n.,v.* climbing buildings, with or without tools and support devices

bunker *n.* underground military command post, as found throughout Australia and Europe, particularly in Britain

burn *v.* ruin for others through lack of subtlety (e.g. "some guys burned the new tunnels by tagging everywhere, now they're kept locked")

Cacophony Society *n.* a group founded in San Francisco, now with international branches, whose members pursue "experiences beyond the pale of mainstream society through subversion, pranks, art, fringe explorations and meaningless madness" and who share some ideals with urban explorers

carriere <French> *n.* a man-made cave, leftover from mining operations

catacomb *n.* subterranean burial grounds and the mazes of tunnels connected to them, as found in several older European cities, including Paris and Rome (strictly speaking, the term "catacomb" only applies to the burial grounds)

cataphiles *n.* those who explore catacombs

catch basin *n.* tank located under the street where water collects before flowing into drains

Cave Clan *n.* Australian drainers who constitute the world's largest urban exploration group

central utilities building or **CUB** *n.* on a college or university campus, the building that supplies the rest of the campus with electricity, heat, cool air and water, usually via steam tunnels

chamber *n.* huge, long room in a drain

chatière <French> *n.* squeeze hole (literally "cat hole") used to enter or exit tunnels

chimneying *v.* climbing by using various body parts to provide force on opposing walls

chud <from *C.H.U.D.*, 1984 horror movie> *n.* you don't want to know what it means (but if you did, I'd tell you it meant *c*annibalistic *h*umanoid *u*nderground *d*weller)

CIHY *n., v.* short for "*c*an *I h*elp *y*ou?"; query often directed at infiltrators

Clannies *n.* annual award night/party held by the Cave Clan in Melbourne and Sydney at the conclusion of the Australian draining season

closed circuit television or **CCTV** *n.* television signals transported directly from a camera to a monitor via wires, without broadcasting

college tunnel *n. see utility tunnel*

combined sewage overflow or **CSO** *n.* in older drainage systems, storm sewers and sanitary sewers may be connected to some degree, resulting in an unfortunate mixing of sewage into stormwater drains during serious storms

crater <climbing jargon> *v.* to fall from a height and hit the ground (as in, "I almost cratered!")

credibility prop *n.* an item such as a clipboard or briefcase, carried or used by an infiltrator to increase appearance of "fitting in"

creeper *n.* one who infiltrates

cut-and-cover *adj.* subway tunnels created by a process of digging down from the top and covering up the hole, as opposed to boring a tube

darkie *n. see stormwater drain*

digestive <from Senor Jojo> *adj.* a full-length expedition that goes in one end and out the other

Diggers *n.* group of underground explorers in Russia

draining *v.* exploring stormwater drains *(see stormwater drain)*

drop *n.* a small waterfall in a drain

elevator surfing *v.* riding on top of a moving elevator

expo <from expedition> *n.* a mission attempted by a group of people

flashlight *n.* American/Canadian word for torch

freighthopping *v.* stowing away aboard freight trains in order to get free transport

geocaching *v.* using GPS units to locate hidden caches of goods based on co-ordinates and clues

grilles *n.* metal bars found in the roof or sides of a drain; rooms made entirely of grilles are called grille rooms

gutter box *n.* small space or room underneath the slit in a gutter into which water falls before emptying into the drain itself

hacking <as used at MIT> *v.* 1. synonym for infiltrating; sometimes known by the full name of roof and tunnel hacking 2. installing or being otherwise involved in the execution of a classy prank

HEPA filter *n.* *h*igh *e*fficiency *p*articulate *a*ir filters, useful in keeping asbestos fibres out of one's respiratory system

hoarding *n.* the temporary wooden walls surrounding a construction or demolition site

infiltration *n.,v.* going places you're not supposed to go in general; covers urban exploration as well as simply dropping in to conventions uninvited and the like

junction *n.* point where two sections of a drain meet; a junction room is a room where two tunnels join into one

labyrinth *n.* a series of connected tunnel systems built for different purposes

lid *n.* another term for a manhole cover

Lift-o-Matic *n.* simple manhole key produced by the Cave Clan

loop *n.* two distinct drain tunnels separating but rejoining further upstream or downstream

Maglite *n.* favoured brand of flashlight/torch

manhole *n.* name for either a hole in the street leading underground or the underground room itself; sometimes used as shorthand for "manhole cover"

master key *n.* a key that opens all, or almost all, the doors in a particular institution

metro *n.* the name for the subway system in Paris and many other cities

mice *n.* slang for campus security guards

mole people *n.* the hundreds or thousands of people who live in the tunnels under New York City, according to a sensationalist book of the same name by Jennifer Toth

mousehouse *n.* slang for campus security office

mummy *n.* tunnel shape so named because it resembles a mummy's sarcophagus (sometimes referred to by water boards as a horseshoe)

outfall *n.* the spot where a storm drain empties its water out into nature; a popular entrance and exit point for explorers

overflow *n.* a drain separate from the main tunnel built to carry excess water when the water level in the main tunnel is high; normally dry

parkour *n.* French sport involving climbing up, jumping onto and falling off man-made structures, often described as skateboarding without a skateboard

physical plant *n.* at a college or university campus, the department which is responsible for maintaining the central utilities building and the steam tunnels; sometimes also used as a synonym for central utilities building

popper *n.* device used to open a manhole cover; the Lift-o-Matic is one kind

rainslot *n. see catch basin*

ramp *n.* in a drain, a slope not steep enough to be a slide

rappel *v.* descend a wall or steep face using a doubled rope

rebar *n.* steel reinforcing rod used in concrete

RCP *n.* round concrete pipe (usually used in reference to the drain shape)

RT *adj.,n.* rapid transit, sometimes used as a short form for "train that runs on a rapid transit system"

sanitary sewer *n.* a sewer that *isn't* sanitary — that is, the kind most drainers avoid

seccers *n.* short for security guards

sewering *n.,v.* exploring sanitary sewers (occasionally misused as a synonym for draining, *see draining*)

shaft *n.* vertical passage connected to a tunnel; *v.* to climb up or down a shaft without climbing tools

shrinker *n.* drain that just continues to get smaller as you head upstream

sign-in <used at MIT> *n.* a small personal mark in an area that one is proud of having found or climbed to, usually dated so future explorers can get an idea of when people have been there; not intended for anyone but other explorers to see

slide *n.* steep section of a drain, steeper than a ramp

skunneling <*sk*ateboarding and *tunneling*> *n.,v.* skateboarding in drains

social engineering <from hacker jargon> *n.,v.* dealing with people (employees, security guards) in a manner that allows you to get past them or obtain information from them

snotsicle <from Action Squad> *n.* small, mucus-like stalactite that hangs from the ceiling of certain moist sewers

spelunking <from caver jargon> *n.,v.* exploring caves, whether natural or manmade; most (natural) cavers prefer to think of themselves as speleogists rather than spelunkers

split *n.* part where a drain divides

steam tunnel *n.* underground passages that house pipes carrying steam and other utilities; found under large colleges, universities and other large institutions

step irons *n.* metal or plastic rungs set into a wall to provide a ladder

storm sewer *n. see stormwater drain*

stormwater drain *n.* underground tunnel that shuttles rain or melted snow from urban areas back out to the wilds of nature where it belongs

stunneling <*st*udent or *st*eam *t*unneling> *n.,v.* travelling through steam tunnels under colleges or universities

tabi <Japanese> *n.* footwear with a split between the big toe and the rest of the foot; ideal for climbing

tag (up) *v.* write graffiti consisting of nothing more creative than an explorer's name

texta *n.* big, thick marker used for graffiti

third rail *n.* the electrified rail that powers most subway systems; to be avoided

tomb *n.* 1. synonym for drain used when the drain is named after someone, from a Melbourne tradition of members naming drains after themselves (e.g. Sloth's Tomb, Bob's Tomb) 2. <used at MIT> an unused space, usually with only one entrance, named by the discoverer

topside *n.* above ground

torch *n.* British/Australian word for flashlight

trainhopping *v. see freighthopping*

tube *n.* subway tunnels created by a boring machine, or a nickname for the London Underground

uberboots <Albertan> *n.* rubber boots that come up to one's knees or higher

Underground, the *n.* 1. the oldest and one of the largest subway systems in the world, in London 2. popular urban exploration mailing list

urban adventure *n.* very much like urban exploration, but with the focus upon experiences rather than sight-seeing

urban exploration *n.* the investigation of manmade structures not designed for public consumption, from mechanical rooms to stormwater drains to rooftops; usually such areas are off-limits

utility tunnel *n.* underground tunnels used to conduct steam, water, cool air, electricity, cable signals and more, also accessible by explorers

vadding <derived from the hacked command for the computer text game Adventure> *v.* exploring — the word adopted by MIT students for real-world hacking

viewing hole *n.* an eye-level hole, usually rectangular, cut into the boards surrounding a construction site to appease curious passersby

water moccasin *n.* poisonous snake rumoured to inhabit drains in the southern US

waterfall *n.* in a drain, a large drop over which the drain water falls

yabbies <from Australian> *n.* fresh water crustaceans found in Australian drains

BIBLIOGRAPHY

Agent K. "Urban Exploration for Dummies" (formerly at *http://uea.ca/drains/drains.php*) on Urban Exploration Alberta, viewed 21 February 2004.

Barnard, Robert L. *Intrusion Detection Systems: Principles of Operation and Application* (Boston: Butterworth Publishers, 1981).

Carnegie, Dale. *How to Win Friends and Influence People* (New York: Simon and Schuster, 1964).

Chamelin, Neil. *Criminal Law for Police Officers, 8th Ed.* (Englewood Cliffs, NJ: Prentice-Hall, 2002).

Deyo, L.B. and David "Lefty" Leibowitz. *Invisible Frontier: Exploring the Tunnels, Ruins and Rooftops of Hidden New York* (New York: Three Rivers Press, 2003).

Horn, Delton T. *Electronic Alarm and Security Systems: A Technician's Guide* (New York: Tab Books, 1995).

Kerman, Scott. *No Ticket? No Problem!: How to Sneak into Sporting Events and Concerts* (Arlington, Texas: Summit Publishing, 1996).

Kim, Ashido. *Secrets of the Ninja* (New York: Citadel Books, 1981).

Mitnick, Kevin and William L. Simon. *The Art of Deception: Controlling the Human Element of Society* (Indianapolis: Wiley Publishing, 2002).

Modes, Wes. "How to Sneak Around" *(http://www.thespoon.com/stories/urban.html)* on Adventuring, viewed 10 March 2004.

Predator. "Approach: A Sprawling Manifesto on the Art of Drain Exploring" *(http://conway.cat.org.au/~predator/approach.htm)* on Predator's Elcheapo Minimum Effort Web Page, viewed 7 December 1996.

Reduxzero. *5100*, issue one. Various articles. 2004.

Weber, Thad. *Alarm Systems and Theft Prevention* (Boston: Butterworth Publishers, 1985).

APPENDIX: URBAN EXPLORATION TIMELINE

This guide is aimed at chronicling the history of exploring neglected and off-limits areas as well as the history of modern urban exploration culture. I'm sorry that this guide is still a little biased towards English-speaking countries, but so far most contributors have been English speakers. If you have any corrections or suggestions, please get in touch.

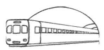

1861

Writing in the Brooklyn Standard, poet Walt Whitman describes his visit to Brooklyn's recently abandoned Atlantic Avenue Tunnel, which in 1844 had been built as the first subway tunnel in the world.

1916

Harry H. Gardiner, "The Human Fly", climbs 12 floors and 211 feet up the side of Detroit's Majestic Building, thereby becoming the first builderer in recorded history.

1955

Guy Debord publishes his *Introduction to a Critique of Urban Geography*, and develops a practice called *dérive*, which consists of travelling through cities and noting psychogeographical variations. In the decade that follows, members of the Situationist International movement argue that society consists largely of passive spectators and consumers of packaged experiences, and suggest that individuals shake up this state of affairs by engaging in creative play.

November 1793

Philibert Aspairt, considered by some the first cataphile, becomes lost while exploring the Parisian catacombs by candlelight. His body is found 11 years later.

1904

One week after the opening of the subway system, New Yorker Leidschmudel Dreispul is killed by an oncoming train while exploring the new tunnels. The Interborough Rapid Transit company responds by erecting "no trespassing" signs throughout the system.

1921

In perhaps the first organized tour of an abandoned building, Dadaists including Andre Breton, Paul Eluard, Francis Picabia and Tristan Tzara organize a trip to the deserted and little-known church of St. Julien le Pauvre in Paris. In promoting the event, the Dadaists offer a series of visits to select sites, "particularly those which really have no reason for existing".

Inspired by the publications of the French resistance that operated through the catacomb network during WWII, Parisian cataphiles begin adopting pseudonyms and communicating with each other through printed paper tracts.

1968

The San Francisco Suicide Club, a group which lists "fringe exploration" among its many aims, is founded in San Francisco. This group eventually becomes the Cacophony Society.

1977

Responding to a challenge by a fire marshal who states "Until you climb a building, don't tell me how to perform a rescue in a high rise building", Dan Goodwin, aka "Spiderman", climbs Chicago's Sears Tower, then the tallest building in the world, becoming the first climber to use suction cups to climb glass windows.

1981

In Australia, Melbourne cave enthusiasts Doug, Sloth and Woody found the Cave Clan, and begin exploring storm drains and other manmade and natural caves. Over the next decade, the Cave Clan absorbs other, smaller draining groups in Melbourne.

January 1986

1959

In Cambridge, Massachusetts, members of MIT's Tech Model Railroad Club's Signals and Power subcommittee engage in semi-systematic excursions into steam tunnels and rooftops around campus, a practice they call "hacking".

1971

Secretly entering Paris' Notre Dame cathedral at night, Philippe Petit stretches a steel cable between its towers. The next morning he crosses this improvised high wire, only to be arrested upon descending. Three years later, Petit duplicates his stunt between the twin towers of New York City's World Trade Center.

1980

Eighteen-year-old rail historian Bob Diamond rediscovers Brooklyn's Atlantic Avenue Tunnel, which had been sealed up and forgotten since 1861.

1985

In Australia, Sydney drain explorer Rolf Adams begins writing the Sydney Pseudokarst ("false cave") series in the newsletter of the Sydney University Speleological Society.

In Australia, Doug publishes the first issue of *Il Draino*, the Cave Clan newsletter.

July 1989

Eric Bagai publishes an essay called "The First Hackers" in a book called *What I Did With My Trash: Ten Years With a TRS-80*. Although not widely read, the essay has the distinction of being perhaps the earliest written explanation of what urban exploration is all about.

1990

After finding a Cave Clan sticker in a drain under Sydney, Predator forms the group's first official interstate branch, the Sydney Cave Clan. In following years, the Cave Clan founds branches in Adelaide, Brisbane, Canberra, Perth and Hobart.

May 1991

In Ann Arbor, Michigan, Dug Song and Greg Shewchuk publish the first issue of *Samizdat*, a zine featuring urban stunts involving tunnels and rooftops. They publish two issues before going on permanent hiatus.

1994

April 1989

The first Annual Cave Clan "Clannie" Awards are held in Melbourne's ANZAC drain.

1990

In Russia, Moscow-area explorer Vadim Mikhailov and his fellow subterranean explorers form the group Diggers of the Underground Planet.

September 1990

Outdoorsman Alan S. North writes *The Urban Adventure Handbook*, a guide in which he encourages people to climb buildings and explore the city as an accessible alternative to climbing mountains and exploring wilderness. Although not widely read either, the handbook inspires a few people to begin using the term "urban adventure" in their writings.

1994

The Diggers of the Underground Planet find Moscow's fabled, but officially denied, "Metro-2" subway system. The seven-level-deep system was built in the Stalin era to allow Kremlin officials to evacuate the city quickly.

February 1994

The newsgroup alt.college.tunnels is founded and the first message is posted. Early posters include later UE fixtures Eric Chien, Ben Hines and Matthew Landry.

Kevin Kelm establishes the website Abandoned Missile Base VR Tour, which quickly becomes very popular.

Wes Modes puts up a website called Adventuring, archiving his writings about freighthopping and buildering. The site brings the term "urban adventure" from North's book to the web.

In the US, Max Action and his fellow University of Minnesota explorers form the group "Adventure Squad", which they later rename Action Squad.

The newsgroup uk.rec.subterranea is founded.

March 1995

1996

September 1996

November 1996

1996

In Russia, the Diggers of the Underground Planet officially register with the Moscow government as the "Center of Underground Research".

April 1996

Ben Hines puts up the website College Tunnels WWW Resource Site, the official web counterpart to the alt.college.tunnels newsgroup.

October 1996

In Ontario, Canada, Ninjalicious publishes the first issue of the paper zine *Infiltration*. In the editorial of the first issue, he coins the term "urban exploration" and introduces the idea of exploring off-limits areas of all types as a hobby.

In response to increasing spam on the newsgroup alt.college.tunnels, Paul Allen Rice establishes a mailing list where student tunnelers can discuss college tunnels and any man-made underground structures, the Underground list.

July 1997

Ninjalicious establishes the infiltration-l mailing list, which is devoted to exploration of off-limits areas both above and below ground.

September 1997

Gunny and Lord Emor of the Melbourne Drain Team establish the Draining webring. In May, Emor hands the ring over to Ninjalicious, who expands the ring's scope by renaming it the Urban Exploration Ring. The renamed ring quickly expands from six to eighteen websites across Australia, Canada, the US and Britain.

February 1998

April 1997

Ninjalicious establishes an Elevator Action-themed website for Infiltration and links his site to the five or six other sites he finds related to exploring storm drains, college steam tunnels or abandoned buildings.

September 1997

Berliner Unterwelten, or the Berlin Underground Association, is founded in Germany.

1998

Explorer and photographer Stanley Greenberg publishes *Invisible New York: The Hidden Infrastructure of the City*, the first of several he will release that showcase his amazing collection of underground New York images.

Yahoo stops lumping 30+ exploration sites into the category Recreation:Cool Links:Recreation and Sports, and creates a new category, Recreation:Hobbies: Urban Exploration.

Ninjalicious establishes the Infilnews mailing list and sends out the first edition of a sporadic e-mail newsletter covering events of interest to urban explorers

Members of the Sydney Cave Clan publish the first issue of the zine *Urbex*. They publish three more issues on paper before switching to an electronic format.

December 1998

January 1999

August 1999

December 1998

Julia Solis establishes a Dark Passage website.

December 1998

German explorers Dietmar and Ingmar Arnold, of Berliner Underwelten, publish *Dunkle Welten*, a German-language guide to the worlds beneath Berlin.

April 1999

Julia Solis and her explorer friends stage an event called "Dark Passage" in the subway tunnels beneath New York City.

2000

Eku Wand and Dietmar Arnold, of Berliner Unterwelten, release *Berlin im Untergrund: Potsdamer Platz*, an interactive multimedia CD offering virtual tours of subterranean Berlin.

Minneapolis-area explorers from Mouser's Under-MN mailing list convene for the first Mouser Week, a week-long festival of group exploration.

August 2000

Max Action finds a vast maze of interconnected utility tunnel systems under Minneapolis and St. Paul that he dubs the Labyrinth, and over the next two years, Action Squad thoroughly explores (and Jim Hollison thoroughly maps) the system.

August 2001

Daniel Joseph Konopka, who had explored with the Chicago Urban Exploration group, is arrested after being found with hazardous chemicals in tunnels under the University of Illinois at Chicago; he is subsequently sentenced to 13 years in prison for storing cyanide in Chicago's subway tunnels. Konopka tells authorities he found the cyanide while engaged in urban exploration at an abandoned warehouse in Chicago.

March 2002

Julia Solis publishes *New York Underground: Anatomie Einer Stadt*, a German-language book about subterranean New York City.

September 2002

August 2000

Canadian explorer Mr. Sable creates a public MSN group and invites members of the Urban Exploration Ring to sign up in order to exchange messages, links and photos. The group, called Urban Explorers, quickly grows to include a membership of more than 100 explorers from Australia, Canada, the UK, the US, Ireland, France and Holland. An Australian subgroup, Urban Exploration Australia, is also popular for a time, until it is censored by Microsoft.

September 2001

Terrorists attack the Pentagon and the World Trade Center, and the US and the world go on high alert. A two-year dark age of urban exploration begins.

August 2002

Julia Solis and her collaborators in New York City form Ars Subterranea, a society populated by artists, architects, historians and urban explorers.

When 922 audience members are taken hostage by Chechen rebels during a performance at a Moscow theatre, Vadim Mikhailov of the Diggers of the Underground Planet leads the Russian authorities into the theatre by a little-known underground route.

In Toronto, Canada, Avatar-X launches the website Urban Exploration Resource, and creates a message forum that can be shared across multiple websites. Several other Canadian websites soon begin to use UER's message board system. Before long, UER replaces the MSN message board as the net's largest and most active exploration message board.

Max Action records and releases versions one and two of "UE Favorite Things", a song which quickly becomes an anthem of sorts.

October 2002

November 2002

March 2003

October 2002

In Toronto, Canada, the first issue of *Catfiltration*, an urban exploration zine for and by cats, is released.

November 2002

Ars Subterranea holds its inaugural event, an exhibit on Underground New York, in Brooklyn's Atlantic Avenue tunnel.

March 2003

Doug launches a full-colour publication called *The Cave Clan Magazine* and prints 100 copies of the premiere issue.

April 2003

The 15th Annual Cave Clan Clannie Awards are held.

Frustrated by infighting between various branches of the Cave Clan, and particularly the increasing independence of the large and important Sydney branch, Doug quits as editor of *Il Draino* and hands the publication over to Beanz.

May 2003

An unidentified satirist debuts the website of the Secret Urban Exploration Ninja Mafia, thoroughly mocking the boasting and illiteracy that have become common on some exploration websites and message boards.

August 2003

The owners of the site Urban Exploration Alberta take most of their content offline after learning that information on their site was used by criminals wanting places to break into for raves and vandalism.

April 2004

More than 65 explorers from North America and beyond converge on Toronto for a successful four-day urban exploration convention called Office Products Expo 94.

June 2004

July 2003

Jinx releases its book, *Invisible Frontier: Exploring the Tunnels, Ruins & Rooftops of Hidden New York*.

October 2003

Explorers John Gray and Mark Gerrity publish *Abandoned Asylums of New England*, a photography book containing more than 220 images of New England asylums.

May 2004

Webmasters White Rabbit, of Underground Ozarks in Missouri, and Mike Dijital, of Abandon Spaces in Massachusetts, take their sites offline after being separately threatened with trespassing charges based on information on their sites.

INDEX